LONG BOMB

LONG BOMB

How the XFL Became
TV's Biggest Fiasco

BRETT FORREST

CROWN PUBLISHERS • NEW YORK

Published by Crown Publishers, New York, New York.

Member of the Crown Publishing Group, a division of Random House, Inc.

www.randomhouse.com

CROWN is a trademark and the Crown colophon is a

registered trademark of Random House, Inc.

Printed in the United States of America

Design by Lenny Henderson

Frontispiece: Photograph is courtesy of Don Buchholz.

The photograph that appears on page 245 is courtesy of James Westman.

Library of Congress Cataloging-in-Publication Data

Forrest, Brett.

Long bomb : how the XFL became TV's biggest fiasco / Brett Forrest.—1st ed.

1. XFL (Football league)—History. I. Title.

GV955.5.X45 F67 2002

796.332'64—dc21

2002024160

ISBN 0-609-60992-0

10 9 8 7 6 5 4 3 2 1

First Edition

To Mickey,
the best reporter I ever saw

"'XFL' stands for nothing at all? That's amazing. Only Vince McMahon would have something which means nothing stand for something."

—Oscar Goodman, mob lawyer, Mayor of Las Vegas

LONG BOMB

PROLOGUE

THE HACKS WHO WRITE the World Wrestling Federation aren't so clever in relating the operatic struggles of the pumped up. Therefore, it couldn't have been their script that floated down from the sky on January 9, 2001, as the XFL machine readied for the league's first game, which would take place in less than a month.

Three days before, on Saturday, January 6, during an NFL playoff game between the Raiders and Dolphins, sixty-two thousand fans looked to the false horizon of Oakland Coliseum. A blimp, a 143-foot-long approximation of the XFL's newly patented black and red football, circled high above the stadium. A plane followed close behind, tugging a banner that read XFL: THE TOUGHEST FOOTBALL EVER. It was difficult to imagine a brand of football tougher than the kind found in a single-elimination NFL playoff game. Unless the coaches handed out shivs. But logic didn't come into play . . . this was advertising. Vince McMahon wanted to take it directly to the competition and win converts for his new football league.

The NFL owned a lot, but it did not own the sky. So McMahon flew his blimp. And the crowd promptly booed.

McMahon didn't care. He ordered another flight the following Sunday, at the AFC championship game, also in Oakland. The blimp's pilot spent the time between games airing out the faux football on a few test runs. On Tuesday, January 9, he took a short practice flight in the afternoon. At the end of the trip, he steered the blimp toward its parking spot at Oakland International Airport. As the huge football attempted to moor, a gust of wind kicked up along the airport's tarmac, buffeting the blimp out of the pilot's control. The ground crew couldn't hang on. The pilot and copilot jumped from the gondola. The blimp was on its own.

The football took off on a Hail Mary, drifting aimlessly across the sky for the next twenty minutes. It drew gawkers. It snarled freeway traffic. In a way, it seemed to fit the XFL's ethos. Everything about this league was supposed to be free-spirited, so why not its four-thousand-pound dirigible? The blimp roamed five miles north over the Oakland Estuary, climbing as high as sixteen hundred feet, until its gondola caught on the mast of a sailboat in a marina. It slammed nose-first into a fish-and-chips shack. Newspaper photographers arriving on the scene captured an easy image of ridicule: the new league crash-landed before its very first game.

Skeptics had to wonder at the timing, since the king of flack ultimately held the blimp's controls. "No," Vince McMahon said when reached for comment. "That wasn't a publicity stunt." Considering that the blimp sustained a couple million dollars in damage, it was safe to say that the bottom-line boss man wasn't fibbing. Not a stunt. And if it was a harbinger, there was no shying away now.

1

EXPLODING THE

FORMULA

THERE IS NO FAILURE LIKE televised failure. It's the most public failure. The most humbling failure.

So it was odd when the two men who had assembled the biggest bomb in TV history began high-fiving on the sidelines of a football field. Yet there they were, clutching cigars and each other, casting back in laughter like the winning quarterback-receiver duo. This was hardly a show of humility. They hugged, released the hug, and then hugged again, as though there were something to celebrate, something that demanded ceaseless glee. They sucked on their cigars. It was as if they had just won the million bucks on *Survivor*.

To Dick Butkus, their display was as crass as a juggler at a funeral. But the face of pro football managed to hold it together. Quietly, he shuffled away from Dick Ebersol and Vince McMahon.

Dick Butkus was so gifted a football player that, to borrow the parlance of NFL Films, "to talk about him is to drain the vocabulary of superlatives." When opponents talked about him, they drained of color. Butkus was the meanest man ever to play pro football. It just happened to be his misfortune to endure six straight losing seasons with the Chicago Bears. He never made the playoffs. And he never asked for a trade. He knew how you were supposed to act when you got your butt whipped. It didn't involve complaints and demands. It certainly didn't involve bear hugs and high fives.

The two men standing near him on the Los Angeles Coliseum field had it all wrong with their grinning and chortling. As Butkus beheld them from the corner of his eye, he knew that the only thing tougher to accept than losing was a teammate unaffected by loss. What did the XFL mean to Dick Ebersol and Vince McMahon? Was it really just another TV pilot in an endless line of "projects"? For Butkus, the XFL was football, and its demise was like getting blown out in the biggest game of the year. He looked like he was passing a stone. Or riding out a mistake.

Butkus and the XFL had always seemed a curious match, football's Prometheus joined with men who dealt in mirage. Nevertheless, the whole venture seemed to teeter on his shoulders, still prodigious decades after he snapped his last quarterback like a wing bone. When you got down to it, the XFL's fortunes could not have settled upon a more fitting barometer. Butkus also knew his way around Hollywood. He lived in Malibu. Had he been the type, he could have bragged about appearing on *MacGyver* three times. If Butkus okayed the thing, then the thing was good.

Butkus was better dressed than his superiors in his double-breasted gray suit to their grubby sweatpants and pleather sleeves. He was more mannered and discreet, just trying to get through the XFL championship game with a modicum of decency, waiting to put the experience in the fish-eye mirrors of his RV as he peeled out of the stadium parking lot one last time. He'd never say as much. But all you had to do was look at that face of a thousand fulfilled threats, of not a single veil, with its many wrinkles and scars folding indistinguishably into one another, and realize that Butkus was accustomed to communicating without words.

You wouldn't guess the meaning by locating the XFL's big-time announcer, who dutifully rumbled from the broadcast position but simmered with the inexpressible rage of a patsy. You wouldn't know it from spying Dick Ebersol and Vince McMahon, who continued a yearlong pageant of public romance, their close conversation cascading above the play on the field. You wouldn't know it if you polled the fans, a twenty-five-thousand-person colony of the lonesome and the die-hard. But you could read it in Dick Butkus's sodden face. The XFL wasn't just a confused flop. It was the kind of embarrassment that made you want to smack yourself for not knowing any better.

For the men in the mesh, selectivity had nothing to do with it. What else were they going to do? Trained to realize the exaltation of the individual, these football players couldn't so easily dissolve into a world of thankless professions where no one called your name on the PA. And why should they, when a league as steeped in hype as this one came begging for their efforts? The XFL was supposed to be much more than a football league. It was a shot at extending the dream, and one of several jackpots awaited—Hollywood, pro wrestling, the NFL—if only the players performed. The XFL promised as much to them as it did to its viewers. And so did recent history.

Driving through the swelling midsection of Las Vegas, a town of winking promises, an XFL quarterback heard a single name, and a story's many details tapped with familiarity along the encoded compartments of his memory. It was the story of a guy with few prospects who spent his weekdays working in a grocery store and his weekends playing quarterback in a pro league that once paid its players in fast food. The story was of victory's essence, of winning when they said all you could do was lose. It was the story of Kurt Warner, the stock-boy quarterback who went from the Arena Football League to the NFL, where he won the MVP trophy. How it happened and why it happened, none of that mattered to the castoffs jacked up on Warner's mythology. The main thing was that it *happened*, and that it could happen again.

A thousand players stood on the outside of the NFL looking in, toiling like ranch hands in one third-rung league or another, watching the dream fade slightly with each passing day. When the XFL blessed them with its creation, it was a reprieve not unlike an eleventh-hour phone call from the governor. Kurt Warner's departed minor-league ghost assumed a very real presence, and XFL players referenced his story only half as much as they dreamed it. They had faith. And they had license. They had another chance at being big shots.

A guy with a nappy head of hair busting out in a parabola, Rod Smart corralled the ladies at the Drink, a meat locker off the Strip in Vegas, telling them what they wanted to hear. His pockets busted out with digits written in flowery script. He was the XFL's poet laureate, and his recognized riff won him bounty of one sort but not another. Attention was his only denomination, and he gladly accepted it.

Kelvin Kinney had done all that was asked. In some kind of perpetual pain, he sat at the plastic bar of a papier-mâché casino, his left foot a similarly lifeless plank. He ordered a glass of Louis XVIII cognac, having approached refinement through years in the NFL's chocolate-on-pillow hotels. No matter how swell he drank, nothing could shake a sense of betrayal. He earned almost $1 million for his last season in the NFL. Now he played for less than $50,000. It wasn't the money that compelled him to further cripple himself. Kinney had given the NFL all he had, and they treated him like a draft dodger, some kind of traitor. He was after something else in the XFL.

Ryan Clement rode through Vegas, talking and talking about Kurt Warner, with whom he shared a position and a fallow period, if not a personal relationship with God. They marked Clement for greatness while the fuzz was still on his face. He was supposed to be the one who made the rifle passes and the fat paychecks. Somewhere it all derailed, and his head grew foggy to forget. Instead of leading the Broncos downfield, he was pinching toes to check the customer's fit.

The car glided under the bulbs of the Strip, which consumed Clement in a blaze of white light. A billboard hung up ahead, standing out in the morass. It was a picture of a man in an oxford shirt holding a check in his hand, smiling broadly. He had good reason. GEORGE HANOVER WON $250,000 AT OUR SLOTS, read the ad copy. In a haze of exhaust fumes and fat, wavy desert air, Hanover's smile existed in a facsimile of motion. He appeared to smile in real time. He was a nobody made somebody, loser then winner. Lost in the gestures of his story, Clement didn't notice the resemblance. As it was for several hundred others, the XFL was Ryan Clement's slot machine, his land rush, his best shot at following Kurt Warner's act with one starring himself.

The players weren't the only ones taking chances—the higher ups were calling for a Long Bomb.

A Long Bomb is a particular type of designed play, when the quarterback steps back and heaves the football as far as he can, aiming for one of his teammates downfield. It's different from a Hail Mary, which is a loser's last gasp, a quarterback's toss into a mess of players from both teams—a prayer, as the name suggests, that has little chance of being answered.

The Long Bomb is something more than a prayer. It's a calculated gamble, an attempt at huge gain against great improbability under intense scrutiny.

As with a casino's big-money wheel, the payout is immense and the odds quite slim. Coaches turn to the play when they want to affect a momentum swing, and like every sweep or screen, it's designed to reach the end zone. The Long Bomb rarely succeeds, and it can leave those who choose it adrift and alone, vulnerable to criticism.

The play is something neither winner nor loser performs exclusively. Instead, the Long Bomb resides in the territory of the risk taker. It conforms to the type of frontier behavior that Americans like to believe is etched onto their genetic code—Lewis and Clark and such . . . "Go West," said Horace Greeley, though "Go deep" would serve just as well. The risk of the Long Bomb, along with the shadiness of the chop block and the savagery of the forearm shiver, is part of the reason football now stands alone as America's game, having clotheslined baseball's Commonwealth, cricket gentility in favor of a pastime more befitting the world's only superpower.

But football has demonstrated no immunity to the particular gentility of our age, the plastic kind, the prepackaged pop and conglomeration of it all, the soul-robbing focus-group denomination dictated by those with myopic horn-rims on the bottom line. The National Football League has a rule on the books that legislates against celebration, and another that requires a player to wear his socks pulled up to his knees: a dress code in the mud designed to uphold the corporate image. It's a bastard evolutionary tract, but evolution of the game all the same.

Witness Super Bowl XXXV, played in January 2001.

The game itself was a tawdry bore, matching two teams with precious few recognizable names in a defensive battle that saw the ball cascade harmlessly from one side of the field to the other in sinister table-tennis mimicry. The game was all temptation and no payoff, played under harsh lighting—like watching Spice at the Budget Suites when you thought you'd bought the real thing. And yet the show went off. MTV threw up a halftime sing-along, a shameful mix-up of every musical genre save the spoons as the NFL and the evening's broadcast partner, CBS, desperately displayed their all-knowing, all-feeling Americanness. On leave from assisted living, Aerosmith joined Mary J. Blige, Nelly, *NSYNC, and Britney Spears on a single stage for a sloppy rendition of a thirty-year-old anthem that would have found a more suitable title in "Stumble Blindly This Way." It was like matching socks in the dark. It couldn't save the telecast. Nor could the fact that New York, the nation's biggest TV market, supplied one of the competing teams. (And apparently there weren't enough fans curious to see how a man who only too recently plea bargained his way out of double murder charges would perform under pressure. Baltimore linebacker Ray Lewis won the MVP trophy.)

By any measure, the telecast was a dismal failure, a staggering disappointment, and not just to the poor millions tricked once again into watching it. No, they were the least affected. The TV creeps, the advertising hoodlums, every ten-percenter who had his grouty little fingernails clawed into America's biggest sporting event—they all lost a little that day. Because in 2001, the Super Bowl, the single most watched event of the TV year, attracted the lowest share (60 percent) of the TV-viewing public in its thirty-five-year history.

There was a reason that America switched off this Super Bowl, which stank of burning offal like few had before it. There was something absent from the game, something even emptier and more unfulfilling about it than usual. The crap, it seemed, had finally reached the porcelain lip. What was missing? Maybe it was the Long Bomb, deemed too hazardous, not cost-effective, too freewheeling, not approved by the focus groups. Maybe it was a lost sense of possibility, the action left unrealized, as though the game was rigged, a sham, like the competition wasn't real, like there was someone somewhere getting one over on the viewers, having an oafish Tammany Hall snigger at their expense. Ultimately, in its equation of promotion over performance, glitz over game, the Super Bowl bore too striking a resemblance to another kind of sports entertainment, one for which a certain pious portion of the audience could not conceive buying a ticket.

And yet there was joy that night as the Super Bowl telecast wrapped with a breathless invitation (which agreed in tone with an air-raid command) to remain seated for the ohmagawd premiere of *Survivor, 2.0*. Yes, there was joy, but it was not in the houses of the NFL, CBS, or their string tuggers—the Advertisers. The joy that night belonged to a princely Connecticut castle, one whose pastoral dusting of snowflakes contrasted sharply with the well-known temperament of the individuals inside. This was the home of Vince McMahon, chairman of the World Wrestling Federation, and on this night the NFL's fumble was his chance at a hundred-yard run. Granted, the

Super Bowl telecast drew 84 million viewers (84 million!) in a country of 284 million people. But for McMahon there was a lesson in the NFL's failure to perform to its own gold standard. There was opportunity, too. As he bedded down for the night, unable to sleep but accustomed to the feeling, he could hardly wait for what came next.

Vince McMahon—bumpkin billionaire, overworker of eyebrows—was about to reinvent football. So he schemed, when he announced plans for a new pro football league in February 2000. It was called the XFL. The letters, McMahon was quick to point out, didn't stand for anything. It wasn't the Xtreme Football League or the X-rated Football League, although those were the dual implications of the ubiquitous twenty-fourth letter, which the American public had come to recognize as the default signpost for "aggressive." No, this was just XFL. McMahon was after an overall feeling, damn the details. Or maybe this was a detail, carefully devised, an abstract sense meant to lure in inquisitive wonder the Chiclet-toothed horde, like moths to a bulb, like sots to a keg. For a period of decades McMahon had been so calculating, so precise and definite, in shepherding his wrestling empire to international influence. With this new venture, everything seemed to hint at something further down the line that no one could see. That fact wasn't lost on the sports-viewing public, which was eager to figure out the conflation.

McMahon would transfer his pro-wrestling approach to the holiest of holies—pro football—and, in the process, make *Monday Night Football* look like it should air on PBS. He would affix microphones to everyone in the stadium save the beer man. Cameramen would roam the field of play and possibly get lost in pileups. Reporters would interview players between downs, mining out-of-breath, cinema-verité comments at key points in a game. Announcers would sit among the fans in the stands. At half time, cameras and microphones would capture Knute Rockne speeches live from the dressing rooms, sending emotional ripples down America's spine. Players would earn scale (roughly $50,000 each per season), but would have reason to answer the gladiatorial call to run opponents through with a stake—there would be a $2,500 bonus per player for each victory. McMahon would amp the game's violence, doing away with the fair-catch rule and several safeguards that the NFL had erected to keep quarterbacks' heads intact. Sex would play a big role, as McMahon explained, since XFL cheerleaders would be "encouraged" to date the players. The XFL would be greater, bigger, better—more, more, more. McMahon predicted that the league would turn a profit inside of three years, claiming that it would attract the young viewers already tuned in to the WWF, along with football fans suffering from the post–Super Bowl shakes, all the while riding the *Survivor* wave. "This experience is the ultimate reality show inside arguably the greatest sport ever shown on television," he said.

By combining the culture of two kingdoms, televising football in the way he produced his wrestling spectacle, McMahon planned to make artifice authentic. This philosophy would enable fans to connect with the game in ways that another, more well-known league was too dainty to attempt. "The NFL would have you believe that it's a golfing outing," McMahon said in the bass voice that had launched a thousand WWF feuds. For a man who made a fortune from fiction, he talked an awful lot about the truth. And he went after the big kid on the block like a wrestler breathing into a bag just to watch it take a new shape. In words that sportswriters would soon pounce upon with prospectors' delight, McMahon said that the NFL was for "pantywaists," for "sissies," and that the XFL would restore football to its origins, when "the whole idea was to kill the quarterback."

This was McMahon—sounding like Charlton Heston, hammered, sermonizing to the Rotary Club—speaking on February 3, 2000, at a press conference in his WWF Restaurant in Times Square. It was the perfect place for this football debutant ball, around the corner from the flagship store of the Walt Disney Company, which in its mastery of character and merchandise certainly proved something of an inspiration. To McMahon, his restaurant was concrete-and-steel proof of how his wrestling circuit had enabled him to enter into what he called the Entertainment Business. He saw himself as much more than a wrestling promoter. And he wanted others to agree. He wanted to be taken seriously.

McMahon himself sounded serious as he explained one of many ways in which his league would succeed where others had failed—the XFL itself would own all league teams, keeping cost centralized and to a minimum. On the field, though, there would be no controls. XFL games would not be scripted, as in the WWF. McMahon displayed the trademark sneer that identified him as the heel on WWF telecasts. XFL rosters, he said, would be comprised of actual football players.

It wasn't long before the public learned that the XFL would air on an actual network, NBC—prideful home of the Olympic Games and Must See TV—and in prime time, Saturday night. NBC would not only air the games but would enter into a fifty-fifty partnership with the XFL. The network had everything to gain and very little to lose, unless prestige meant anything anymore. By mid-2000, NBC was the one major network on American TV without pro football or a reality series. NBC execs believed that the XFL would shore those two holes. The league would also allow NBC to experiment in the historically low-rated Saturday-night slot that network sports chairman Dick Ebersol had loudly described as a failure. The XFL would resuscitate NBC on many fronts. Ebersol compared the league to the advent of *Saturday Night Live,* which he had helped develop in the mid-1970s. His colleague, NBC sports president Ken Schanzer, likened the XFL to *The Rocky Horror Picture Show,* where everything was fair game. McMahon said, "The way we're going to cover this is going to revolutionize not only the way football is covered but sports itself."

The XFL was starting to sound pretty important, especially to those who consumed alms with closed eyes. Even a skeptic's anticipatory hackles stood on end. The scope of this idea was wide enough that its ultimate result—success or failure—could only be commensurate. If it worked, competing networks would fall over one another in copying the XFL formula. If it didn't work—man, what a car wreck. There was no keeping it under wraps. NBC and the WWF were so adept at generating hype that the league had a larger profile than Hitchcock before its players assembled for a single practice. "XFL" was the most searched term on the Web engine Lycos. Bettors flooded Las Vegas sportsbooks with phone calls about the XFL even while the Super Bowl was in progress. Family groups and censors prepared battle plans to combat what they saw as a coming storm of temptation and vulgarity.

The NFL also had its eyes open. Not that the ruler of all pro sports leagues was worried about a rival operation populated by players it had already dumped. NFL commissioner Paul Tagliabue was overheard wondering at an owners' meeting, "Is it real or is it scripted?" He had good reason to laugh off McMahon's challenge. The NFL had ruled pro football without a real threat for thirty-five years. It had the biggest TV contract in sports, the most invasive licensing phalanx, and a plodding weekly routine that had become the very backbone of the American male's fall social calendar. But in recognizing the XFL as more TV studio than football league, NFL officials realized they had to tweak their own product to stay ahead of a unit catering more directly to the increasingly fickle eye of the TV audience. As part of its 1998 contract with the networks, the NFL had granted increased access to sideline reporters. Now the league was looking for other ways to spice up its televised product. The NFL allowed TV producers to affix cameras to on-field officials' hats. Suddenly, there were more shots above sideline huddles. And ABC hired Dennis Miller as a commentator on *Monday Night Football*, the NFL's weekly showpiece, even though the comedian had no sports broadcasting experience. The show's then–executive producer Don Ohlmeyer admitted that Miller's hiring came in response to the XFL, which was still six months from its first game.

Ohlmeyer had gone so far as to consider conservative commentator Rush Limbaugh for the job. That was the state of trepidation around the NFL, which had seen its overall ratings shrink by 9 percent from 1999 to 2000. The numbers reflected a general sports trend. The 2000 World Series earned the worst ratings in the history of the event. The 2000 Olympics in Sydney, Australia, delivered the lowest ratings of any Summer Games. *Monday Night Football* posted its worst ratings ever in 2000. Yet the aggregate sports audience remained huge. With the XFL, McMahon gambled on the idea that fans still wanted to watch but their desires had changed quicker than the traditional sports leagues and stodgy TV networks had modified in accommodation. McMahon believed he found the answer, and it was difficult to shout him down. Why had *Monday Night Football* posted such lousy ratings in 2000? Because *WWF Raw Is War* outperformed *Monday Night Football* in head-to-head telecasts throughout the 2000 season.

The WWF's upward trajectory imbued McMahon with the bottomless confidence of a boy-band member, and he continued taking chances in preparing his new league. He and Ebersol had studied Dennis Miller's performance on *Monday Night Football*. To the football fans located outside

Miller's urbane geographic circle, the comic's weekly pas de deux on ABC didn't make a whole lot of sense. His references to Disraeli and Yalta were the type of pitter-patter that would get you slapped around in half the sports bars in America. This was football. Where was the gristle? Ebersol and McMahon planned to provide it.

They called a press conference in November 2000 to introduce the color commentator for NBC's main XFL telecast, a person Ebersol referred to as "one of the most interesting and colorful leaders in America today." For once, the TV executive wasn't exaggerating. The XFL hired Jesse Ventura, governor of Minnesota, who was more widely known as a former WWF wrestler. The governor, generally referred to as "The Body," was another piece of a puzzle that would explode the TV sports formula.

This was perhaps the loudest press conference on record. McMahon and Ventura had been steroid pincushions for years, while Ebersol just looked like a strung-out ex-weightlifter. With their overgrown baritones competing for a single parcel of airtime, it was hard to tell whose ego took up the most space. One was an elected official, another a billionaire, and the third considered himself an oracle. They opened themselves to questions.

A reporter on the teleconference phone line asked after the propriety of a governor peddling cheerleaders. "I'm not buying in to that," Ventura boomed, his voice a cannon. "I'm here to do football." Another reporter questioned the way the game would be presented. "It's honesty," said McMahon. "Something you in the media don't know a whole hell of a lot about." A reporter asked if the XFL had devised a doping policy—at this confluence of wrestling and football, it was worth thinking about the pharmaceutical history of both sports. The three-headed monster didn't know what to say. There was a lot of huffing and puffing and mouth-breathing into the press-conference microphones. It was tough to tell just whose voice came through, since potency oozed from collective pores. The three voices reverberated as one of them explained that illegal drugs would not be tolerated in the XFL. Just what did that mean, the reporter wanted to know, since many forms of performance-enhancing drugs were legal with a prescription? The question hung on the buzz of the teleconference line. No one ventured an answer. A click snapped through, and a moderator quickly apologized for the technical difficulty.

The teleconference ended, but not before the two partners declared their indefatigable commitment to Governor Ventura and to each other. In the ensuing months, Dick Ebersol took pains to spread the gospel of the XFL, especially as it pertained to Vince McMahon. During a January press conference in Pasadena, he lavished McMahon with the kind of overblown praise reserved for obituaries. "I don't think I've ever had a partnership that meant more to me in business, one that was more honorable," Ebersol said. "And if I was run over by a truck, I'd like him to raise my kids." This was dialogue straight from a WWF pay-per-view. But there was genuine strategy involved.

Ebersol's game plan had nothing to do with a football league. He knew that McMahon wasn't beloved by the press, and that their opinion would now matter in ways that it never had with the WWF. Ebersol was trying, by proxy, to rehabilitate his partner's tarnished reputation; to turn McMahon's image from filth into family. "I'd like him to raise my kids"? Ebersol was no media darling, either, but he was trying his best to rub a little NBC polish on someone he knew the press disliked even more than himself.

It all played into a larger scheme, at least as far as McMahon would have had it. No matter the heights of WWF success, in many minds, pro wrestling clung precariously to a rung one up from porn and cock fighting. Regardless of his accomplishments, McMahon would always be something of a pimp. He desperately sought a stature that, for all his financial success, he could never seem to attain. For years his minions had lobbied the Museum of Television and Radio in midtown Manhattan to host a gala for McMahon, whose track record as an independent TV producer ran for more than twenty highly rated years. The museum steadfastly ignored the proposal. McMahon would never say as much, but he longed to be taken seriously. And if the guys in the black ties wouldn't invite him, he would push his way in.

The XFL was an invitation of McMahon's own design, a fake ID that would grant him entry to a party where everyone was legal and on the up-and-up. The XFL was different from the WWF in one critical sense—it was genuine competition. This was America's game, real football and not pantomime. The XFL was a grandiose idea. And if it worked, well, it wouldn't silence McMahon's critics, but it would make them seem more shrill and, in that way, easier for him and his new fellow partygoers to ignore, chattering as the critics were, like uncredentialed paparazzi roosting beyond the wrought iron. They would remain there, shouting vainly against a tidal wave of good cheer for the man they believed to be a fraud and a counterfeit.

The XFL wasn't just McMahon's attempt at expanding his wealth, influence, and WWF empire, although it certainly was that. This was an exertion of another of his visions, one of sport's next step. If all went according to plan, no amount of criticism or envy could deny the achievement.

The XFL was McMahon's shot at legitimacy. It wouldn't be easy.

It'd be a Long Bomb.

2

THIS. IS. THE
XFLLLLLLLLLL.

THIS GUY KNEW A THING or two about ceremony. Vince McMahon scheduled the first game of his new league to coincide with the first anniversary of his flash XFL press conference at the WWF Restaurant. February 3, 2001, would mark the start of the football revolution. This was more than a display of organizational might, a brag about how NBC and the WWF could whip up an entire football league quicker than it took the networks to develop a half-hour sitcom. The timing made a different kind of sense. February 3 fell on the weekend following the Super Bowl, thus positing the XFL as a critical continuance of America's football watching. The situation also played perfectly into McMahon's theory that people were ready to watch something new. February sports ratings had always been slight, marking the time between the Super Bowl and the Final Four when the NBA and NHL slithered along the underbelly of their interminable seasons.

McMahon had his T minus ten, the When to begin. What about the Where? . . . Vegas, baby.

In full militarism, Vince McMahon goose-stepped onto the turf at Sam Boyd Stadium, a horseshoe in Henderson, Nevada, ten miles from the Strip, home to the University of Nevada–Las Vegas Runnin' Rebels football team and countless Styx concerts. McMahon's shoulders swung as though coat-hangered inside a black XFL varsity jacket, and his pompadoured head shivered with each stock stride. McMahon looked like a choleric landlord come to collect past-due amounts, and he stuck a puffy red microphone before his face. His mouth opened, and the cleft in his chin protruded to reveal gathered skin. He had waited many years for this particular football moment, striding the field and bellowing much as Patton would have: "This. Is. The XFLLLLLLLLLLL . . ." The audio of his microphone so thundered that his pronunciation trailed off into diffused crowd dither, and those in attendance took a moment to gather their senses after a cathartic display of rainbow lightning from the edge of the stadium. The fans cheered him, this magnanimous XFL McMahon, in contrast to the greeting that the odious Mister McMahon usually received in the WWF ring. He had stumbled upon a new character to play.

The sun drooped here in Vegas, unlike back east, where a crucial number of viewers as yet uncounted by the Nielsen elves watched in darkened prime time. The stadium nearly toppled from the moment's weight as the crowd warmed to the thought of their Las Vegas Outlaws taking on the New York/New Jersey Hitmen in the first XFL game. A new league. Unknown players. A debut TV show. A single element would have been enough. Where to look? Harder still on TV, for once play began, NBC's cameras flew crosswise, lengthwise, anything-wise above, across, over the field, everything but through the turf, down into the grass for comments from the chinch bugs crushed under the weight of the cleats atop them. No, this wasn't the NFL.

NBC opened the XFL era with a montage. These were slogans zipping across the screen atop an assault of driving guitars: SMASHMOUTH. PASSION. NO FAIR CATCH. CONTROVERSY. PAID TO PLAY. PAID MORE TO WIN. It felt like subliminal advertising—except that it was written across the screen in big red letters. The next bit of overt symbolism came in the form of Dwayne Douglas Johnson, better known as The Rock, the WWF's most famous wrestler. Johnson's turn as *SNL* host on March 18, 2000, earned the show its biggest ratings of the season. Having proved his mass appeal, Johnson then moved on to movies and signed a $5.5 million deal with Universal Studios, for which he would appear in *The Mummy Returns* and, later, *The Scorpion King*. Did McMahon need any more proof that his empire had entered a golden age?

The NBC telecast depicted The Rock on videotape against a black backdrop, his black shirt unbuttoned to the waist at the bottom edge of the screen. This was a football league, but it was also a chance for McMahon to juice the other components of his Entertainment Business. Johnson's mouth opened to pure wrestling oration. "The Rock says he's all psyched about the XFL," he intoned, greedy for air. "Oh, wait a minute. The Rock isn't psyched. He's pumped about the XFL. No, no, no. The Rock isn't pumped. The Rock is geeked about the XFL." This endured, The Rock's odes digressing and compounding, giving NBC time enough to cut to a shot of him pronouncing from the big-screen marquee of the Mandalay Bay casino, down on the south end of the Strip, as daylight traffic coasted past on the roadway beneath his outsize image. The Rock yelled still as the telecast cut to the packed Sam Boyd Stadium, where fans watched him on the thousand-square-foot liquid-crystal screen that stood at the horseshoe's open end. "The Rock simply says: Just bring it." He finished, then leaned toward the crowd and lifted his right eyebrow. This was his signature gesture of defiance, and as with everything else under McMahon's reign, it was copyrighted to the boss man. The Rock was a telegenic Big Brother peering out at the world. He was also a big brother helping along a younger brother in Police Athletic League spirit, WWF urging on XFL, newly minted Hollywood actor lending star power to the no-names under the helmets.

Fireworks exploded the length of the field. Video of violent tackles and moist bikinis cut jerkily across the TV screen. Crowd shots revealed the standard enthusiasts, highlighted by an old-timer in a torn poncho who bent back at the waist and hooted, careful not to spill his double-fisted cargo of Coors.

Then it was to the NBC announcers, as Governor Ventura uttered his first words as XFL color commentator. "The thing I love about the XFL is the heart and soul that these players show for the love of the game of playing football and the opportunity of continuing to play the game they love here in the XFL." Ventura was so fired up on his elliptical phrasing that he bumped into his smaller broadcast partner with an unintentional elbow and nearly knocked him over. They both played it off as though nothing had happened.

NBC cut to a shot from the field, where Dick Butkus, director of XFL competition, readied for the start of play. "Ya know, in the past, all football games started with a coin toss," he said, the Sam Boyd crowd buzzing in anticipation, flattered by the presence of a football legend in their own backyard. "No way, Jose." Then viewers got their first look at *the XFL difference*, as two players engaged in the Scramble, a whistled sprint for a ball ten yards distant. The play came in place of the standard kickoff, and it was decided upon by McMahon and Ebersol only the day before the game. Las Vegas won the Scramble, and the crowd belched in rapture.

It was to the cheerleaders next, with low-angle shots so front-row as to enumerate the gaps in their fishnets. They weren't so much dancing as wiggling, like they were being tickled. George Thoroughgood's song "I Like Girls" played over the PA, reinforcing the point for only the dimmest of viewers.

NBC quickly shuttled to segments from each locker room, where coaches speechified. "Let's get out there and play this game the way I know we can play it," said one leader of men. "Let's get after their butts," said the other. Twin brothers in inspiration.

The patented red and black XFL football bounded off the kicker's toe, revolving high into the desert-honey sky framed by jagged peaks. Hype finally in the wake, the game settled in, with Las Vegas driving the length of the field for the league's first score. There was good and there was bad. These were opening moments. Unhappily for Ebersol and McMahon, after all their machinations, their annum of innovation, the XFL's first points came by way of a tired old field goal.

Get me rewrite!

There was plenty riding on this game. Since the announcement of the NBC-XFL partnership, the league had only grown in importance to the network. NBC was in the midst of a downturn that started with the 2000 Summer Olympics.

Dick Ebersol knew he would have trouble in Sydney, since the fifteen-hour time difference between the East Coasts of Australia and the U.S. meant that America would be working or snoozing when the Games were on. With this one, the TV execs couldn't dictate the starting times as they had for nearly every major sports event over the past several decades. Ebersol's solution only compounded the Olympic problem. He chose to air all the action on tape delay, which not only put the Games in prime time but allowed his cronies to edit the events into sparkling human-interest dramas. Viewers were left to watch soft-focus *General Hospital* drivel such as the searing portrait of a husband-wife equestrian team that strung out over an hour, as Ebersol's editors alternated between tension and exposition as a way of injecting emotion and sheer thrill into a horse jumping over a stick. It was this way with every sport—sentiment easily detectable in its manufacture.

Critics tarred Ebersol for it, and vigorously, too, betraying a general antipathy for a man who never seemed to have much time for most reporters; and whose arrogance, much like his beloved Olympians' achievements, always seemed to outdistance previous records. Viewers leveled their own criticism, making the Sydney Games the lowest-rated Olympics (a 13.9 prime time average) since 1968, the year ABC legend Roone Arledge began to turn the Games into a bankable TV franchise. The numbers were so low that NBC had to dole out free spots to its advertisers, a common practice when programming draws below stated expectations. As the Games ended, another problem reared its head. The economy took a dive, and NBC profits with it. The calendar turned to 2001 and the XFL approached, as NBC sketched plans to lay off six hundred employees. The network wasn't alone. CNN cut four hundred jobs, and several other media companies announced similar plans.

It was no secret that NBC had been having troubles. The coveted demographic of youthful viewers who willingly spent money on the ephemeral products that advertisers dangled before it was moving along to the WB network. Whispers had it that *Friends*, NBC's entertainment lynchpin, would only be around for a season or two more. The network had struggled with a long line of sitcom flops and had just dumped Garth Ancier as president of its entertainment division after only seventeen months. In his place, NBC chairman Bob Wright promoted from within. Jeff Zucker, thirty-five, had served as executive producer of the *Today* show since he was twenty-six, and to great success. Zucker's *Today* ratings often surpassed the viewership for competitors on ABC and CBS combined. Zucker's will for achievement went all the way back to his college days as president of the *Harvard Crimson*, the school newspaper. The president of the *Harvard Lampoon* at the time, Conan O'Brien, felt the need to goose Zucker by stealing an entire edition of the *Crimson*. Zucker called the cops and years later, as head of NBC's entertainment division, got his revenge on O'Brien by becoming the talk-show host's boss.

Zucker also inherited the XFL. And a new network battle. On January 3,

2001, Zucker's first day on the job, CBS announced a prominent programming switch. The second installment in the suddenly mammoth *Survivor* franchise would air opposite NBC's Thursday-night slate, where *Friends* ran just thirty minutes to *Survivor*'s full hour. It was an attempt to topple the colossus that was NBC's Must See TV. Thursday's prime time was the most valuable terrain on TV, a night when advertisers paid top dollar in order to influence viewers' upcoming weekend activities, such as going to a movie or shopping for a car. NBC had cast a spell over the night, ruling it nearly without interruption since the network's bulletproof mid-1980s lineup of *The Cosby Show, Family Ties, Cheers, Night Court,* and *Hill Street Blues.*

The CBS challenge forced NBC into emergency mode. Jeff Zucker responded by ordering roughly ten extra minutes from *Friends* and prodding *Saturday Night Live* executive producer Lorne Michaels to produce another twenty minutes of fresh *SNL* material, extending the *Friends* timeslot to a full hour: anything to hold off the *Survivor* charge. NBC resembled a fort whose inhabitants had failed to stock up for winter. It was strange—a network with countless hours of programming at its disposal chewing the pulp from just two shows. "Very interesting," said one *Friends* producer. "It's like we don't have anything else we want to put on the air."

For all this, Vince McMahon was the savior. Before the XFL, NBC had been broadcasting movie reruns on Saturday nights, a signal that the real estate, while still valuable, was worth very little indeed. What did NBC have to lose? If McMahon's XFL worked, and worked big, it could deflect *Survivor* and maintain NBC's strong place in the weekly ratings battle, if not on Thursday night. It could also stem the tide of decreasing revenues that plagued the network. McMahon needed momentum for his own company, which traded publicly. Since the first XFL press conference, WWF stock had fallen from $22 to $15.14, and quarterly earnings dropped by 25 percent—in large part due to start-up costs associated with the XFL. It could all go either way, depending on how many people watched.

Heading into the first game, the XFL sales force had sold 70 percent of TV advertising at $140,000 per thirty-second spot. Since the unproven league had yet to play a game or earn a ratings point, advertising contracts included clauses that allowed companies to cancel orders without penalty if the product failed to match expectations. Ebersol and McMahon guaranteed advertisers that the games would average a modest 4.5 rating on NBC. If the XFL could maintain that average throughout its twelve weeks, it would not only guarantee a future for the league but would go further to solidifying the joint reputation of Ebersol-McMahon. If the XFL couldn't make the bar, the future would become as murky as a frat boy's fish tank.

So much for numbers. What about dreams? For this was McMahon's dream. But was it the right dream for a man with the luxury of selection? Football twines with the American identity, but no matter how beloved, too much of something renders it tedious. It wasn't a simple prospect, siphoning attention from Masonically devoted NFL fans. Not to mention the college game, which preceded the pro game, having anointed its first champion in 1869. Who needed another football league?

For a solid third of each calendar year, it is easier for John Madden to pass through the eye of a needle than for an American to escape a vision of football. High school teams play on Friday, colleges on Saturday, pros on Sunday and Monday. As the seasons progress toward winter, the schedules distend into Tuesday, Wednesday, and Thursday. Cable and network programming stock endless games, with windowsill satellites plunging cavities that fans may have missed. While games hasten toward completion in the eastern time zone, competition gets under way out west. So elemental in its stress of land conquest, the game echoes earth's very rotation. It's all on TV. During the 2001 season, ESPN alone aired 132 college and pro football games in four months, averaging roughly one football game every day. ABC, CBS, and Fox did the rest. And that's just football. According to ESPN researchers, from September 2000 through August 2001, networks and cable channels pumped 25,750 hours of sports programming into American TVs. That makes nearly three days' worth (70.5 hours) of TV sports zapped into the American household every day.

Each year, the NFL stages 259 games, excluding the preseason. There are 617 collegiate football teams (115 in Division IA; 502 in Division IAA, II, and III), each with their own schedule of roughly ten games. Don't forget high school football, for which folks in Florida, Texas, and Nebraska would gladly sacrifice a cycle of virgins. How much is enough? The endless hand-offs; the wearying, clapping break from the huddle; the inertia of the off-tackle no-gainer.

Then there are the minor leagues of pro football. For years NFL teams have used the college ranks as a convenient developmental pool. Still, minor pro leagues survive. A hybrid of football and hockey, with indoor football played on a fifty-yard field surrounded by plastic retaining walls, the Arena Football League has inexplicably kicked around for the last fifteen years like a closet affinity for *MAD* magazine, largely through the barnstorming approach of its owners. And in 2001—could this have been true?—it spun off into a second circuit, Arena League 2. Moments like these reinforce the belief in America's ability to support anything with a logo and a TV commercial. Then there's the Canadian Football League, even older than the NFL, which the truest of fans can locate buried amid the sand dunes of the cable box. There's also NFL Europe, which has existed in one of several incarnations since the early 1990s. The NFL likes to call it a pro developmental league, but in reality it's a purgatory from which very few players escape, suffered instead to survive schnitzel and cow-foot soup among a disinterested population they cannot comprehend.

With so much football already out there, and with the NFL standing atop the pile, founding a pro football league appeared to be a madman's prospect. The last time anyone tried it was 1983, when the United States Football League earned surprisingly solid TV ratings on ABC and ESPN after signing college stars such as Heisman Trophy winners Doug Flutie and Herschel Walker. But the USFL (1983–1985), like the All-American Conference (1946–1949) and the World Football League (1974–1975) before it, evaporated after a few seasons, unable to sustain acolytes in a culture of monotheism. The NFL's stranglehold trapped all oxygen. How can the Wichita Whatevers compete against the likes of the Dallas Cowboys, whose cheerleaders even are transcontinental icons?

Only one rival operation ever earned a tomorrow. By the late 1960s, after forty years in business, the NFL had finally marched out from its citadels in the Northeast and Midwest to develop a fan base in the wider country, where baseball had held a monopoly. Thanks to TV, there was suddenly room to grow, and the NFL, with just fourteen teams, ached for a larger presence.

The American Football League came along, and with a different style of play, which emphasized passing and the Long Bomb. Fans loved the new league, and in 1970, the AFL and NFL merged, with the winners of each league meeting in what became the Super Bowl. Heady days . . . Fast-forward thirty years and note the evidence of saturation, with thirty-two NFL teams and more on the way. What American fan hasn't consumed some portion of the football speedball—two Saturday college games, two pro games on Sunday, one more on Monday night—and barely lived to tell the terrible tale? Did America need more football on TV?

With the XFL, viewers resolved to give it a shot, to toss another pinch on the spoon. They just had to make sure it wasn't cut, or there were going to be some problems. That was the XFL's dilemma—it *was* cut, impure. Its rosters were composed of guys who couldn't make it in the NFL, and the atmosphere wouldn't have the pomp of college ball. So why should fans watch when the football junkies already had plenty of options? The only way they would was if the telecast—and the vision behind it—matched in innovation Vince McMahon's whirling publicity that induced everyone to have a peek. Straight football wasn't going to do it. Not on NBC. Not in prime time.

3

A LONE

DESERT SPECIES

FIVE HOURS BEFORE KICKOFF of Game One, Sam Boyd Stadium's dusty parking lot began filling with RVs and SUVs, and the stench of charred meat sliced the air. The flesh eaters had arrived, eager for the kind of barbarism depicted in a hyperbolic TV ad that showed a wrecking ball clobbering an XFL player. The curiosity of violence and the mondo life combined to shutter the ticket windows. All thirty thousand seats were bought and paid for. Out on the access road, scalpers were getting $75 for the $15 tickets.

McMahon and Ebersol couldn't have chosen a locale more apt for their XFL coming-out party. Perfect size, half as big as the seventy-five-thousand-seat bowls of the older cities, Sam Boyd Stadium couldn't fit another backward-capped Napster disciple or twitching grocery-mart video-poker addict. NBC knew that Vegas would sell out. It was essential proof of importance—the background shot of a packed house—that could keep the popularity-obsessed coveted demographic from switching to the WB.

There were other reasons to recommend Vegas. The setting indicated not only the tenor of the league but its very chances. If the XFL had been a lock, a guaranteed success, its debut may have occurred in the columnar confines of the capitol or the legitimizing machine of the country's westernmost beachhead. But like most confident gestures, this one contained elements of doubt, nods to chance.

There was also more sublime justification at work. There was style; there was personality. For all his wealth, all his clout with people like Barry Diller and Sumner Redstone, Vince McMahon shared more with the hoods who built Vegas from the sand up than the Disneyites who bought a few lots and started paving things for the stroller derby. He found comfort among the castoffs, not the coddled. That was his particular charm: He grew up in a double-wide and then found himself extra-large, counted among the cultural heavies of the day. How did he do it? Well, there was the hagiography, and then there was the story the public will likely never know, for McMahon guarded his inner child with litigious fists.

Anyone could guess at seamy details. While admiring the guile it must have taken to beat the long odds of his *naissance,* one also wondered at the twisted mores in McMahon's wake. It was the same head shake that greeted the wise guys who constructed a vision of Vegas, the mobsters, the "classy" version of which was easy to cherish for the same reasons lending McMahon a striver's irresistibility. The general public forgave them their trespasses in exchange for their illusions, falling hard for the dice shooter—especially since the bottom-liners didn't. Vince McMahon had certainly achieved. And so had Bugsy Siegel with his Flamingo Hotel, which invented a mode of western leisure. Even though Siegel had killed a few guys, his admirers couldn't help but shiver at his own murder, carried out by unfulfilled creditors who had no use for his dreams. Big ideas carry prices appropriately sized. So McMahon laid out his big idea in the desert, plunking down his cash on the felt.

Hours before kickoff, he was still trying to improve the odds. McMahon hustled through Sam Boyd's empty stands wearing reading glasses and carrying a yellow legal pad, working out the final pieces as the NBC technicians counted down to show time back in New York. From the outset, McMahon relied on his ability to change busted parts on the fly, as he did in his wrestling league, where the fans were more open to changes in the story line than the audience for NFL football, though the crowds most certainly overlapped. McMahon was on to visions, not details, and he didn't have any hang-ups about uniformity. While discussing one of countless bits of minutiae before Game One, McMahon turned to NBC's Ken Schanzer and said, "Look, we'll do it this way, and if it doesn't work, we'll change it—ya know, 'cause we can change it."

Schanzer smirked. After twenty years with NBC, he knew the importance of getting things right the first time. "Vince, I know that," Schanzer said. "I know we can do that. But my view is that we have one half of football. If we don't grab 'em in the first half, I think we're done. If we have one good half, we'll live to see a second half." Schanzer desperately hoped everything would come together, but he realized there was a chance that all the circus bits might not mesh. He knew that the technical crew could have used a few more days of practice. He crossed his fingers. Schanzer was guarded, though optimistic enough about the pull of viewer curiosity to lay down a little money. He bet XFL president Basil DeVito that Game One's rating would nearly double their hoped-for 4.5. He said it would top an 8. The stakes: a futures bet on the Kentucky Derby. It was a trebled wager, one bet contingent on another, one good half leading to the next, just as he was hoping.

As game time approached, Dick Ebersol was a picture of relaxation. He trusted his lieutenants and had relinquished the majority of artistic control to McMahon. Ebersol smoked a cigar with Jesse Ventura, then strode the sidelines in a pair of beat-up loafers and an XFL hat. He stopped at the fifty-yard line to take in the scene, as the throngs could be heard yelling outside the locked gates of the stadium. They chanted the letters of the league, disputing NFL commissioner Paul Tagliabue's claim several days before that the XFL was "basically a nonissue" and "not what we worry about." The new league was getting plenty of attention on that first night, and not just among the tailgaters. Up in the press box it was standing room only as the sportswriters and TV critics squirmed all over one another to get at the catering.

Rod Smart ambled across the parking lot toward the Outlaws locker room, loose as he could be before the biggest game of his life. This was his first real shot at the pros. He had attended the San Diego Chargers training camp after finishing college in 2000, and made it to the last cut. But he never really had much of a chance, tolerated by the San Diego coaches mostly for his fresh legs, which kept the Chargers' defense in tackling dummies for the duration of the preseason.

Smart grew up in Lakeland, Florida, a place that sits on the edge of dreamland. But there was very little Disney in Smart's upbringing. Football got him out of all the bad stuff, at least this far. But he could never forget that as a kid, he got his jets from racing his mom during visiting hours at the pen. He ended up getting a football ride to the Western Kentucky University.

The Hilltoppers, they're called, not that the name fit Smart very well. He hadn't climbed any mountains. There was a nickname on the way that made more sense.

Smart had almost made it across the parking lot when Ben Snell, another Outlaws running back, bolted from the locker room. "Yo, that shit is tight," Snell said.

"Whatchu mean?" asked Smart.

"They got our nicknames on our jerseys."

"Not me . . . I got Smart."

"Go take a look."

Smart was confused. As far as he knew, he would be wearing his last name on the back of his jersey. When he peeked inside the locker room at number 30 hanging at his stall just inside the door, he saw something else spelled out in white block letters. He ran from the locker room to join Snell in uncontrollable laughter in the parking lot. They ranged about like sailors at port, grabbing on to each other to keep from falling over. It was the last thing Smart ever expected to see. He ducked back into the locker room, where the rest of the Outlaws prepared for the first game.

Who signed up for this league, anyway? Actors, bouncers, wrestler wanna-bes, misguided dreamers? An application form posted on XFL.com during the recruiting process did little to silence the skeptics that were mounting in the press. "Do you wear glasses?" it wanted to know. "Do you have an agent? Do you consider your speed to be great, good, average or slow?" It was football as correspondence course, and more than forty thousand people asked after nearly 400 spots. Over the midsection of 2000, the XFL named its eight teams: Birmingham Bolts, Chicago Enforcers, Las Vegas Outlaws, Los Angeles Xtreme, Memphis Maniax, New York/New Jersey Hitmen, Orlando Rage, and San Francisco Demons. They sounded like the names not only of comic book characters but of comic book characters who tried a little too hard. The league hired general managers and coaches, and in October 2000 held its draft, which parceled 379 players to the eight clubs. To the surprise of many, it turned out that they were actually real football players, not fabricated figments of McMahon's teeming sea of WWF cartoon characters. There would be no Helmetless Fred, the hardheaded kook who slammed his shaved skull into the turf to psych up before every play. No

Double-Duty Johnson, the groupie hound who was late to every game with a knowing grin on his face. No Enduro, man of endless capacity whose only exploitable weakness was a ticklish rib. These players were culled from every minor league, and from the practice squads of NFL rosters. There were 14 former NFL first-round picks, and even a Heisman Trophy winner, Rashaan Salaam, who went to the Memphis Maniax. Mike Keller, the league's vice president of football operations, said that the worst team in the XFL "could beat the hell out of a CFL team. And our worst team could beat the best college team. Our best team would be able to compete with the lower twenty percent of the NFL." It was a misguided statement, but there was an element of truth to it. Nearly every one of the players had either played in the NFL or been a part of a major college program.

These weren't schlubs. And they weren't *Survivor* rejects, either, hoping to cash in with a guest appearance on *E!*. In our culture of being instead of doing, this XFL was something of a reversal. *Survivor* contestants were famous for simply existing, like child monarchs, winning cash the size of a mountain for deeds the level of a ditch. The XFL guys fell somewhere between the two ills, fame and wealth. The XFL players weren't getting rich but they had a salary, and a pretty good one for a few months' work. Like a scarred boxer who gets his head into a fight by getting it smacked around, each had endured this all before, for years, though most of them outside of view.

No one ever sees what happens to the college football star who disappears. That's just it: He disappears, left to fend for himself—no one to buy him a car, slip him untraceable sums, take his exams. Where does he go? And what does he become, robbed forever of the special status that cloaked his deficiencies? The men who populated the XFL were the disappeared. Though many of them still found themselves locked in arrested development— absent from appointments, unwittingly rude, rich with back-row gags—the signs of a certain kind of failure were there. They squinted at the dying light of their football careers and, while resolving to keep one scrunched-up eye on that sliver, trained the other on the future's questionable prospects. This game couldn't keep them on the dole for long. And what else had they been trained to do?

They were nobodies, and their stories multiplied and overlapped in such a way as to become typical and mundane. Welcome to the desensitized zone. Some guys played a few games in the NFL before being waived. Other guys bounced from one NFL practice squad to the next without seeing any real action, kept around in case of injury to the real stars. Still others went high in the NFL draft only to crash and burn, ill equipped to handle the very real pressures of the pros, so different from the unpaid existence of college sports, where "job competition" has as much real-world meaning as "work-study."

No matter the level, the football preparations looked the same. Down in the Sam Boyd locker room, the Outlaws got their bodies into it. Some guys stretched. Some guys sat in the trainer's room waiting for a tape job. And plenty of guys swallowed pills. Percocet to numb the coming pain, speed for revving up, inhalers filled with any number of concoctions for general eye-popping effect. "And they didn't have asthma," one Outlaw would say later. "There were plenty of guys popping a handfull of pills—five or six at a time—into their mouths thirty minutes before the game." Where were NBC's all-access cameras? Not capturing this for the folks at home who had been pledged complete coverage. This helped explain the "technical difficulty" on the November 2000 teleconference, as Ebersol and McMahon didn't mind averting their eyes from anything that would prompt these guys to impersonate the wrecking ball in the TV ad. XFL players taking performance-enhancing drugs? No way. Yes, and Barry Bonds and Mark McGwire subsisted on meat and potatoes.

The cameras missed Rod Smart, too, as he stripped buck naked and slipped into his brand-new jersey. That's all he wore, the jersey and a pair of sneakers, filled with pride in the words scrawled across his shoulder blades. To celebrate, he climbed his locker stall, slung his legs through the top of it, and hung upside down. He hollered like a beast, his unit dangling toward the floor. A few teammates yelled at him. Others ignored him. They had seen Smart's act before. This was how he got jacked up just for practice. Later, he put his jockstrap on backward and asked the trainer to tape his groin, making a fool of himself to offset the tension in the locker room. At least that's what everyone figured, since Smart didn't lend himself to easy examination.

They all had their pregame routines. Defensive end Kelvin Kinney sang in falsetto, much too loudly, unable to hear the terrible noise he made beneath a pair of headphones. "I know that you're in a better place," he screamed off-key. "I wish that I could see your face." He was a ripped specimen with a shaved head shaped like a bullet. Kinney was the varsity player come down to teach the JV scrubs a thing or two, the kid who professed to care less than the next, though his heart wouldn't hear of it. Kinney had played six years in the NFL for the Redskins, the Raiders, and the Lions. He had fresh memories of chasing down the Jim Browns of his era. It wasn't lack of skill or desire that knocked him out of the NFL, but something painfully beyond his control.

The Outlaws were about ready to take the field, leaving behind their lair, which was ripe with the mentholated stench of Bengay. Before the team walked onto the field, behemoth guard Pat Kesi ran to the bathroom and heaved his pregame meal into a toilet. The locker room filled with the putrid smell of half-digested food, causing several teammates to spit up involuntarily.

The teams ejected from the locker rooms beneath the LCD screen. Fireworks spouted up and out, overlapping in final salute and finishing in a smoky "X" that dissipated in the wind, with the knife-edged Frenchman Mountain hanging like a living room oil in the great desert beyond. Quarterback Ryan Clement led the way for the Outlaws, who played to the roar of the crowd, engaging in the customary palms-heavenward supplicating mock-flight motion of the arms. They wore black and gold, the fabric of their jerseys constructed with heavy outer stitching, like something from Karl Kani instead of Starter or Champion.

Jesse Ventura was in the broadcast booth, joined by play-by-play man Matt Vasgersian, a nasal-voiced 33-year-old with dark, bristling hair. Vasgersian, who had four years experience calling games for the Milwaukee Brewers, was the best NBC could get, since most experienced play-by-play men were wary of attaching themselves to Vince McMahon. Vasgersian deliberated over the XFL job for the same reason, wondering whether it would do more harm than good to his career. He was no WWF shill. But for this job he might have to be. When Ebersol hinted at work with NBC down the road, Vasgersian bit.

NBC would air two games each week, one national Saturday-night game with a backup regional telecast running simultaneously. McMahon inked deals with the overair network UPN and the cable channel TNN to air the league's remaining two weekly games on Sunday afternoons.

Jerry Lawler would handle color-commentary duties on NBC's secondary game. Lawler was well known in wrestling circles, having spent thirty years in the business, the last decade in the employ of Vince McMahon. At fifty-one, he still wrestled occasionally. He was known as "The King," and he entered the ring wearing a crown, albeit one that looked like it came with a side of fries. A native of Memphis, Tennessee, Lawler had gained national fame in 1982 in a bizarre set piece with comedian Andy Kaufman, who had been wrestling women for a few years. Kaufman's protracted wrestling "comedy" was little understood at the time, least of all by earnest tough guy Lawler, who became an easy target for Kaufman's belittling taunts directed at southerners. Lawler pile-drove Kaufman during a match, slapped him out of his chair on *Late Night with David Letterman,* and threw flaming paper in his face in the stands of an arena. Lawler was a perfect foil for Kaufman. And though no one knew it at the time, Kaufman and Lawler were in cahoots all along. The episode served both men well—Kaufman puzzled the intelligentsia, while Lawler solidified his hero status in Memphis.

Lawler did have a colorful history, but the real draw in the announcer's booth, of course, was Jesse Ventura. Unlike Dennis Miller, Ventura came to his announcing job with a résumé. After his formative broadcasting years in the WWF, Ventura had spent two seasons as a radio analyst for the Tampa Bay Buccaneers and another with the Minnesota Vikings radio team. He also hosted a Minneapolis sports-radio talk show and volunteered as an assistant football coach at a high school in Minnesota. Ventura had played football in the mid-1970s for North Hennepin Community College, in his hometown of Brooklyn Park, Minnesota. He wasn't very good; yet he would pull off his helmet after every tackle and wave to the crowd. This stunt was more in line with the reasoning that landed him the XFL job.

As governor, Ventura called legislators "gutless cowards." When he met with the Dalai Lama, he asked him if he'd ever seen *Caddyshack. Playboy* published an interview in which the governor advocated legalizing prostitution, blasted the obese by saying they "can't push back from the table," and said that organized religion was "a sham and a crutch for weak-minded people who need strength in numbers." Ventura's in-state approval rating hovered around 70 percent. This was why Ebersol and McMahon wanted him, for his ever oscillating lower jaw—and the way his forthright approach connected with the public. They didn't bring in Ventura to diagram plays on the Telestrator. They brought him in to be Jesse, the announcer who riled fans on WWF telecasts in the 1980s by continually saying, "The pleasure is all yours."

Matt Vasgersian was meant to hold the telecast together. His first on-air task involved a simple setup—introducing the evening's go-to guy, the coach of the New York/New Jersey Hitmen. Rusty Tillman looked like an old-time football coach, with a beer gut, rosy cheeks, and a tight white flattop. He had spent almost his entire life in the game, the last two decades as an assistant coach in the NFL, and had a reputation for wearing his emotions for public viewing. He threw water bottles, kicked trash cans, and went nose to nose with players in order to motivate. Tillman was pushing fifty, and he wanted to be a head coach in the NFL. Job offers had never come. As he watched peers pass him by on the way to the next level, Tillman began to realize what was holding him back.

"In football you get labeled," Tillman said. "And it's real tough to change the image that is created. I had this image of a wild man. And it really wasn't me anymore. As you grow up, you learn how to channel your energy in a different way. The XFL was a chance for me to prove I could be a head coach in the NFL." Two things had to happen—the Hitmen had to win, and Tillman had to carry himself with the dignity befitting a governor.

There was just one problem. Weeks before the first XFL game, the league staged a few scrimmages in Orlando, dry runs for both the players and the broadcast crew. Tillman knew it was only a practice, not for broadcast, so he had a little fun—he threw water bottles, kicked trash cans, went nose to nose with his players. He was his old self. Ebersol and McMahon loved what they saw. Without bona fide star players in the XFL, this was exactly what they needed: someone with a little verve whose colorful antics would keep viewers entertained. "At the rehearsal game, the best single personality was Rusty Tillman," said NBC's Ken Schanzer. "The one thing we were certain of on Night One was that Rusty was gonna give us a great game. He was gonna be miked. We were gonna go to him all the time." Ebersol told Tillman he was going to be "the first star of the XFL." What that meant wasn't clearly defined. Ebersol and Schanzer told Tillman to be himself. From what they had seen in Orlando, that was all they would need.

As Vasgersian introduced Tillman to a national audience, the camera depicted the coach pacing the sidelines before the game's first play, squeezing play charts in his fist. "He's fiery, he's animated," Vasgersian said. "At times you think he's completely wacked out of his mind." Tillman responded by tripping over a camera cord.

Before the game's first play from scrimmage, the Las Vegas offense huddled around quarterback Ryan Clement, the 284th pick in the XFL draft. This was a far cry from the future that everyone had mapped out for him. Clement had been a prodigy, starting for Denver's Mullen High School varsity as a fourteen-year-old freshman. He piled up huge numbers throughout his prep career. By the time he finished high school, Clement had thrown for 9,273 yards (third all-time in the history of U.S. high school quarterbacking). He went on to start at quarterback for football powerhouse University of Miami. He was headed to the NFL.

The microphone imbedded in Clement's jersey picked up his call for the first play, "Trey left ninety-seven slant. On one." The Outlaws broke the huddle and hunched over the line of scrimmage. On the screen was something other than the stock football shot. The camera hung in the air above the field, behind Clement as he scanned the defensive scheme. It practically peeked over his shoulder as he took the snap. This angle, the single most striking thing in the XFL telecast, was a technology called Skycam, or as the league rechristened it, XCam. It came courtesy of John Gonzalez, the director of the telecast and an Emmy-winning NBC veteran. Gonzalez was also in charge of twenty-six microphones and twenty-seven cameras, each more than any network had used in any Super Bowl.

Clement took the snap and scampered through the line to his right, gaining a handful of yards before taking a hit and landing hard on his right shoulder. The play caused Ventura to launch into XFL salesmanship. "And you notice right away there's no sliding in the XFL," he said, the saliva congealing at the back of his throat. "Our quarterbacks get treated like fullbacks. They're required to play the game here."

This was an allusion to the NFL's policy of preventing defenders from tackling quarterbacks who willingly slid to the turf at the end of a run. It did look ridiculous when a quarterback engaged in a baseball slide to avoid punishment in a game that was predicated on one's ability to survive it. The slide rule may have been dainty, but it developed over a number of years during which the NFL lost quarterbacks to cheap shots, which diluted the overall quality of the product. (With backup quarterbacks, teams had trouble scoring.) Ventura had a point here, but he was selling the XFL, not describing it. Like all announcers, he wore an earpiece, and into that earpiece Vince McMahon barked orders and fed Ventura lines. This was how McMahon ran WWF telecasts.

Clement picked himself up off the ground and walked toward the huddle with a cameraman walking right beside him on the field of play, casting a shadow on his uniform. John Gonzalez switched to a wider shot of the field, which included the image of a cameraman in black clothing and a black hockey helmet, darting toward the sidelines. He looked like a streaker from the stands. Vasgersian called him "Bubba Cam."

A radio report from a disembodied voice transmitted over the telecast— "Solo right three-twenty-four Dakota"—and Clement held his hands over the earholes in his helmet to hear. Vasgersian chimed in. "What you're listening to is the sound of coach-to-quarterback communication." Gonzalez tapped in to the play-calling that came from Vince Alcalde—the Outlaws' offensive coordinator who sat up in the booth above the field—and transmitted through the sound system in Ryan Clement's helmet. That was great, but what did "Solo right three-twenty-four Dakota" mean? Only a former player could unravel the code; to the average fan it was altogether meaningless. Although neither announcer offered an explanation, the radio report did bring fans further inside the game, providing an inkling of the complexity of the quarterback's position. The crowd was yelling, Clement was catching his breath from the last play, his shoulder was burning, his teammates were looking to him for guidance, and with his hands over the earholes of his helmet, he was trying to decipher Alcalde's squawk.

The on-field cameraman, Bubba Cam, stuck his lens into the huddle over Clement's shoulder as the quarterback recited the next play to his teammates. This was a TV first—the camera was in the huddle. This was sacred ground equaled only by the pitcher's mound. Fans have always wondered what goes on in the huddle between plays. There was the story from Super Bowl XXIII, when Joe Montana, in the middle of the winning drive as time ran off the clock, pointed to the Joe Robbie Stadium stands and exclaimed to his 49er teammates, "That's John Candy!" There were no comments like that in this huddle, though if Clement had looked up to the stands, he could have seen David Spade.

Clement dished the ball to Rod Smart, a compact tailback who didn't reach his five-foot-nine-inch listing in the team media guide. Smart rushed for a first down. He trudged back to the huddle, where his introduction to prime time awaited. "What's that on the back of his jersey?" Vasgersian asked the governor in a coy tone that betrayed rehearsals.

"I'm not sure," Ventura said, his tone projecting an image of inquisitive fingertip touching pointed chin. "Ya know, they can put any name they want on the back of their jersey. So you got nicknames. You got everything out there."

As further chance for self-expression in his new league, McMahon decreed that players could place anything they chose in the name slot on the backs of their jerseys—a phrase, a nickname, haiku—anything, as long as it fit the space.

"I know you got nicknames," Vasgersian retorted, "but that seems to me a phrase." This was so clearly a setup. The two announcers sounded like parents talking to a three-year-old in overenunciated syllables.

Smart wandered around the far side of the huddle, where the on-field camera closed in on the back of his jersey. There in huge letters was his personalized nameplate: HE HATE ME.

"He hate me?" asked Ventura.

"He hate me," confirmed Vasgersian, who was equipped with his own metastreetwise take. "Don't be a playa hata?"

"Who hates him?"

"Everybody, apparently."

"Who?"

"He."

"Oh, he."

The two announcers did their best to share the audience's surprise at

Smart's nickname. This was the way of star building, not so disconnected from the "brand building" that McMahon always stressed with the regularity of a parent potty-training a toddler. Following the acknowledgment of his nickname, as if on cue, Smart got the ball again. This was how NBC edited the Olympics. The intro, the big buildup, the stunning performance, the emotional payoff, the Wheaties box. This was Smart's chance. He took the handoff from Clement, and before he could take a single step, a New York defender wrapped up his ankles and planted him four yards behind the line of scrimmage.

Time for a more predictable component of the broadcast.

The Las Vegas cheerleaders hopped and twirled on the sidelines like pogo sticks. All ethnic bases were conspicuously covered, like in an ABC cop drama. The women jogged from the grass to their metallic perch that hung on the edge of the stands. They ran up a set of stairs, with the camera following them like something out of www.upskirts.com. This was no different from the NFL, which televised abundant flesh minus commentary, as if sneaking it in without verbal acknowledgment absolved involvement in the skin trade. Columnists had criticized McMahon for his talk of cheerleaders, but the XFL was merely taking a stab at forthrightness. Although the chief of XFL cheerleading undercut one of the league's very tenets, the availability of its women.

Jay Howarth, at thirty-eight, was perfect for the job. "All I do in my life comes from first being a cheerleader," she had once said. She had cheered for the Denver Broncos and San Francisco 49ers, and she selected the women who represented the XFL based on "their sporting ambitions to be champions." Howarth was fiercely loyal to her cheerleaders, and she let it be known that she wouldn't expose them to an agenda-driven press, which had been coalescing against the new league. "I will not have my girls' words be mangled," she griped one day. "I will not have my girls misquoted."

The XFL cheerleaders embarrassed themselves just fine on their own. During a CNN segment that aired a week before kickoff and featured just that type of agenda-driven unwashed magazine writer for a talking head, a league cheerleader summed up the cultural importance of her peers thus: "I think the XFL cheerleaders are going to start a new stereotype." Or perpetuate an old one. A few weeks before the league's first game, the Outlaws pink-slipped one of their cheerleaders, who it turned out worked as . . . a working girl.

Play continued on the field, and while the NBC crew recovered from Rod Smart's missed opportunity, Vasgersian milked Ryan Clement's Everyman desire: "Ryan Clement's the kinda guy that would play football, according to his coach, for a cup a coffee." To prove this, the screen wiped to a previously recorded shot of Clement in the Las Vegas locker room. Beside him was the blond bob of cheerleader Crystal Aldershof. She looked Clement up and down with moist, parted lips. "Quarterback Ryan Clement knows how to score," Aldershof said. "Especially against an eight-man front," Clement retorted, with a stiffness that revealed many takes. He nervously passed an XFL football from one hand to the other, as though talking to a woman for the very first time. He handled the football more adeptly than he did the metaphor. "When the free safety slides over and my receiver gets a nice, free release, which causes the defense to collapse, therefore allowing us to penetrate for the touchdown." Aldershof and Clement grinned at each other like four A.M. losers, the only ones left at the bar, the point finally realized.

The word "penetrate" hung in the air as the telecast returned to an on-field shot. It wasn't the sexual innuendo that was so galling; the allusion was so clunky that it compounded the lack of humor. The segment was worse than the flattest late-1980s *SNL* skit. The discomfort protracted as neither announcer remarked on the segment, a sulfur whiff left unacknowledged. The only thing roughly resembling commentary hung wordlessly in the top right corner of the screen. It was NBC's logo, a peacock, barely discernible underneath a large "X."

There were several such segments throughout the telecast. This was McMahon's attempt to interject the WWF's highly successful sexual play. It all came courtesy of the fertile mind of Shane McMahon, Vince's son, who longed to make his mark on the XFL. There was a better sketch, if NBC really wanted to knock down a few walls. One of the Outlaw cheerleaders, a redhead who went by the name of Charidy LaFontaine, was the lead dancer in Midnight Fantasy, the topless review at the Luxor hotel and casino. It would have made for good TV. LaFontaine put on clothes to be an XFL cheerleader. NBC wasn't interested, though John Gonzalez cut to a shot of

LaFontaine dancing in the stands, while a drunk perv in a seat behind her howled like a lone desert species.

After the Outlaws kicked a field goal, roving reporter Fred Roggin located Rod Smart on the Vegas sideline. "All right, here with Rod Smart," Roggin said, his hand placed firmly on Smart's jersey in the proprietary manner of the on-field interviewer. Smart promptly trotted away and into a team huddle. Roggin chugged after him, the camera following in dead air. "Rod has HE HATE ME on the back of his jersey," Roggin continued, grabbing a handful of Smart's jersey and tearing him away from the strategy session. "Rod, why do you have HE HATE ME on your jersey?"

Smart took cool account of Roggin, apparently prepared for his moment. "'Cause they hate me," Smart declared, pointing across the field at the New York bench. "Look how they looking at me."

"They hate him, Body," said Vasgersian, his voice oozing with inflammatory joy.

"I'm waiting for the first one that has HE LIKES ME," retorted the governor, concluding the repartee with a thud.

On the opposite sideline, reporter Mike Adamle approached the prefab star of the night, Rusty Tillman. Adamle wanted the coach's insight to the game so far. This was Tillman's first chance at delivering on his promising practice run in Orlando. "We just gotta play better special teams," Tillman snarled. Then he stalked away from the microphone as though there was nothing for which he held greater derision.

Later, the camera found Tillman nervously shuffling through his crib sheets, lifting his head long enough to look at the field for a second at a time. "What do we got?" he yelled at an assistant, asking for an update on the game. "Second down? And what? Call time-out!" He looked frazzled, overwhelmed by the task of commanding an entire army for the first time. It was clear that he didn't have the head space to be the star of a TV show. He was trying to win a football game.

New York did very little with the ball on its first possessions, giving its punter a workout. During one runback, an official tossed the first flag of the game. The referees wore microphones, too, and, for the first time ever, viewers gained access to their huddle:

"Twenty-nine, personal foul."

"So we're gonna go . . . We're gonna go."

"From—"

"We inside the thirty? We're inside the twenty-eight, so we're gonna go to the fourteen . . . Personal foul?"

"Yes, they do."

"Gonna be personal foul, first and ten."

"Number twenty-nine."

"Continuing action, right?"

Fans had finally heard the refs, who were dimmer than anyone could have imagined. It was not unlike the time when the absent-minded ref at a University of Michigan game forgot to close his microphone after announcing a call. Following several exhalations, 110,000 fans were treated to the disclosure that "I don't know what the hell's going on out here."

Play continued and several microphones picked up the muffled sound of huffing and puffing. "Lot of heavy breathing out there," Vasgersian said. "Sounds like a prank call." This was the kind of free hand that McMahon had hoped his announcers would bring to the proceedings. Vasgersian was coming through. But when the camera moved in for an extended shot of the Outlaws cheerleaders jiggling to a Beastie Boys song, he reached a crossroads. John Gonzalez held on to the image of the women bouncing up and down and rubbing against one another. The picture dominated the screen for a whopping fifteen seconds. Until this point, Vasgersian had been the perfect shill for McMahon. But as the cheerleaders bounced away, he couldn't think of the right thing to say. With the telecast hanging on dead air, McMahon raged in Vasgersian's earpiece. "Say something!" he demanded. Finally, Vasgersian chimed in. "I feel uncomfortable," he said. "Man alive! Allrighty then. Those suits are something else." He sounded like a fraternity pledge paddled into submission.

Clement drove the Outlaws near New York's twenty-yard-line. It was third down when he threw a pass over the middle. The ball slammed off a pair of New York shoulder pads and popped into the air, coming to rest in the hands of tight end Rickey Brady at the back of the end zone. It was the Outlaws' first touchdown, and the home crowd erupted. Vasgersian leveled his own assessment. "Sloppy seconds!" he yelled, regaining the paycheck spirit.

The Outlaws lined up to run a play from scrimmage. This was another component of *the XFL difference*. As Dick Butkus had said, "During the extra-point kick in the NFL, you can get up and go to the bathroom." In the XFL, teams had to convert the extra point on a play from the two-yard line. Rickey Brady dropped an easy pass in the end zone, and microphones picked up his apology to Clement.

Gonzalez returned to the New York sidelines and a shot of the designated star. Rusty Tillman was coaching. There were no water bottles flying around. He crouched in front of his defensive unit. "Can you tell when he's audibling?" he asked, referring to Clement. "I can tell from the sidelines. When he audibles, I want you to go to two. 'Cause he's audibling most of the time to quick passes. You're showing it too early." This was the authentic take, instruction on the fly. It was good stuff, but it could have used some dressing, perhaps an announcer with the ability to point out Clement's audibles as they happened. There was raw material here, but it wasn't being fully exploited.

No, NBC was more interested in turning the lens on David Spade, who sat smugly in the crowd in a Foghat shirt and a baseball hat pushing his latest movie, *Joe Dirt*. This was an attempt to legitimize the XFL effort—if David Spade thought the game was worth not only watching but *attending*, well, then the thirteen-year-olds should be compelled to stay tuned. It must be pointed out that not only had Spade drawn an NBC paycheck for a dozen years (first with *SNL*, then with *Just Shoot Me*), but he was no stranger to the Vegas tables, having grown up in nearby Phoenix. This was shabby cross-purposing. It wasn't Jack sitting courtside at the Lakers, and it did little to legitimize the game. The real story was playing out on the field.

New York quarterback Charlie Puleri dropped back to pass, and the ball slipped off the back of his hand. It was a glaring signal of ineptitude. This kind of play was hardly a surprise, given that the league had afforded teams just one month to practice before the first game—a minuscule amount of time, considering the two-month training camps that experienced NFL teams endured every summer. Rusty Tillman had hired his offensive coordinator on December 26, six days before training camp.

New York prepared to punt, giving fans a chance to see more of the XFL difference. With no fair catch, there was about to be some ass whipping at the expense of a minimum-wager. Vegas wideout Mike Furrey had volunteered for danger duty, if the XFL wrecking-ball ad was to be believed. Furrey caught the punt, and two Hitmen immediately clobbered him. The tackle didn't generate the loudest sound of the play. That honor belonged to an article of yellow laundry that arced over the rolling pile of bodies. A ref whistled New York for violating the five-yard halo surrounding the kick receiver. The penalty dashed the hopes of the league's wrecking-ball commercial. The protective halo, which the NFL used and with which McMahon had taunted the NFL, was an XFL rule that hadn't made the headlines. What about all the talk of pantywaists and sissies playing in that other league? The halo rule undercut the whole point of the wrecking ball. What was the purpose of licensing headhunting if you retained rules that protected the intended?

Rod Smart grabbed a screen pass from Clement and rumbled fifty yards to the New York twenty-one-yard line. "HE HATE ME with the biggest gain of the night so far," Ventura yelled, offering this up as analysis. Fred Roggin grabbed Smart on the sideline chalk, using the fifty-yard play as another chance to polish the star. "HE HATE ME," Roggin said. "Talk about the play." It was a bone-chilling query along the lines of "How do you feel?," and the subject reacted accordingly. Smart looked up at the game clock, then, without a word or a glance at his beleaguered inquisitor, he sprinted back onto the field. Roggin was left in a cloud, and Vasgersian could be heard giggling at his colleague's embarrasing misfortune.

Vegas managed another field goal to go up 12–0. The screen then filled with the threatening image of scar-browed "Stone Cold" Steve Austin, the WWF wrestler. He wore a camouflage jacket and cap, identifying with his fans in the tree blinds. At first Austin's eyes didn't meet the camera. He wagged his head back and forth, his eyes focused on the floor. Something was going to happen, something hostile. When Austin lifted his head to the lens, he was ready for menace, and his voice was laced with hatred. "I hear the guy that runs the NFL, Paul Tagliabue, said that the XFL was a nonissue." Austin sneered, peering into the camera as though someone had just keyed his F150. "A nonissue? Hell, I think that's an insult to football fans everywhere, and an insult to men knocking heads on the football field. You know, Mr. Tagliabue, you might be careful, or that nonissue just might bite you on your ass." Austin paused for effect as the word "ass" hissed off his tongue. "And that's the bottom line. 'Cause Stone Cold said so." His eyes honed to coal-black points. Here again, McMahon took advantage of fans' awareness of his wrestlers, though unless they strapped on the pads, it was difficult to see just what they meant to the XFL.

This was a strange way of cross-marketing the brands. Doubtless there were those in the audience who cheered the effrontery, but the majority of viewers had to wonder at the insult. To be a potential fan of the XFL was to be a football fan already, which meant holding some affection for the NFL, the best of all football leagues. Disparaging the NFL before a fan base that had grown up on the league was like Krushchev bagging on Stalin. The public may have agreed in principle, but in the end it was a loser's tactic.

Camera operators ran in and out of the picture like drunks on a dare. Meantime, Fred Roggin corralled Rod Smart again and asked him about the team's inability to score touchdowns in the red zone. "Well, they givin' us different looks," said Smart. "So we're gonna have to just come in red zone as a team and make something happen. This is the second time it happened. But next time we're gonna make something happen." Asking football players to extemporize is like discussing foreign relations with an actor. Either you get silence or daftness as they display the narrowness of their talent.

As the game drew toward halftime and New York persisted in anemia, Ventura took the opportunity to criticize Tillman's coaching. "I wonder what Tillman's plan is. He must want to wear out Vegas's offense." This also served as a knock on the coach's TV performance, as Ebersol, McMahon, Schanzer, and the rest were at a loss to explain his lack of sparks. Vasgersian attempted to resurrect Tillman's profile, practically urging him on: "Rusty Tillman is one of the most animated coaches in the XFL." Tillman wrinkled his nose.

Without Tillman carrying his expected weight, Ventura had nothing to play off of. So he filled his time by continuing to sell the league.

"Great thing about the XFL is we have freedom of speech," he said.

And later. "That's the great thing about these players. They've given up careers to come and play." (What careers those were was never revealed.)

It was the pro-wrestling tone that viewers knew to be disingenuous, even if it came from a governor. With no villains or charmers in the XFL, the bluster latched on to the only target it could find—the telecast itself. That became the thing the viewers had to buy.

Ryan Clement hit wideout Nakia Jenkins on a twenty-seven-yard slant, splitting three defensive backs on a perfectly timed throw. Jenkins cruised into the end zone for a touchdown. Clement leaped into the air. After all the years of being down, Clement felt vindication. He nearly busted out in tears, but he quelled his emotions by hustling down to the end zone and giving the New York defensive backs an earful. "All day long," he yelled in an earhole. "All day long."

With three minutes left in the first half, Vegas led 19–0, and Rusty Tillman remained too busy with his ailing team to be a TV personality. Halftime approached, and with it Tillman's chance at redemption via a speech that would both rouse the troops and hold the TV audience. "We'll be there to see it," said Ventura, as though pushing pork through the statehouse. " 'Cause in the XFL we go into the locker room." It sounded like he was giving directions to a foreign tourist.

The telecast reached halftime. Burger King had purchased exclusive rights to the all-access halftime camera, and it was the fast-food logo that plastered over initial shots of . . . players eating orange slices. "Let's get it done," Tillman yelled to his team in the locker room. "They're not beating us. We're beating ourselves. Do what you're supposed to do." In the first instant of the halftime cam, viewers learned that in private, coaches offered the same clichés they spewed in public. Tillman broke out the blackboard and began diagramming plays.

In the Vegas locker room, cameras revealed . . . players listening to music on headphones. It was hard to see the "coveted demo" getting fully charged by this. The halftime cam had the feel of a documentary, a delicate genre as yet unplumbed by the WWF/WB fanbase.

Not that there wasn't plenty of action in the locker rooms. It just wasn't the kind that NBC preferred to put out there. There were several players with their heads draped in towels, taking deep breaths. They were getting jacked. "Guys were snorting these little capsules. Everybody passed it around," one Outlaw would say later. "You just break it and then sniff it all in. It makes you feel like Superman."

Instead of hitting the medicine cabinet, NBC cut to the chalkboard, where Tillman continued his exhortations, bordering on plaintive whines. Nineteen points down and Tillman was pleading with his troops? This certainly wasn't the Tillman of epic tantrums. This was the Tillman who wanted to show NFL general managers that he could connect with his players. He was trying out. This was all X's and O's. If it had been Vince Lombardi, every letter would have carried the weight of an MLK sermon. But listening in on the secrets of unknowns isn't so interesting.

"Well, the locker room at halftime," said Vasgersian, in a voice that betrayed his underwhelming reaction to the centerpiece. "Both of them a little more mellow than we thought." Rather than bolster the content and lend meaning to what he had seen, Vasgersian opted for the fast-food employee's response: I just work here. Ventura tried a little harder. "We thought we'd get the explosion outta Tillman. Well, he's coaching tonight instead of yellin'."

There wasn't much to work with, so John Gonzalez cut to a shot of a dozen guys in yellow sweatshirts yelling incoherently into the microphone clutched by an unidentified female crowd reporter. "There's actually more animation there than in that New York locker room," Vasgersian said, again telling it like it was but certainly not flattering the content. Ventura smiled ruefully into the camera. "It better change, or he'll be down forty to nothing by the end of the game," the governor said, referring to Tillman. "But ya know what I love? People are having fun. That's what football's all about— fun and heart." Fun and heart? What was this, the Pinewood Derby?

By the opening of the second half, the sun had disappeared in Vegas, and the bright stadium lights pooled on the players' helmets. Tillman's halftime adjustments had no immediate effect, and minutes into the fourth quarter, the score remained 19–0. The sideline camera tried once more with Rusty Tillman. He was being pantsed on national TV, and the camera moved in on his nose. "Get outta my way," he yelled into the lens. "Get outta my way!"

New York was getting bageled, so NBC played its only card and switched to the secondary game, the Chicago Enforcers visiting the Orlando Rage. Surrounded by cheerleaders dancing in the Citrus Bowl booth, Jerry Lawler greeted the prime-time-network audience. It wasn't long before he displayed the qualities that had kept him in wrestling checks for three decades. "I love the XFL, I love America," he squealed over a shot of cheerleaders between plays. "It's the land of milk and honeys."

There was more:

"I got a fifteen-yard penalty for roughing the cheerleaders during the break."

"I like to use the terms 'wide receiver' and 'tight end' around cheerleaders."

"They had backfields in motion all night."

The nonsense detracted from what was a very close game that saw the home team come out on top. Sideline reporter Jonathan Coachman, another WWF shill, approached Orlando coach Galen Hall. But Hall, apparently of the Tillman school, turned his back and walked in the opposite direction. Had anyone read their McMahon manual of Cooperation and Personality?

The clock stopped with one second remaining in the game, and fireworks exploded at the end of the Citrus Bowl. "We have premature pyrotechnics," said Lawler's broadcast partner, Jim Ross. Lawler couldn't resist. "Story of my life," he said, and the audience needn't have summoned much imagination to believe him.

4

XFL RULES!

IN AN INTERVIEW TENT behind Sam Boyd Stadium, Vince McMahon made a sizable miscalculation. He lorded over the proceedings, assuming his Mister McMahon WWF character as the only way he could suffer through the ignominy of availing himself to the reporters with whom he shared such strong mutual distaste. He issued a statement, then opened the floor to what was a very reluctant gallery. Rather than make any attempts to cultivate a media throng that was poised to blanket the country with its multipronged assessment of the XFL's first game, Mister McMahon huffed and puffed and tried to blow the tent down.

"Where are the questions?" he said, glowering. "There have to be some more questions." He glared at the reporters. "This is it? Somebody's got a question out there, doesn't he? Come on. Bring it. Bring it." The more he talked, the more he sounded like The Rock or Stone Cold.

McMahon had constructed his wrestling monolith without the approval of the mainstream press. In fact, he brought the WWF to power despite the media's best efforts. This press conference was a chance to sneer without recompense. What could the writers possibly do to him? McMahon's football creation had just aired on NBC in prime time before a packed house. The governor of Minnesota was his announcer. A guy wore "HE HATE ME" on his jersey. McMahon had succeeded in bringing his football vision to life. Yet he was more defiant than jubilant. "You're not going to write about it without asking *anything,* are you?"

Finally, a reporter lobbed a question, asking McMahon if he thought there had been enough sexual content during the game. "I like sex," said the boss man. "I mean, I've been married thirty-four years. My wife is here. Yes, I like sex. I don't think there's ever enough sex." The interview tent filled with the sound of furious scribbling. Chicka-chicka-chicka. This was just the type of comment that the morals watchers couldn't pass up. It was perfect fodder for people who didn't read to the jump page. But did it mean anything?

McMahon's comment was as calculated as all the rest he spat out when a situation ran by his rules. What he said mattered less than the way he said it. His game was all bluster, and his words were not meant for exact quotation. McMahon could never battle silkier speakers on their terms. His tactic had always been to ratchet the volume, sink the pitch, and intimidate with intonation. His swagger and the newspaperman's reaction to it were the kinds of things that fed his popularity. The critics failed to grasp this. They gulped his line about sex as they had all the others, with rabid little eyes, excited at the meal, unaware that on tonight's telecast and in tomorrow's paper they would only fan the flames.

"What you saw was an honest game tonight," McMahon said. "You heard honest commentary. We turned our cameras and microphones to our fans. The fans are a really big part of everything we do. You saw a lot of honesty out there, which you don't get in most other sports. I think the viewer experienced the game. Comments were made by coaches and players on the field. You could hear what they were saying. That was the first time you could ever experience that from a fan standpoint. We opened the game up to the fans. That's what it's all about. We'll continue to listen to the audience. That's what we're all about. We really could care less about the negative comments from the media. The fans here in Las Vegas looked like they had a good time. That's what it's all about."

Evidently it was all about the fans. Something said so many times, in such a routine monotone—could it possibly be true? And on whose side would The Fans ultimately sit? Lip service wouldn't do the trick.

Rusty Tillman also held a postgame press conference, standard procedure for a head coach. Reporters who had listened to the game's telecast asked Tillman about Jesse Ventura's disparaging remarks, since the coach hadn't heard them down on the sidelines. On the short end of a 19–0 blowout, Tillman had enough negative thoughts running through his head. Now this, the governor getting on his case. The coach looked spent. His face was flushed a beet red. He laughed off Ventura's comments and moved along to the next question.

Ebersol and McMahon had trumpeted their goal of a 4.5 rating as eminently attainable. When the Nielsens came in, their 4.5 seemed ridiculous. They got a 9.5.

In one single blow, the XFL was worthwhile programming, if not yet a legitimate challenger to the ratings gobbler of the NFL. The first-night rating earned 81 percent of ABC's *Monday Night Football* average for the 2000 season. The XFL beat the *MNF* average among an important group, men aged 18 to 34 (a 10.2 rating to a 9.5), and crushed ESPN's overall Sunday-night NFL coverage (7.2) by 25 percent. And there was heavy symbolism in another piece of information. The first weekend of XFL games aired against the NFL's Pro Bowl, the annual postseason all-star game from Hawaii. The Pro Bowl earned a 4.7. It was the lowest number in the seven years that ABC had been televising the event.

Up in Manhattan's GE Building, the centerpiece skyscraper that loomed over Rockefeller Center, NBC officials didn't embark on much of a celebration. "We were too busy getting the numbers out," said one NBC staffer. Game Two was only a few days away. And at WWF headquarters in Stamford, Connecticut, Vince McMahon knew his task didn't end after just one night. The numbers were huge, but there were eleven weeks to go.

At Legio's restaurant in Hawthorne, New Jersey, John Gonzalez ordered a plate of fettuccine bolognese and another of chicken milanese. Gonzalez felt like he had earned two dinners after having worked for ten months putting together the XFL telecast. He was proud of his staff and their ability to mesh such a complicated setup. It wasn't long before two teenage waiters walked up to his table, having spotted his XFL hat. They gushed with enthusiasm. They asked where they could buy an XFL hat. They wanted tickets. "The XFL rules," they said.

There's an old saying that you can eat only one steak at a time. With the XFL, NBC was after the whole cow. As Gonzalez sat back and ate from his two plates, he couldn't suppress a grin, believing he had "lightning in a bottle." He could only imagine what the future held. "It's like they wanted to touch me because I had an XFL hat on." And they belonged to the coveted demo. "This is it," thought Gonzalez. "This is gonna be huge."

For NBC, the XFL's performance worked wonders. The game registered an 86 percent increase over the network's Saturday-night movie franchise. And the XFL enabled NBC to withstand CBS's *Survivor* and hold on to the top spot among adults aged eighteen to forty-nine for the week. It was a huge upset win for NBC, which was supposed to crumble under *Survivor*'s assault. "I feel like Gloria Gaynor," Jeff Zucker told reporters. "I will survive."

When the papers came out, the general sentiment was less sanguine, as the oracles unleashed their judgments.

New York Post: "For however much longer the XFL lasts, there's really only one scorecard worth keeping. It's the one that notes all the sell-outs who lent their names, careers, reputations and consciences to this predictably unmitigated garbage."

Chicago Sun-Times: "I have just one request for any 12-to-34 male who thinks the XFL is the future of sport. Dude, may you rot in Vince McMahon hell."

The New York Times: "Like a blight that has crept from the low-rent fringes of cable to network prime time, the XFL mingles violence, voyeurism and even politics into one trashy Saturday night show that suggests how the lowest television culture is gaining mainstream respectability."

Los Angeles Times: "Now we know what the X in XFL stands for. Xceptionally Xaggerated Xpectations. Xtravagantly Xcruciating Xecution."

Even Hunter S. Thompson took a crack, writing on ESPN's website: "We are stuck with this fraud for a while. But it is a lot better than being in Prison."

Dick Ebersol didn't spend much time worrying about the criticism. He was a young staffer at ABC Sports when *Monday Night Football* debuted in 1970, and he watched the program prove all the early newspaper skeptics wrong. Ebersol did release a statement of his own after the XFL game, moving quickly to spin the debate, stressing the difficulty of broadcasting a 19–0 game. "The fan and viewer come first for us, and the fact that a vast and overwhelming majority of them stayed through a blowout is a testament to their interest and to the product. A blowout is every producer's greatest fear, but in this case the unique and original manner of producing the game obviously attracted a lot of very early fans." Ebersol and McMahon realized that a portion of the audience had come to the programming out of curiosity and, their appetite sated, many viewers might not return. Yet if they could retain half—just half—of the opening night's audience over the remainder of the season, their risky experiment would pay off.

Ken Schanzer won his bet with XFL president Basil DeVito, since the game's rating topped an 8. DeVito had to buy a Kentucky Derby futures ticket on the horse Monarchos for Schanzer, which he picked up at the Las Vegas Hilton. Schanzer may have won his bet with DeVito, but there was something about the whole situation that didn't sit right.

Schanzer lit a cigar using the faux-antique two-handed gas-lamp contraption that dominated his desk, which sat in a corner office on the fifteenth floor of the GE Building. He could see all the action down on the street below, but he was insulated from the noise. His cigar kept going out. Schanzer continually relit it, puffing and puffing. He pursed his lips and blew a series of smoke clouds toward the ceiling.

The XFL had exhausted its only chance to make a first impression, and Schanzer was worried. He realized the possible ramifications of televising a blowout, a horrible first game. As he had told Vince McMahon, Schanzer believed that the XFL needed one good half of play in order to hook viewers into watching the next. His thoughts turned sour. It couldn't have been worse, he thought.

Schanzer wasn't pulling skepticism from thin air, nor was he one to disparage a project that he had worked so hard to develop. He stared at the Nielsen numbers on his desk, and he knew he had a problem on his hands. When the Outlaws-Hitmen game opened at eight P.M., the national rating was 11.7. Within an hour, the number had dropped to 10.1, a loss of a couple million viewers. By the end of the game, the rating had fallen to 8. As the 9.5 proved, the XFL had greatly benefited from advance hype. By the end of its first telecast, the league's hype had worn off, and its audience had decreased by a third.

Two floors above Ken Schanzer, *Saturday Night Live* executive producer Lorne Michaels looked out at the world with an opposite view. Michaels was expecting big things. When the first XFL telecast ended, affiliates along the East Coast segued into their local newscasts, as they did every evening at eleven P.M. After a half hour of news, stations returned to network programming—*Saturday Night Live* for NBC, which aired a rerun of the March 18,

2000, show, hosted by The Rock. The rerun earned a 7.4 rating, excellent for a repeat showing, and in line with the show's recent numbers. After years of poor ratings and pitiable writing, *SNL* was recovering. Skits were sharper. Ratings were up. The show had regained not only its sense of humor but also a measure of relevance.

SNL's February 10 show was going to be the biggest, most hyped show of the year. Singer/actress Jennifer Lopez was set to host, and she was riding a two-pronged wave of unconscionable stardom. In the week leading up to the *SNL* appearance, Sony released the album *J. Lo*, a follow-up to her platinum debut; and *The Wedding Planner,* a romantic comedy starring Lopez and Matthew McConaughey, opened in theaters around the country. *SNL* was shaping up to be a perfectly timed bonanza for both the network and the singer/actress. Ads for the show ran continually during the week. And if Lorne Michaels needed any more help in getting people to watch his show, he would get it in the XFL. It would be nearly impossible for Game Two to duplicate the 9.5 rating of the first game, having sated the fickle and curious. But if the XFL's Game Two between Los Angeles and Chicago could register anything near that number, a sizable audience would be tempted to put away the remote control and stay on for *SNL*.

Ebersol, Schanzer, and Jeff Zucker had talked about this scenario countless times in devising the network's approach to the XFL. "Saturday night was a dead zone on network television," Schanzer said. "You were going on a night when you couldn't draw flies. If you could create a beachhead on Saturday night, you could create another night of television." How frustrating it was, the inability to infuse prime-time Saturday with any value. Ebersol quipped that "the real star programmer on Saturday nights across America is Blockbuster Video." This was one reason why the XFL wound up airing on Saturday night; also, NBC didn't have any room on weekend afternoons, which were booked solid with the NBA, golf, and tennis. By placing the XFL on Saturday night, NBC planned on drawing the young demographic that was liable to watch *SNL*. On the eve of the second XFL telecast, everything was aligned for a dominating night: from eight P.M., when the game began, to one A.M., when Jennifer Lopez's turn on *SNL* ended.

For Ebersol and Michaels, it was an old arrangement. Dick Ebersol was director of late night and weekend programming at NBC in 1974, when

Michaels approached him with the idea that became *SNL*. Within a year, the show sent their careers through the roof. Their relationship didn't share a similar trajectory. They bickered, and Michaels packed up in 1980, putting Ebersol in charge of the day-to-day operation of the show for five seasons. Michaels eventually returned to the program as executive producer, and by many accounts, the two men managed to patch things up.

Michaels was supportive of the XFL project when he first learned of it. He knew he could use a strong lead-in to his show. He had only one concern. Having spent more than twenty years in live TV, Michaels realized the inherent problems of the format. You couldn't control everything. And where a football game was concerned, that included the hour of its completion. What if the game went into overtime? What if it delayed the beginning of *SNL*? Ebersol took Michaels's concerns into consideration, though he wasn't going to let anything get in the way of his new football invention, the project that he likened to *SNL* itself. Besides, Ebersol had heard this argument before. In 1969, when then–NFL commissioner Pete Rozelle shopped *Monday Night Football* to the networks, he went to NBC. The network turned him down, largely because of the vocal objections of Johnny Carson, who insisted that nothing be given the ability to disrupt the starting time of his *Tonight Show*, the program that tucked millions of Americans into bed five nights a week. Thirty years later, *Monday Night Football* was the second-longest-running show in network TV history and Johnny Carson himself was tucked into bed. Ebersol wasn't about to duplicate NBC's previous gaffe. He took Michaels aside and personally guaranteed his old colleague that the XFL wouldn't delay *SNL*. With that, Michaels's anxiety was assuaged. And after the XFL's first ratings performance, he was happy to have the league as a lead-in.

Sitting behind his desk, Michaels anticipated the convergence. The XFL would provide a sizable preshow audience, and Jennifer Lopez's star power would take care of the rest. *SNL* would prove that it was back on top. The show's last original telecast, hosted by actress Mena Suvari, had scored an 8.3 rating on January 20. Michaels could only imagine the numbers that Lopez would pull.

He wasn't the only one looking forward to another week of the XFL.

5

NOT READY

FOR PRIME TIME

A HOT BREEZE TWIRLED a leftover beer cup across the parking lot at Sam Boyd Stadium, its massive scoreboard casting a long shadow against the blacktop. A separate football field stood across the lot from the stadium. The close-cropped lawn of neon green had been engineered out of the desert dust, with its farthest blades abutting rock and sand. The Las Vegas Outlaws sprinted through practice drills.

They had been on prime time. They blew out their first opponent. They knew the ratings. The whole experience left them feeling like kings. They were starting to believe the XFL hype.

Media outlets across the country had grown particularly interested in Rod Smart. The Outlaws' PR man, Trey FitzGerald, kept reaching into his pocket throughout practice, answering continuous calls on his cell phone. Everyone wanted to talk to HE HATE ME.

A mountainous Outlaw had to laugh. "Kelvin Kinney?" he asked. "Nah, I ain't Kelvin Kinney. See that dude way down the far end there about the five-yard line? That's Kelvin Kinney . . . I'm Rich." Kinney wasn't fooling anyone with his skeptical slit-shut eyes. His teeth marked him anywhere. They were a jumbled mess of Scrabble tiles, highlighted by a single hovering golden square, located in the upper reaches of his six-foot-seven, 270-pound frame.

Kinney was full of bravado. "Lennox Lewis?" he asked, and he bragged about his days as a Golden Gloves champ in West Virginia. "Lennox Lewis? Come on, I'll take Lennox Lewis." He set to shadow boxing, a jab, an upper cut. "I'll get a shot at him through the XFL. I could take him."

"You ever seen Lennox Lewis?" a teammate asked. "I stood next to him once, and he's a big dude."

Kinney wasn't impressed. "*I'm* a big dude, too."

A few players talked big about a new Denzel Washington movie that was supposed to start shooting around town in a few weeks. "I'll get my agent to get me in there as an extra," one guy bragged. "It's some kinda gangster movie. I'd make a good gangster. I'll get in there through the XFL." The league was going to provide them all with a free pass to some kind of stardom.

Fifty feet above the practice field, model airplanes looped through the sky. Buzzing from their miniature engines pierced the air. A couple of locals had parked their pickups in the brush beyond the practice-field fence and set up shop. There was nothing the Outlaws could do. It was public land.

Outlaws head coach Jim Criner looked up at the sky from beneath his panama hat and cursed the model airplanes. It was hard enough putting together a team of strangers in the short amount of time that Ebersol and McMahon had given him. Tack on the constant temptations of Vegas and the effect of the national spotlight, and the last thing Criner needed was something that made it hard for his players to hear his orders during practice.

Even without the distractions, Jim Criner was twisted tight as a cornrow. He kept his opinions of his players locked in a mind that changed with the wind. With a featureless face, Criner resembled a 1940s film-noir bagman who doesn't make it to the end of the picture, doubled under in a crack of smoke, pitched and rolled into the ditch to die. Given the choice of two coaches on opening night, NBC had a no-brainer in going constantly to Rusty Tillman. Slapstick wasn't Criner's game. And there were good reasons why he wanted to avoid the spotlight.

By the early 1970s, Criner had been an assistant coach at BYU, Cal, Utah, and UCLA. He landed his first head-coaching job in 1976, at Division IAA Boise State, then a few years later made it to the big-time of Division IA, with Iowa State. His career was on an upward swing, and Criner couldn't have foreseen what happened next. With a few games remaining in Iowa State's 1986 season, the NCAA accused Criner and his staff of providing loans, rent money, and cash payments to players and recruits. Iowa State fired Criner. He maintained his innocence, but was left with little chance of ever coaching in college again.

For five years, Criner fished. In a pond in Montana. And he missed football. In a few years, he was a head coach again, with the Scottish Claymores of NFL Europe, where he went on to win a championship. When the XFL called, Criner knew it was another step in recovering his fallen reputation.

The Outlaws disembarked from a plane in Memphis, Tennessee, where they would face the Memphis Maniax in the second game of the season. They ambled down the jetway and through the terminal toward baggage claim, past the food court, where a group of women was eating. They were the University of Texas women's track team, and they perked up at the sight of fifty muscled men. The Longhorns noticed the similar design of the Outlaws logo on a few jackets and asked a Vegas coach to point out Rod Smart. They huddled around Smart as he marched along with the team. "Rod, we don't hate you," they cooed in his ear. "We love you!" Smart returned the sentiment, escorting each and every woman through the concourse. He was starting to understand the power of NBC and HE HATE ME.

The Outlaws were scheduled to play on the Sunday-afternoon UPN telecast. The big NBC show, the ratings barometer, would operate some distance away in Los Angeles, where the hometown Xtreme were going to take on the Chicago Enforcers. It would be the first pro football game of any significance in Los Angeles since the Raiders and Rams left after the 1994 NFL season. How many people would care enough to watch? What percentage of the opening-night bonanza would return for a second viewing? How many had the XFL hooked?

Vince McMahon wasn't taking any chances. He had access to the same numbers as everyone else, and he knew that ratings for Game One had dropped steadily throughout the telecast. He also knew that WWF stock had slipped by more than 10 percent (even as the market remained steady) in the last week. As he was wont to do in the WWF, McMahon made a few changes on the fly, a demotion foremost among them. McMahon booted Matt Vasgersian to NBC's second telecast. He was accustomed to dealing with a certain type of announcer in the WWF, and Vasgersian's Game One refusals to sell himself like a vendor of street Rolexes had cost him the top job. McMahon brought in someone he could trust to inflate and exacerbate. Longtime McMahon lieutenant Jim Ross moved up from NBC's regional

telecast, bringing years of WWF experience (and a season as the Atlanta Falcons radio color commentator) to the national show, along with his ever
present ten-gallon hat.

The Rock stepped onto the field at the L.A. Coliseum, opening the telecast just as he had in the XFL premiere. He was once again ready to erupt,
looking slick and robust—fresh, perhaps, from a Burbank storyboard meeting. He emerged from a cloud of smoke and wasted no time in mocking the
"NFL suits" who fled Los Angeles six years before. The Rock had an ingenious plan for what the businessmen could do with the suitcases they had
packed back then. "Turn them sideways," he said, "and stick them straight up
your candy ass." When the fans cheered, it was less for The Rock's sentiment
than for his third-tier cuss. Some things still managed to arouse. If The
Rock's tirade was meant to forge solidarity with a populace that supposedly
felt abandoned by the NFL, McMahon had failed to realize that in this
sprawling basin of a million entertainment options, pro football had been an
afterthought for some time.

As McMahon picked a fight by proxy, the cameras picked up shots of a
structure that sat behind the east end zone. It was a hot tub enveloped in full
beach regalia. There was sand, a lifeguard stand, and a silk-screened mural
that looked like a Dick Dale album cover. Three women in bikinis splashed
around the tub. They weren't Xtreme cheerleaders, who were positioned
elsewhere in the stadium, wearing a fabric approximating chain mail. No,
this was a different group of women, and they looked of the rented variety.
These women, in fact, stripped at the Spearmint Rhino on East Olympic
Boulevard. For all the people who couldn't stand McMahon, this was ammunition. For everyone else, it was about time. There was a run on the beer
stands.

The game began as the week before. The Scramble. Ventura's booming
voice. But as the telecast entered its thirteenth minute, something new and
unexpected was added to the broadcast. The TV screen went black. Inside
the production truck parked in the stadium parking lot, John Gonzalez felt
his abdomen contract.

Gonzalez was the one man Dick Ebersol believed could execute the technical end of the XFL job. A twenty-five-year NBC veteran whom everyone called Gonzo, he had won two Emmy Awards, for his coverage of the Summer Olympics in 1988 and 1992. His real passion was football. And he was devastated by NBC's loss of the NFL. For Gonzalez, it was a "mourning period." Not only had he directed four Super Bowls; he had worked on every NFL weekend since the start of his career. Pro football was a part of his life, and without it, he felt a little lost.

Not that Gonzalez was by any means single-minded. He was a wine buff. And he was trying to publish a few novels he had written, which betrayed an appreciation for storytelling that was evident in his TV work. His track record, coupled with his work on the Gravity Games and with MTV Sports— both of which attracted the young viewers Ebersol coveted—made him an obvious choice for the XFL. Gonzalez had spent nearly a year shaping the technical components of the XFL telecast.

In the production truck at the L.A. Coliseum, his head was pulsating. After so many hours invested into the manifold pieces of the XFL, he couldn't believe that he didn't know why his live broadcast had just gone dark. He knew the location of every wire and transponder pertaining to the telecast. As the production truck's pandemonium engulfed him, Gonzalez racked his brain. Years before, while directing the Orange Bowl, he had watched images similarly disappear from his monitors. It turned out that a power switch had corroded and fallen out of a stadium wall, zapping the telecast of all electricity and forcing announcer Paul Maguire to call the game from a monitor back in New York. It was for just that reason that Gonzalez always provided his own power source at games—separate generators that ran off their own fuel. What had gone wrong?

In New York, NBC technicians placed a standby slide over the national broadcast. The slide stayed on the screen for a minute and a half, a lifetime in the business. Wayne and Garth public access territory. The engineers behind the dials at the GE Building finally switched to the backup XFL game, Orlando and San Francisco, where Matt Vasgersian was enduring the adolescent squeals of his new broadcast partner, Jerry "The King" Lawler.

In L.A., as the production truck reverberated with the howls and gulps of caffeinated production staffers, Gonzalez underwent Orange Bowl flashbacks. This just can't be happening, he thought to himself. It's impossible that this is happening. When a staffer finally figured out the problem, it had such a simple solution. Someone forgot to top off the generators.

By the time NBC returned to the L.A. Coliseum, the network had been away from the main game for more than twenty-seven minutes. Whatever percentage of the TV audience persevered through the blackout had missed three touchdowns. Chicago led the game 12–6 near the end of the first quarter. The queasy feeling in John Gonzalez's stomach didn't fade when the picture reappeared on the monitors before him. After twenty-five years in the business, he knew the fickle nature of TV viewers, the temptation of the remote control. He believed that few people would have waited out the standby slide. You're on to another program, he thought, and you get trapped there.

There wasn't much time for speculation. There was a game to broadcast. Halftime came quickly, with the sizable crowd of 35,813 lubricating a stadium made infamous in the days when the L.A. Raiders played there and their fans turned the place into a weekly Devil's Night. It looked like old home week as drunken scuffles broke out throughout the stands. Most fans managed to keep out of trouble. They watched either the tight game on the field or the loose women in the hot tub, who groped one another in lesbian pantomime.

Most everyone seemed to be enjoying themselves about the time a huge Chicago player failed to get up off the field after a play in the third quarter. Octavious Bishop, a 330-pound tackle, writhed on the turf. He had broken his left leg. It took trainers nearly fifteen minutes to determine the extent of the injury and hoist the piano-size Bishop into an ambulance. The Coliseum went dead quiet, echoing the graveness of the injury. As the delay strung out, the big screen at the end of the stadium remained dark. Where was the vaunted WWF "in-stadium experience"? Fans grew restless. They began throwing food at one another, then escalated to beer bottles. One fan stood up, held out his arms, and presented himself for a pelting. Apparently a submissive. The strippers in the hot tub couldn't hold the fans' attention, distant and unreal as they were.

One fan, a forty-six-year-old paraplegic who had brought his nephews to the game, got caught in the crossfire. In the midst of a tussle, a few sloshed fans slammed into the man's wheelchair, which was parked in a handicapped section. The man flew off his chair and fell headfirst into a concrete walkway six feet below. The fall opened a gash on his face, and the man lay in a puddle of his own blood before paramedics could reach him. Newspapers would report the incident the following day as though it had been a direct extension of McMahon's condemnation of pantywaists and sissies, as though McMahon had provoked the behavior. But could you really blame him for the drunken actions of a few unfortunates who were unable to grip the lowest rung of the evolutionary ladder? Some people are always looking for a reason to act out. And if McMahon was responsible for this ugly peek at anarchy, then what of the NFL? That league sells beer, too, and if you've ever sat in the 700 level of Veterans Stadium for a game between the Eagles and the Giants, you have surely witnessed the combustive force of MGD and ennui.

Back at *SNL* studio 8H in the GE Building, Lorne Michaels fought hard to maintain his studied schoolboy air. Jennifer Lopez was getting ready in her dressing room. The doors were about to open to the live audience. Michaels was full of expectant excitement before the biggest show of the year. Yet when he looked at the XFL game playing out on the monitor in front of him, he saw a considerable amount of time left on the game clock. Octavious Bishop had just consumed fifteen minutes with his busted leg. The L.A.-Chicago game would have to finish by eleven P.M. for everything to come out on time. Not to worry. With three minutes left in the game, the Enforcers held a comfortable lead, 25–13.

L.A. had the ball, urged on by its quarterback, Tommy Maddox, a former UCLA star who had pulled his club within field-goal range several times during the game, only to watch placekicker Jose Cortez miss the boot. Maddox vented his anger on the sidelines, yelling into the mike embedded in his jersey, "If he can't make it, let's don't kick it." NBC would go on to hype this quote as a breakthrough in televised sports on par with instant replay.

Inside of three minutes, Chicago committed a personal foul that gave L.A. excellent field position. Maddox connected on a touchdown strike, and after a missed extra-point try, the score stood at 25–19. There was 2:36 on the clock. Lorne Michaels started pacing. It was coming up on eleven P.M. He hit the phones, calling his bosses to alert them to the possible situation.

L.A. regained possession of the football. Maddox marched the Xtreme down the field. With only twenty-three seconds on the clock, L.A. running back Ken Oxendine scored on a one-yard plunge. The rowdy Coliseum crowd suspended the donnybrook to put their hands together for the home team. On the extra-point try, L.A. had a chance to take the lead. The fans held their breath. Lorne Michaels stopped pacing and glared at the screen in front of him. John Gonzalez prayed that his generators would last through the play.

The Xtreme failed to convert, leaving the score tied at twenty-five. The play clock ran out. Overtime.

Lorne Michaels couldn't believe what he was watching. All he could think of was Dick Ebersol's personal guarantee. Michaels tore through the underbelly of Studio 84. He got on the phone again. He lost hold of his temper. As the studio audience began pouring into the studio, Michaels threatened to scrap the whole show and air a rerun in its place.

NBC could have preempted the L.A.-Chicago game and dumped out to local news on time. There was, however, a discouraging precedent: the *Heidi* Game. On November 17, 1968, NBC broadcast a game between the Oakland Raiders and the New York Jets. With less than a minute left in the game and the Jets leading by only three points, NBC switched to its seven P.M. program—*Heidi,* a kid's movie about an irresistible Swiss girl. After NBC left the game, the Raiders stormed back, scoring two touchdowns in nine seconds to win 43–32. Twenty minutes after the game, NBC gave the final score in a crawl along the bottom of the screen. Fans raised such an uproar that the NFL subsequently inserted language into its TV contracts guaranteeing that games be shown in their entirety. Joe Namath played in the *Heidi* Game, and though Tommy Maddox provided a poor facsimile, NBC executives were loath to inaugurate a J. Lo game.

L.A. received the ball first in the extra period, with four downs to score from the twenty-yard line. They popped it in the end zone. Chicago answered, sending the game into a second overtime. McMahon and Ebersol, while concerned about the overrun, could not have been disappointed with the show they were producing. If only this game had played out on the league's first night, instead of the 19-0 blowout.

It was 11:25 P.M. in New York, and Lorne Michaels had decided to go ahead with the show. He would begin *SNL* at its usual time, 11:30, taping it to air whenever local news broadcasts finished. Tommy Maddox threw a touchdown pass to open the second OT in L.A., right about the time Michaels, Jennifer Lopez, and *SNL* cast member Will Ferrell traded lines in the show's opening skit. The premise involved—what else?—Lopez's infamous hindquarters. Ferrell pretended to help Lopez settle in to her dressing room, merely taking the chance to ogle her butt. Michaels saved the day, "firing" Ferrell on the spot and restoring Lopez's dignity. "This is NBC," he apologized. "We can't have people running around here like it's the XFL."

Chicago failed to score in the second overtime, and the game finished, mercifully. L.A. came out on top, 39–32, in a thrilling comeback. The time was 11:42 P.M. in New York, which meant that *SNL*'s biggest show of the year would begin at 12:12 A.M., a staggering forty-two minutes late.

When Ryan Clement dropped back to pass in the first quarter in Memphis's Memorial Stadium, defensive end Shante Carver was looking to make it onto the weekly XFL highlight reel that circulated through league stadiums. He drove Clement's right shoulder into the turf. This was the same shoulder that Clement had landed on at the end of the league's first play from scrimmage. The shoulder separated. Clement's backup, Mike Cawley, entered the game. He didn't have to do much, since the Vegas defense dominated the Maniax just as it had the Hitmen. Kelvin Kinney recorded a sack, while the defensive unit stuffed Memphis. Despite Mike Cawley's 3-for-13 performance and Rod Smart gaining just 22 yards on 12 carries, the Outlaws took the game 25–3.

The team boarded the flight home after the win in Memphis, holding a perfect 2–0 record. Players talked about hosting the championship game at the end of April, but they would have to get through the next few games without their top quarterback.

When the Nielsen numbers showed themselves, it was clear that the XFL delay had affected considerable damage to *SNL*. Jennifer Lopez scored a 6 rating. This was not how it was supposed to go down. Mena Suvari had managed an 8.3 a few weeks before, and she was barely a star. Even The Rock's rerun a week earlier had scored 7.4. Lorne Michaels was devastated by the lost opportunity.

And when the numbers for the XFL came in, there was further anguish in the GE Building. The XFL's Game Two earned a 4.6, a monumental 52 percent fall from the week before, and just a hair above the 4.5 that NBC had promised advertisers. Ebersol and McMahon had allowed for a drop in ratings, but this was alarming. There was more unsettling news in the form of demographic breakdowns. Among men aged 18–34, there was a 60 percent dropoff from Week One; for males 12–24 there was a 70 percent plunge.

Vince McMahon spun as best he could. The numbers showed that at eleven-thirty, *SNL*'s scheduled starting time, NBC's rating swelled from a 4.9 to a 6.6, a 34 percent increase. The XFL issued a statement claiming responsibility for the eleven-thirty ratings spike, by virtue of the game's exciting finish. Yes, and Al Gore invented the Internet.

Word of Lorne Michaels's temper tantrum fell into the hands of an eager press. Reporters took pleasure in drumming the demise of the XFL in the wake of its ratings dive. The Michaels angle was gravy. It all combined to make NBC look like a stricken giant, plagued by internal bleeding.

Ebersol and McMahon wondered what had happened between Weeks One and Two to turn off so many millions. They had put on a great game. The two teams represented the second- and third-largest cities in the country. There were babes in a hot tub.

John Gonzalez had his own theory. He asked his two young sons how they had reacted to the blackout. As soon as the screen went blank, they were off to MTV—and their father was the director. It didn't give Gonzalez much hope. He believed that a larger crowd had been watching the game only to change the channel away from the standby slide.

The game's first half hour registered a 4.8 rating; its second half hour a 4.5. Nielsen doesn't track numbers in increments smaller than thirty minutes, and since the blackout had occurred during the first fifteen minutes, there was no way to compare pre-blackout numbers to post-blackout numbers. No one would ever know the true impact of the technical difficulty. What was clear was the media pounding. A broad brush painted the league as a very uncool enterprise. By extension, disliking it became cool.

Los Angeles Times: "XFL a Problem Child." *New York Post:* "It's Getting Late Early for Fast-Fading XFL." *Hollywood Reporter:* "NBC Takes a Sack."

In the week following the overrun that kept J. Lo on TV well past the bedtime of the adolescent crowd that created her, Dick Ebersol and Lorne Michaels made up as best they could. "We just got trapped that night," Ken Schanzer said. "Lorne understands what can happen with live television. Was he angry? I think he got over it." Michaels's dyspepsia abated only when Ebersol made a few concessions. From then on, XFL games would kick off five minutes earlier. Ebersol scrapped the first-person, on-field player intros that the league had been using. The game clock would begin running from the moment an official spotted the ball, even if the previous play had gone out of bounds or fallen incomplete. Ebersol also promised to shave five minutes off the halftime break, thus limiting his chance at capturing Knute Rockne in action.

These were minute changes, but they added up to more than just a twenty-minute cushion. The entire gesture reinforced the XFL's position in network hierarchy. If NBC believed in the XFL formula—and the network had cause to, since the league had a whopping 7.1 average rating after two weeks—then it may have shrugged off the league's insouciance. Ultimately, the XFL had to play by the rules just like any other prime-time program with scattered, partisan support in the GE Building. Had NBC lost faith? McMahon's crew attempted its spin on the *SNL* appeasement. "We would have wanted to tweak it after a week or two no matter what," said XFL president Basil DeVito. "That's how Vince is. He's never satisfied and always wants to make it better."

NBC brass had begun to question the league, and any further ratings decline would push the XFL into a kind of purgatory, where its very future would come into question. Game Three suddenly became pivotal, as NBC wondered what numbers the league could pull over the long haul. "We always felt we were gonna get a big rating the first night," Schanzer said. "And then the second week, we would fall. The big issue was the third week. Where would you settle?" If the Internet could provide a signal of public appeal, the outlook wasn't good. During the week leading up to Game Three, the term "XFL" plummeted from the fifth most popular search item on Lycos to number twenty-five—just behind "the Bible" and just ahead of "marijuana." It looked like the coveted demo was bypassing a new hobby in favor of some old standbys.

6

THE MAN IN THE ORANGE GLOVES

IT WAS MIDAFTERNOON, a few hours before game time, and like the Hanson brothers applying the foil, everyone in and around Sam Boyd Stadium saw to their prebattle rituals. Outlaw linemen huddled at midfield in the empty bowl, staring solemnly at the ground, soberly enacting game strategy in their faded jeans, mimicking ballerinas as they glided through formations and ripped the air with their arms in slow motion. The clouds moved slowly above them in patches. Technicians and sound crews, guys carrying clear, bulbous sound catchers, scurried down the white chalk of the sidelines, running final tests, taking direction through their headsets, nodding at disembodied voices. The woman who would sing the national anthem cleared her pipes through the stadium PA. "How's that sound?" she asked.

In the Las Vegas locker room, a few Outlaws sat in the trainer's room waiting to get taped. A couple others hunched in their dressing stalls in their jeans, bobbing their heads to the music pumping from their CD players, rubbing their hamstrings loose, cracking Juicy Fruit and twisting the kinks out of their necks. Mike Cawley, the backup quarterback, was getting the start in place of Ryan Clement, whose shoulder was still a week or two away. Cawley stretched his throwing arm, trying to stay loose. No one said much. The room was tight, stifling, the tension pushing beads of sweat out of the guys' foreheads. An NBC camera crew was there, zooming in on a few faces, though most of the guys ignored the intrusion, refusing to play the part.

If the cameramen really wanted good footage, the curtain was about to come up. Actually, it was coming down, as Rod Smart stripped naked at his stall. Here again was his pregame *Folies Bergère*. He poked his head through his jersey and threaded his legs between the slingshot elastic of his jockstrap. He slipped into his Nikes. No pads, no pants. Then he walked the room, pausing every now and then before a lineman or a receiver. With the words HE HATE ME facing the teammate and his butt cheeks popping out of his jockstrap, Smart stretched: deeeep toe touches, lateral inner-thigh stretches, knee-to-chest hamstring pulls. His face was serious, his ass hirsute. And the players, shocked by the grotesque vision, were paralyzed. A few guys pretended it wasn't happening. Others shoved him aside. The nervous NBC camera guys turned away, professing higher priorities in nervous body language. They were missing groundbreaking sports video.

There wasn't much time to get a handle on Smart before something equally incongruous entered the field of vision. Out of nowhere, and proceeded by an actual puff of smoke, courtesy of a cigar, Governor Jesse Ventura crossed the threshold and marched briskly into the locker room. A handful of unsmiling Minnesota security types in trench coats traveled in his considerable wake. Ventura landed in a lion's den, where all eyes immediately focused on him. The Outlaws began to wonder at his purpose. The governor stiffened and pulled on the cigar jammed in his fist. He folded his arms and looked over the outfit as if preparing to give a rousing speech. The whole thing felt awkward. Ventura wasn't before his constituents, either Minnesota voters or wrestling fans holding fluorescent placards. This wasn't a research trip for the announcer in him. He didn't chat up the players or gather insight for the broadcast. He wasn't checking up on injuries and their status. He wasn't taking notes.

He just stood on the worn carpeting, allowing himself to be checked out like a thirteen-year-old girl at the food court. He seemed drawn inexorably by the feeling that this was the place to be, maybe missing the communal perspiration of his days with the Navy SEALS, or in the WWF. The players, possessing sharply honed instincts for those out of position, sensed it was time to pounce. Anything to forget about Rod Smart wiggling in the corner.

Kelvin Kinney nudged the guy at the next stall, defensive end Antonio Edwards. "I bet I could whip his ass right now," Kinney whispered. He called out in a voice as throaty and overgrown as Ventura's: "Hey, Jesse." The whole place perked its ears. "I thought they called you 'The Body.' What happened?" The room exploded with laughter. Ventura's face flushed. He stomped toward Kinney. "I'm fifty-two," said the governor. "I don't work out anymore." Then he gestured to the man in the trench coat standing at his elbow. "You gotta deal with this guy." The trench coat opened and a gun poked out. "Okay," said Kinney, backing away. "You win tonight."

Ventura was messing around, of course, and he knew that if the players were messing with him, then they must think he was okay. But he knew when it was time to go. He turned on his heel and made for a door down a skinny hallway, where he walked out into the light. The NBC cameras didn't get a single shot of the business, preferring to focus on stock images of cornerbacks bobbing to their music and athletic tape wrapping round and round stationary ankles. So fascinating, so in-depth, so "in the moment."

The sun hung low, forcing squints from the few tailgaters who didn't hide behind wraparound mirrored shades. Ten thousand cars packed the desert plane below the concourse entrance to Sam Boyd Stadium. Vast barbecue pits smoked between every few cars. Impromptu touch-football games sprung up everywhere, tight spirals and wounded ducks littering the late-afternoon sky. Kids in tricked-out Jeeps offered others the chance to share in subwoofer pride as Creed and Papa Roach blasted contiguous square acres.

High up in the press box above the field, the league fed a catered dinner to members of the media. Jeff Shapes, a league press director, soured on doling out the free meal. He had loose, messy black hair that fell down in front of his eyes every so often, and he was forever compelled to shovel it back on his head. It lent him a self-defeating quality, which suited his task of convincing pro sportswriters everywhere that the XFL was the real deal. "The coverage we're getting, it-it-it just doesn't make any sense," he sputtered, sweeping his hair from his eyes.

Ebersol and McMahon were frustrated by all the negative press. Especially painful was a column by Bill Plaschke in the *Los Angeles Times* on February 11, the morning after the L.A. game. Plaschke wrote very little about the game, instead focusing on the strippers splashing in the hot tub behind the end zone: "With about six minutes left in the first quarter Saturday, the Xtreme's Tommy Maddox scored the first touchdown by a Los Angeles pro football team in the Coliseum in more than six years. I missed it. I was talking to Cindy, Shanna, and Roberta." Plaschke mentioned rowdy fans, a woman who flashed her breasts, and what he called "dirty-dancing cheer-leaders." He also wrote, "As with anything touched by Vince McMahon, you have to wonder. Was it real?" This was not the type of coverage Ebersol and McMahon had hoped for after a game that appealing. But could they really have been surprised? They began to understand what they were up against, and an attitude of victimization began permeating the paid staff.

"These sportswriters, they just take potshots," Shapes continued. "They're saying that the football's horrible. It's not horrible. It's not the NFL—but it's not horrible! That's just gratuitous." He swept back his hair. "If you don't like it, just say so. There's too much wrestling for you. Too much of the cheerleaders." Sweep. "Don't just say it's because the football's awful. 'Cause it's not."

Good argument. Wrong crowd. The pro sportswriters were never going to jump on board with the XFL. They saw, one and all, an interloper, McMahon, elbowing his way onto their idea of hallowed ground without paying his dues. Plus, it was an easy line to write: "Wrestling charlatan fails at football." Dash that off in two minutes and be home in time for SportsCenter, where your nascent hunches will be confirmed by anchors who work for a network that has no purpose in speculating on the usefulness of the XFL, since it broadcasts the NFL. Even if a pro hack did find something redeeming in the XFL, what did he gain by admitting it? Only the derision of his peers.

The reporters maintained a solid front. Meanwhile, down on the field, another man tried his best to stand out. The Man in the Orange Gloves. He must be visible at all times—hence his equipage: fluorescent orange, elbow-length Rita Hayworth jobs—yet remain unseen, part of the scenery of the game, one of the shapeless throng that composes the sidelines. The Man in the Orange Gloves tells the referee when to suspend the game for a TV commercial and when to begin once the network has appeased its true owners. His tasks may seem trivial, but during Game Three of the XFL, in that climate, with the overwhelming need to finish the game before eleven P.M. Eastern time—so that all NBC affiliates could break for local news (at one half hour per) and then be free, clear, and not just ready and waiting but damn well excited to televise the God-almighty program that was *SATURDAY NIGHT LIVE* at eleven-thirty—there couldn't be one weak link. The Man in the Orange Gloves was the junction between sport and broadcast, the socket connecting both types of bloody competition, network and football.

Fine. Perfect. Three hours to play this thing. Plenty of time. And all kinds of chances to highlight the things that John Gonzalez needed to highlight. The Bubba Cam. The sideline interviews. The cheerleaders. And, of course, Rod Smart. With Rusty Tillman dropping the ball, Dick Ebersol and Vince McMahon had switched their focus to the Vegas tailback. He was now going to be the XFL's first personality. Smart's on-field numbers didn't warrant much attention. In his first two games, he gained 66 yards rushing on 25 attempts, an average of 2.64 yards per carry. That was barely worth putting him in the game, let alone highlighting him on a prime-time national telecast. And an outspoken personality wasn't cause, either. Remember Game One and his wordless scamper onto the field, which left Fred Roggin holding a ten-pound bag of dead air. But in this league, one didn't need to be a shining physical specimen, a gifted performer, to be worthy of attention. There were other things to contribute. In the WWF, the jealous wrestlers whispered that The Rock couldn't really wrestle, technically speaking, and didn't deserve all the attention (just as they whispered about Jesse Ventura and Hulk Hogan long before him). But The Rock's gift of charisma and enunciation, a very rare combination among all the beef in the WWF, was what made him a star.

Same went for Smart, who caused a stir not with playing-field perform-ance but with words, not from his mouth but from between his shoulder blades. HE HATE ME—no one was quite sure what Smart meant by it. Even he couldn't and wouldn't say for sure. Not yet, at least, and not on national TV. That was what made his nickname so irresistible: its abstractness. He was like a classic-rock guitarist who scored a hit with one tasty lick.

The nickname, if you could call it that, had caught on. *Sports Illustrated* interviewed Smart. During Monday's *Raw Is War* WWF telecast, wrestler Chris Jericho entered the ring wearing Smart's jersey. ESPN's website polled fans on which sports feud they wanted to see end. Was it Kobe Bryant–Shaquille O'Neal? The dispute between Philadelphia Flyers general manager Bobby Clarke and holdout star Eric Lindros? The winner was HE HATE ME and whatever defense he played against. Milking the formula, ESPN switched the poll later in the day, asking fans to choose their favorite Valentine's Day name in sports. HE HATE ME won in a landslide, beating

New York Mets manager Bobby Valentine, Cleveland Indians general manager John Hart, and golfers Fred Couples and Davis Love III, among other names more prone to longevity. Mr. Smart would do well to protect himself in the marketplace of slogans and trademarks.

The first thoughts of many in the press box led straight to domain registration and the need for www.hehateme.com. (The experts remained unaware of a site with a similar theme, www.hehatemesucks.com, where fans could buy the official Hehatemesucks T-shirt [$17], or read the Hehatemesucks top-ten list. "Stomp out the hate," said the site. "Show how much you hate HE HATE ME.")

"He's gotta do it."

"Does he have an agent?"

"No, no, no, he should have a publicist. That's what he needs."

"He should get in one of those 1-800-Collect ads. Something like 'My mom would hate me if I didn't save her a buck or two.'"

Dick Butkus dug the last bits of beef sausage from his teeth with a wide, fat toothpick, preferring to stay out of the debate. He assumed a grimace that allotted him a five-yard bubble devoid of people. The players flooded onto the field, and Butkus clocked the hang times of practice punts with the stopwatch in his free hand, pretending not to listen to the talk of opportunism when there was some real damn football going on around here. But Butkus had a history of Hollywood dialogue. ("Tastes great. Less filling.") Right then, somewhere in the ageless land of syndication, where time was as slippery as Kirk Cameron's Dep squeeze bottle, someone was watching Butkus perform as Coach Mike Katowinski in the sitcom *Hang Time,* or as Ed Klawicki, the lovable rockhead who ran the local diner in *My Two Dads.* Ultimately, even Butkus couldn't avoid donating his thoughts on Rod Smart's showbiz career.

"He better copyright that quick," Butkus said, gesturing with his toothpick. "But actually, if he writes like that, he's probably not smart enough." Everyone had a big laugh, cackling disproportionately as you do to the jokes told by people of such size. No matter how smart he may have been, HE HATE ME had his mind on things besides websites and T-shirts. His agent back in New York, however, was figuring out a few ways to capitalize on his client's new status.

The pregame warm-up ended, and the teams jogged to the locker rooms for a final rest before play began. And so it was time for the cheerleaders to assume both the field and their distinctive choreography. Not to say that the dancing was original. The gyrations were distinctive—as in characteristic—in employing the same kind of kinetic, hands-out, shadowboxing moves that the members of *NSYNC had used to such great effect. Those confections punched the air with small, pillowy fists and spun and twirled while wearing faces that said they were actually tough guys dressed as wankers just for the money. Apparently, this was how Jay Howarth and Vince McMahon wanted their girls to dance. Silly Dancing, not to be confused with Difficult Dancing or Sexy Dancing.

As for appearance, the Outlaws cheerleaders were of the Christina Aguilera school, done up in eight coats of paint like an old barn. The uniform made them look like an Old West buckaroo gang in yellow and black. There was a sheer yellow top, which drew attention to the handiwork of the accredited local plastic surgeonry. The tops of their breasts boomed out of the clothing in perfect orbs, like scoops of ice cream. Black fabric hugged the hips and the upper thighs, leaving visible a small yellow triangle that covered the crotch. A sign in the crowd read NICE BITCHIN CHEERLEADERS, the capital letters aligned to constitute the name of the proud peacock broadcasting the event.

The L.A. players ran from the gate first, with the hometown fans booing their arrival. Finally, a reason to release the bilious Coors-and-sausage fumes. An NBC producer in a headset greeted the Xtreme players, ordering them to run toward the cameras and away from the firework stanchions that lined the playing surface. The players blithely obliged, jogging past The Man in the Orange Gloves, who stood with his arms folded, eyeing them as biblical adversaries to his final goal of appeasing oh great Yahweh, Lorne Michaels. What if one of them had a devastating injury that consumed fifteen minutes as he lay prone on the field?

Fireworks interrupted his thoughts as the official NBC telecast began, salvos timed perfectly and exploding with millisecond delays down the length of the field and then bursting in huge, sparkling plumes above the entertainment-center scoreboard, ending in overlapping shots: a two-story "X," up, out, fading away. The sky was nearly dark, and the stadium choked in fireworks smoke as the Outlaws sprinted onto the field. One of Gonzalez's Bubba Cams quickly located Rod Smart and zoomed in on the back of his jersey, the words HE HATE ME bouncing up and down on the screen. Cut quickly to shots of fans holding signs in the crowd, as Gonzalez couldn't mask his eagerness, unwrapping all his presents as fast as he could. There was the lyrical, HE HATE ME 'CAUSE HE AIN'T ME, and the obligatory, HE HATE ME FOR PRESIDENT. And one couple, a middle-aged man and woman, each held a sign. One read HE HATES ME, the other SHE HATES ME. Everyone strummed air guitar.

The Outlaws' nervous quarterback, Mike Cawley, took a few final warm-up throws on the sidelines. If the first two games were any indication, he wouldn't need to score many points, since the XFL's top defense backed him up. The Las Vegas defense had allowed just one field goal in its first two games, while scoring two touchdowns of its own. Kelvin Kinney led the league in sacks, with three.

The referee absent-mindedly cradled the football as the players jogged into position. The Man in the Orange Gloves feverishly wound his hands like a clock in a time-travel movie, desperately trying to get the ref's attention. *SNL* was waiting!

Rod Smart ran toward the huddle with the cameras glued to his back: Gonzalez pounding it into the viewer's head. Smart's mediocre stats appeared on-screen. His actual name was nowhere to be seen. NBC had wiped him from the county register. Smart, now formally known as HE HATE ME, had become a model and proved an axiom of McMahon's marketing. Most XFLers were in the league for one reason: to get noticed by scouts, football and otherwise—to get their names out there. Here was Smart with the most recognizable name so far, and it wasn't even a name. He had found distinction in obliteration. Most of the guys with personalized jerseys chose things like "Death Blow" or "Hit Squad" or "Super-C"—predictable, wearying signs of stunted masculinity. But HE HATE ME, what the heck was that? It sounded psychotic, paranoid, like Smart was scared of the bogeyman under his bed. You wanted to give him a reassuring talk. "Whoever's doing all this hating, he doesn't really hate you, and if he does, well, then that's his loss, 'cause you're a great person." Vince McMahon must have been holding his sides. This particular experiment was working. But why withhold the capper from the locker room, what would have been the first lap dance by a running back in TV history?

The national telecast's new play-by-play announcer, Jim Ross, offered an assessment of the L.A. quarterback. "Tommy Maddox, the Gunslinger," he yelled. "The spirit of the XFL lives within his shoulder pads." Jesse Ventura's best line of the night came sometime later. "Defense versus offense," he said. "Ya gotta love it." Maybe the governor had been too busy pulling Rusty Tillman's chain, which he had continued to do during the league's second NBC telecast, even though the coach wasn't on it. New York lost again and Ventura took a few potshots at the coach. He was getting under his skin. Tillman even asked Hitmen general manager Drew Pearson to call the league office and get Ventura to cut it out. Pearson made the call, but Vince McMahon said he was continuing with the developing angle.

The L.A. defense took the field, and looking closely, viewers could see that Rod Smart hadn't charmed everyone with his lyricism. Two L.A. players had their own responses. The back of number 53's jersey read "I Hate He," while number 46's said "I Hate He Too." It made for good TV—this predictable human response, a backlash instead of an attempt to develop a new franchise, thus propelling HE HATE ME ever higher—and it presented a challenge for Smart, who had raised his head only to prompt others to clothesline it clean off. In this game, once again Smart wouldn't deliver, rushing for a meager 24 yards on 15 carries, an average of 1.6 yards per try. McMahon's laughter began to fade. His WWF writers couldn't manufacture Smart's dominance as though he were Stone Cold. It did them no good to stand on the sidelines (as they did at wrestling matches) with ears attuned to the crowd reaction each time Smart carried the ball or appeared on the Jumbotron. This thing wasn't scripted. Smart had to produce on the field, write his own follow-up riff to the one-hit wonder of his nickname. There was no one feeding Smart touchdowns or lyrics, as with Britney Spears, requiring only that he stand on the "X" and look purty.

Smart's lackluster play, combined with an inexperienced Cawley at quarterback, made the Outlaws offense sputter all game long. The Vegas defense came through as advertised, squashing nearly every L.A. drive. Midway through the third quarter, the score stood tied at nine. Vegas couldn't capitalize on L.A.'s troubles with Cawley skipping passes off the turf and launching throws over the heads of wide-open receivers. It made for some pretty awful football, pretty awful watching, as one series after another resulted in a punt, a punt, another dreary punt. The product wasn't cutting it.

An L.A. player lay prone on the field in the peculiar pretzel posture that signaled something more than a bent finger. Amid the pile of padding and shiny fabric, there was a foot sticking out at an odd angle. A Bubba Cam moved in for a closer view. The player's face had gone gray in shock. The Bubba Cam operator walked to within a few steps before several L.A. players pushed him backward, shaking their heads and hands, telling him to back off, the players themselves guardians of good taste. On the telecast, Gonzalez cut to a replay of the injury, slowing the tape and highlighting the snapped ankle. This wasn't such a television anomaly; the same thing happened on NFL telecasts. As Gonzalez ran through several different angles of the injury, the tortured player and the L.A. trainers received a visitor, The Man in the Orange Gloves, who stood over the scene with his hands on his hips.

NBC cut to a commercial, a cheeky ad for *SNL* with two cast members exhorting the XFL to get moving already. It seemed timed to the situation, especially given the costly extended injury time-out from the previous week. When the broadcast returned, trainers had carted the L.A. player off the field, and play resumed. The third quarter ended with the score still tied at 9.

The day clock read ten-fifteen P.M., EST, which left forty-five minutes to play the final fifteen on the game clock. No problem. But into the fourth quarter and up in the press box, there was a sense that it wouldn't be so easy to finish on time. "*Heidi* Game, Part Two," someone said.

A few series later, there was not a lot of time left on the game clock—9:03—but that wasn't the problem. Las Vegas's defense had stifled Los Angeles and its quarterback, Tommy Maddox. Meanwhile, the Outlaws offense couldn't shake its anemia. Cawley had the ball in his hands again, and he stumbled, tripped, and bumped into his teammates, looking like a guy yanked from the stands in a pinch. It wasn't all his fault. Everyone on the Las Vegas offense appeared out of sync. Maybe the cheerleaders were throwing them off with their pitiful timing. Another Cawley throw hit the turf, forcing a Vegas punt and preserving the tie as the clock counted toward an extra period. Vegas called time-out, the Man in the Orange Gloves threw his hands up in the air, and an *SNL* ad popped up on-screen. Another punt just before the six-minute mark, and another L.A. injury left a player lying on the grass.

Vegas had the ball again, and things were finally looking positive, with Rod Smart wiggling his butt off-tackle for fourteen yards and a first down. But the Outlaws couldn't sustain the momentum, and another punt came with 3:23 left on the clock. Time: ten-forty.

Things were getting tight in the broadcast booth as the game reached for the dreaded word: overtime. L.A. moved the ball on the first two plays of the next possession, setting itself up with a third down and one yard to go near midfield. Maddox looked like he was about to take control of the game. But the Xtreme couldn't convert the third down, spurring another wintry, sorrowful punt. Instead of scooting to the edges of the stadium bleachers, the crowd sank back in a stupor. The kick buried Las Vegas at its own ten-yard line with 1:48 to go in regulation. Time: ten-forty-five. They had fifteen minutes to get it done.

Cawley threw incomplete on first down. On the next play, he dropped back and fired for an open receiver streaking down the middle of the field beyond the first-down marker. The pass sailed over his head and bounced off the turf. Dozens of Outlaws fans mustered enough energy to boo. The XFL execs upstairs fidgeted in their seats. This game would have to be decided somehow by someone, with just over a minute to go. The Outlaws finally managed a first down, and they called time-out. Time: 10:49 P.M. EST.

The game didn't look like it was going to make it, with only eleven minutes to go before the affiliates were scheduled to break for local news. A thick cloud of fireworks smoke hovered over the Vegas huddle as the players broke for the line of scrimmage. Cawley took the snap and threw a strained pass to a receiver over the middle. Everyone in the stadium could see where it was going. Interception. The Outlaws tackled the L.A. player at the Vegas forty-one-yard line. Time: ten-fifty.

While there was no evidence of a fix, Cawley's was a curious throw, one that prompted many bettors in the sportsbooks to make eye contact for the first time all night. The game clock read 1:11. The Xtreme earned a first down with thirty-one ticks on the clock, then called a time-out with one second left in regulation. Time: 10:53 P.M. EST.

On the sidelines, The Man in the Orange Gloves used his accessories to pull at his hair. An *SNL* ad covered the bottom third of the screen during L.A.'s time-out. Time: 10:55 P.M. EST.

L.A. placekicker Jose Cortez trotted onto the field and positioned himself for the field-goal attempt, which measured forty-eight yards—no easy task for an NFL kicker, let alone a guy who was laying roof shingles a month before. The snap came, and Cortez booted the ball. It fluttered end over end, gleaming in the stadium lights before clearing the crossbar as time ran out on the game clock. Whhhhheeeeewwww. A many-voiced gasp rattled the press-box windows. Game over. L.A. had won. Players stormed the field. And there were a few moments to spare in the telecast, enough time for Bubba Cam shots of the ubiquitous prayer circle and of Jose Cortez playing to the crowd in grand relief. The Man in the Orange Gloves wore a smile as bright as his most distinguishing article of clothing, and a look of relief that outdid Cortez's.

It was sighs all around. What very few people knew was that there was little need for suspense. During the previous week, when Ebersol was making his concessions to *SNL,* NBC execs had quietly promised Lorne Michaels that they would preempt any XFL game that ran beyond eleven P.M. Since the game never got to that point, everybody won. There would be no *Heidi* Game, Part Two.

The stadium emptied with the singular emotion of the defeated fan. Beer cups flew onto the field. A tussle broke out in the southeast corner of the stands, attracting a buzzing swarm of yellow-jacketed security. The desert air seemed humid all of a sudden, stretching out the fans' slump-shouldered exit up the aisles toward the concourse.

A trio of Outlaws coaches, having spent the game upstairs calling plays via headsets, squeezed into an elevator in the press box. They stank of dejection—caps askew, shoe gazing, swearing under their breath. The elevator opened to the concourse, where hundreds of fans milled about, not wanting to leave, not knowing which way to go. The coaches waded through the drunken masses, some of whom noticed something oddly coachlike about the three men in identical maroon sweatsuits. In the milling about, there was also a noising about, a murmur, whose timbre sounded something like rage. The volume increased, then increased still further, sloshing around like the beer that fueled it, gaining momentum and coalescing toward expression. Did they want more drink, though the stands had closed for the night? Was this thing heading toward faceless violence? Were the coaches in some kind of danger by being vaguely responsible for this general dejection? The sound gathered, and syllables began to join in something resembling a chant. In their hurry toward the locker room and away from the fray, the trio of coaches momentarily halted, struck by the noise. They looked over their shoulders with concern. They were stuck, at the mercy of whatever it was that was going to happen in the crowd. Then the chant achieved clarity, the words became discernible, the three syllables so simple: "L.A. sucks! L.A. sucks! L.A. sucks!"

The coaches disappeared into the crowd while the chant continued, gaining force and decibels. As the fans in their Outlaws jerseys and Outlaws hats circled about, badmouthing their conquerors and rallying behind their team, for a brief instant everything felt major-league. These people cared.

Down in the conference room adjacent to the Outlaws' locker room, XFL PR man Jeff Shapes couldn't help but smile. "Finished just in time," he said, giddy as he swept back his hair. "How 'bout Cortez? Last week he was a bum, this week he's a hero." Shapes laughed as he said, "He's Jennifer Lopez's cousin. He's gonna host *Saturday Night Live*."

In the locker room, the Outlaws existed in a painful ether much different from the one inhaled from the broken capsules before the game. "We'll get 'em when it counts," coach Jim Criner told his team, alluding to the rematch scheduled for later in the season. Criner was worn out when he emerged from the locker room, his head reddened and sweaty. The dream of an undefeated Outlaws season and what would have been an automatic NFL gig was so stale that it offended. Criner grabbed a seat behind a card table and began answering lobbed questions. The press went easy on him, but not for long. Why did you pass so late in the game? Why didn't you just wait for overtime? Couldn't you find a better quarterback? The questions and Criner's choked answers fell short of embodying any drama or tension—the coach on the ropes defending his decisions, and his precious, try-hard players—considering that the conversation included just four people, rendering the tiny white-

washed side room immense and ringing it in echoes. There was no one there.
A black camera tripod was propped up against a door with a sign attached:
PROPERTY OF NBC—DO NOT REMOVE. As though a thief could hide in this
meager gathering.

Criner soldiered on. A few more people funneled through the doorway. A
couple more reporters. A few workmen with walkie-talkies. And then came
a woman, a middle-aged woman with shiny gold earrings and a big rock on
her finger. Who was this woman, what was she doing here, and why was she
smiling like she was on Paxil? She walked in and stood to the side of the
room, not really listening to the reporters grasp at analysis and Criner spill
clichés. She fiddled with the Velcro enclosures of her jacket, which was extra
large and red and black, a brand-new Gore-Tex ski jacket with the XFL logo
sewn over the breast. Her eyes were bright and wide. She mumbled things in
people's ears and laughed, then listened and laughed again. She walked out
of the room. Then she walked back in. And then it came in the show of
respect from the men wearing identical XFL jackets, the slight, unconscious
bows almost Asian in deference. This woman, this fifty-something, proper-
looking, polite-seeming, demur, even—this woman was Mrs. Vince McMahon. The woman who shared his bed and rubbed his forehead and told him
that all those mean people out there, they didn't know what a special, sweet
person he was. No, no, no. That didn't do her justice. She was also Linda
McMahon, CEO of the XFL and WWF. Tonight she was taking in that
which jointly belonged to her. And what did she think?

She thought that "it was a great game, one that our fans surely enjoyed."
She believed that "our fan base is growing." And she was glad the game
ended succinctly, since "we have to remember the people at the network."
She was friendly. She was humble. She was gracious. She was full of shit.
Not completely full of shit. But there was enough of a cubic-zirconia twin-
kle in her eye, a static HAL lamp, a register: POWER ON. There was a gleeful
smile, one that didn't quite suit the occasion. The smile was maybe conjured
up from memories of her son Shane's junior high school graduation ceremony, or of surveying a garden freshly planted, no longer on bended knee.
The smile was pleasant, suburban. It was a seeming smile, a receiving-line
smile, a smiling smile.

And it was turned down by the arrival of her husband, Vince, who thundered from the labyrinthine underpinnings of the stadium, vast and swift and big-shouldered, projecting stores of venom so that no squirrel reporter would dare approach him. He sent out other signs, too . . . that five minutes before *SNL* was a cushion. But not much of one. McMahon just got by. As he stalked around in his black XFL varsity jacket, as he paced, as he sweat in big globules, it was clear what was happening underneath the hair, through which he ran his beefy, steroidal fingers. He exhaled, tilting his dimpled Travolta chin slightly skyward, relieved that, tonight anyway, his league hadn't caused a ruckus at NBC. It was hard enough making everyone happy by drawing solid ratings. Stepping on the tender toes of Lorne Michaels—the single, fey heirloom of a lost and golden, pre-*Survivor*, pre-*Who Wants to Be a Millionaire* NBC age—that was another headache, for which the medicine may have been too harsh. So McMahon paced and pondered, glad to avoid one trouble but anxious about another potential leak in the ship. He would soon get his hands on the overnight ratings, which offered a glimpse at the final Nielsen numbers. He would see if he had once again faltered but delivered, or if he had to kick in for wholesale changes.

Twenty feet away in the shunted half-light of the stadium's withering postgame bulbs, fans gathered on a mound covered in crabgrass, as the players sprinkled out of the locker room. The quick and fortunate Outlaws had already made it to their cars undiscovered. Some players got stuck in the mix, hounded for one autograph after another by fans who weren't quite sure which one was which but didn't seem to mind anyway, caught up in the thrill of proximity. Other Outlaws were toweling off in the sweaty, steamy Bengay innards of the locker room, taking their time behind the placards that restricted entry to a chosen few, delaying and reveling in the adulation that awaited.

Once Vince McMahon appeared, the mood on the crabgrass mound shifted decidedly. This *was* an unexpected treat, the chairman himself. It took several minutes for the fans to approach McMahon. They shuffled on the crabgrass, papers and posters in hand, their chests pulling them toward McMahon's signature, their feet rooted to a spot in unvarnished fear. The combined effect left a hill populated by shaking and disturbed, indecisive physical mumblers. Meanwhile, the Outlaws continued their sporadic exits, but now passed unseen, unaccosted, as the eyes of their fans were trained on the boss man. Several players looked put-off as they passed by people who were supposed to pay homage. This was a problem when the guy upstairs, the shareholder, the check writer, was the one who awed the fans, rendering the players' physical feats a sideshow folly that was barely worth the price of admission. Was the football so subpar that the CEO rated all the attention?

Finally, one fan made a move. He was a chubby kid, about fourteen, dressed in a black and gold Outlaws jersey and baseball hat, the horns of a desert-withered, skeletal steer forming an "O" on his forehead. The kid strode to McMahon and handed him a poster, rousing the CEO from his thoughts of TV ratings and overtime periods and the coveted demo. McMahon signed absentmindedly. Maybe because his head was filled, he didn't bite off the kid's. This was a surprise, and it encouraged a dozen other fans. As the zealots embarked on their pilgrimage, the Las Vegas locker room belched its last Outlaw, whom the evening swallowed without ceremony. As he shuffled toward the parking lot, his head cast down and harboring unknowable sentiment, HE HATE ME couldn't find any love.

7

HE HATE ME
'CAUSE HE AIN'T ME

WHEN ROD SMART SKULKED into that Vegas night, it would have been hard to get any kind of odds on his boss, who stood nearby signing autographs, even knowing who he was. Vince McMahon, along with Dick Ebersol, had been gassing on and on about his skill in creating stars, explaining how that intangible expertise would extrapolate to considerable ratings for the XFL. He and Ebersol would manufacture fame from anonymity, he said, since they had done it all before. It wasn't quite working this time around because there was one important difference. In the Olympics, where Ebersol polished icons, fame emanated from actual achievement; without gold medals, Olympians wouldn't get endorsement deals and spots on Leno. In McMahon's world, where a pro wrestler's character was often indistinguishable from his actual persona, public favor came before backroom kingmaking. A wrestler could never make it if fans didn't react to him. In these two worlds, celebrity, while enhanced by TV, remained organic.

Rod Smart, XFL poster boy, operated by the same inescapable principles. Here, the great star-making machine of Ebersol and McMahon threw a rod. Smart's play didn't warrant much attention. Neither did the words that came out of his mouth. Smart stood out thanks to a single ingenious phrase, which McMahon and Ebersol furiously packaged for the strong-arm sell. But once you got past the nickname and the newspaper sidebars, there wasn't much about Smart that was worth watching. Through the first three weeks of the XFL season, HE HATE ME was a flimsy facade.

Yet there was great irony in the peddling of Rod Smart. Because there was indeed something vital and genuine there, something very much organic, if only NBC dug deeper than a facile five-second interview.

Rod Smart opened the door a crack to see who it was, then wider, enough to allow a shaft of light to slice the darkened stoop of his rented second-floor apartment on Nellis Boulevard, up the street from Sam Boyd Stadium. "Um, yeah, come in."

Rod Smart's apartment was as comforting as a storage closet. There were some rented chairs and a few rumpled issues of *The Source* magazine. With bare white walls, the place looked like the brochure pictures down at the rental office. There was a single loaf of bread in the fridge. Paper towels and empty Gatorade bottles littered the kitchen countertop. It looked like the plumbers had just left after installing the fixtures.

There was too much going on for Smart to go shopping for anything more than frozen pizza. But the distractions were welcome, the type and variety of a teenager's moistened meditations.

Smart crumbled to the carpet in jean shorts and a blue T-shirt, a screwdriver twisting in his palm. He was assembling a cabinet for his TV. The apartment was still tucked away far from the Strip, out where Vegas turned into just another southwestern wasteland, the motel chinch bugs trading places with the desert Gila monsters. The only sign of action peeked out from Smart's back bedroom, where cheetah-print sheets gave it all away.

The phone rang and Smart punched the cordless. "Oh yeah, girl," he said in the honey-coated voice that he had refined for a single objective. "Of course I 'member you." Yes, Rod Smart epitomized *the XFL experience*.

About a month earlier, an Outlaws PR staffer stopped by Smart's locker a few days before the first game. Smart never listened closely to the incidentals of team meetings. So when the employee mumbled about putting something on the back of his jersey, Smart didn't know what he was talking about. "What do you mean?" he asked. "Smart. My name. What else?"

"But you can put anything you want," said the man.

"For real?"

The whole concept dazzled Smart, especially since, as a running back, he was bound to get plenty of airtime. He met up with the other Outlaws running backs that night, his friends Chrys Chukwuma and Ben Snell, and the three ribbed one another over games of pool at Snell's place. For guys who couldn't tread NFL water, this was a rare chance at a splash. Chukwuma wanted his jersey to read "Chuckwagon"; Snell came up with "Thoro," as in thoroughbred—the two nicknames matching wishful visions of their own running power. Smart couldn't come up with anything, and his friends wouldn't let it lie, goosing him every chance they got.

Smart's cordless rang again, interrupting the home improvement, and he pulled his nappy parabola of hair out of the TV cabinet. "Nothing," he said into the phone, assuming the Voice. "Just chillin'. Oh, hold on a second." He clicked over to answer his second line. "'Member me," he said. "I met you at the Boulevard Mall. You was shopping for some shoes."

Smart made a few easy promises and then returned to the cabinet.

"Oh yeah, so they tell me you can put anything you want on the jersey," he explained, looking up from his project to emphasize points here and there. "So I'm thinking about Lakeland, where I grew up. Back home, we call Lakeland 'L Town,' so I was thinking about that, too. But I thought, 'Man, I gotta come up with something different, something that'll catch some attention.'"

The phone rang again and Smart answered.

"'Member, I was in the Drink the other night, and I grabbed your hand," he said. "You gave me your number, but you said you was being watched." The Voice kicked in and Smart smiled, knowing it was in the bag. He grabbed a seat on one of his rented chairs. "H-h-hold on a minute," he said, clicking over for another call. "Aw, hey baby," he said, talking so long that he forgot about the first caller, who had hung up by the time he returned. He phoned back and apologized. The Voice smoothed it all out.

"I'm a friendly person," Smart said, once he hung up, laughing at his own joke. "I like to get to know people." When he met women, Smart would tell them he worked for an Internet company, relying more on personal charm than the aura of athletic celebrity. He didn't need any built-in advantages. He kept his Nikes like new, maintained a scraggle of scruff along his jaw and returned messages on his two-way pager with the devotion of the Internet techie he pretended to be. He had a nonchalant way about him that women craved—and that coaches couldn't get a handle on.

So it was a few days before the first game, when a local reporter grabbed

Smart after practice. Smart still hadn't figured on a nickname, and time was running out. The pressure was on, too, since Coach Criner had just named him starting tailback for the first game. Everyone back home in L Town was going to be watching. What to wear? With the model airplanes buzzing over the practice field, the reporter had a question of his own: What did Rod think about nearly being cut from the team? Smart looked at him funny. "Cut?"

From the start of training camp, Smart had felt like an outsider. Coaches deconstructed him for his shiny Nikes. He killed in practice, and they criticized him for his hair. They cut him down at any sign of individuality. He didn't know it at the time, but with one scrimmage left, he was on his way back to L Town. In that final practice, he ran for an eighty-yard touchdown. It saved his job. He never knew how close he had come. And here was Coach Criner spilling it to a reporter. Smart's anger overtook him. These motherfuckers really are nasty, he thought. They didn't appreciate his style, the fact that he had style, unlike the rest of the drones on the team. After all the talk of equal pay, the lip service about the emphasis on talent and not favoritism, it turned out the XFL was just like the NFL. It was like the life that Smart had always known back in Florida, where a kid with a teenage mom in and out of prison never had much of a chance at fitting in. Smart knew he was good enough to make the team, but the Outlaws coaches were treating him just like everyone else always had.

When Outlaws PR man Trey FitzGerald stopped by his locker, Smart handed over a piece of paper with three words scrawled on it: HE HATE ME. The epithet had less to do with the opponents Smart would face and more to do with the opponents he had always faced. "This is what you want?" FitzGerald asked, puzzling over the words as though reading Mandarin.

He wasn't alone in his bewilderment. When the NBC production crew showed up in Las Vegas the day before the first game, they asked the starting tailback to shoot an interview for the telecast. Smart walked into the locker room, where NBC producers had hung a few of his teammates' jerseys as a backdrop. There was Chrys Chukwuma's jersey: "Chuckwagon." And Ben Snell's "Thoro." But when Smart saw his number 30 he was confused. All it said was "Smart."

He turned to FitzGerald. "Man, what the hell?" he asked. "You said we could put anything." FitzGerald explained that the XFL office in Stamford had decided against allowing him to wear HE HATE ME. Smart was steamed.

Stamford hadn't endorsed HE HATE ME because no one could understand it. FitzGerald had called Billy Hicks, the league's vice president of administration. But Hicks flat-out denied the request. Was HE HATE ME a racial epithet, a jab at the NFL . . . a gang thing? Billy Hicks didn't have any idea, and rather than take a leap of faith, the XFL office reneged on its vow of self-expression. The league that had professed a free-spirited ideal was legislating just what could and couldn't be said, what was acceptable—the very indictment McMahon leveled against the NFL.

Smart wouldn't let it drop, but there was little FitzGerald could do. The PR man did have an idea. He knew that Billy Hicks and Vince McMahon were somewhere in Sam Boyd Stadium that moment. He suggested that Smart track them down and plead his case personally. Smart found Hicks and McMahon on the field, with groundskeepers and pyrotechnicians flitting around them. Smart introduced himself, then explained the meaning of HE HATE ME. "It's like, if I have a good run, I get up and look at the defense and say, 'They hate me.'" Hicks and McMahon exchanged glances. "And if I'm not getting the ball enough, I look at my coach and say, 'He hate me.'" The executives had a laugh. McMahon looked at Smart. "We'll think about it," he said. As far as Smart knew, the prime-time viewers on NBC would know him simply by the name his mother gave him.

When Smart arrived at Sam Boyd Stadium on game day, Ben "Thoro" Snell bolted from the locker room with news of the modified jersey, and the two friends had a good laugh in the parking lot. McMahon changed his mind at the last minute, finally willing to take a gamble on his own outspoken devotion to outspokenness. And when every TV and newspaper story about the XFL's first game led with mention of HE HATE ME, using it as a device for good or ill, it was clear that everyone had made the right move. Rod Smart had his quarter hour.

But he had no power. During the practice week between Games One and Two, Smart got an idea based on visions of his newfound relevance, the countless interviews he had given, all the attention that went straight to his parabola. He wanted new words on the back of his jersey for the second game. "I want to change it to 'Who Is He,'" he told FitzGerald as the team departed the irrigated practice field one afternoon. "'Cause I want the people to know Rod Smart, and not just HE HATE ME, but Rod Smart." He sounded like a graffiti artist who sold his first painting for a million bucks. When the Outlaws entered the locker room in Memphis, Tennessee, for Game Two, Smart couldn't believe what he saw on the back of his jersey: HE HATE ME.

He chased down FitzGerald in the hallway. "Man, what about 'Who Is He'?" FitzGerald said that the request had arrived too late in the week for Stamford's approval. The following week, the same game played out: Smart requested Who Is He and FitzGerald claimed that the request had overshot a vague deadline. There was no way McMahon was going to ditch a nickname that had grown so familiar that sportscasters ceased to employ anything else in referring to the player who wore it. Smart relented.

"I thought everybody must really like that," he said, spread out on the carpet in his apartment. His phone rang once more. "I said, 'I guess I'll stick with it.' Apparently they weren't gonna let me change anyway. Guess the league hate me, too. I guess everybody found themselves a new hero, and it was me."

A set of knuckles rattled against the front door and Smart welcomed a guest. This woman couldn't get through on the phone, so she just showed up. She took a seat on the couch, where she crossed a pair of smooth legs.

Not only did McMahon prevent Smart from moving beyond HE HATE ME, stymieing the freedom of expression that he had championed, but he also maintained ownership of the riff. McMahon exerted his proprietary force much as he had with the names, characters, and even the gestures of his WWF wrestlers. With the XFL, McMahon applied the WWF formula: *I own everything, in case anything turns out to be something.*

Rod Smart wasn't blind to opportunity. He and his agent wanted to print HE HATE ME T-shirts, maybe put him in a few commercials. One call to Stamford dashed any hope at big dollars. McMahon highlighted the small type on the XFL player contract that Smart had signed before the season started. If McMahon owned The Rock's raised eyebrow and Stone Cold's 3:16, he certainly owned Rod Smart's HE HATE ME. And so it was. Vince McMahon tossed around favors like a man with no arms, claiming freedom of expression, though it was merely corporate double-speak for "anything that'll make me money." He shut out the man who devised the single most recognizable component of the league. Without lucrative possibilities, Smart took what the nickname and the TV exposure granted him.

His female visitor, bored now by talk of football, laid *The Source* back on the coffee table and stretched out her thighs. Looking for something that would speed the night to its purpose, she plucked Smart's two-way pager from between the couch cushions. She scrolled through his messages and discovered a way to end one conversation and begin another. "Dear HE HATE ME," she read, laughing aloud. "I sent you my panties in the mail. Love, Becky." She didn't mind coming here after so many others, and she walked to the back bedroom. Smart followed. The "esses" and "effs" of their whispers sounded like the noises that the cheetah sheets were about to make.

It was time to go, back out on the stoop in the same sliver of light where the evening began, through the clandestine portal. HE HATE ME scratched apologetically at his parabola. The air was charged with anything but hatred, more like the whiff and essence of it all. Smart peered over his shoulder at the legs that angled across the cheetah skin, glowing in the soft light of an unseen bulb. He grinned like a kid getting a bike for Christmas. "I didn't know she was gonna come over with no panties on."

Vince McMahon wasn't so lucky. When he learned the ratings for Game Three, his relief at having finished in time for *SNL* vanished quicker than Jon Lovitz's career. Las Vegas–Los Angeles—featuring the biggest (nick) name in the league, the second largest TV market in the country, and a bladder-busting last-second finish—delivered a number that shivered the very foundation of the XFL: 3.1. This was a stunning two-week turnaround, a 67 percent drop in viewership since Week One. More detailed numbers showed that the XFL had also suffered a 75 percent plunge in a key demo, men aged 18–34, since the first game. Game Three ranked as the lowest-rated prime-time show on any of the four major networks during the week, tying for eighty-ninth place overall with UPN's *Star Trek Voyager.* (Ratings on UPN and TNN reflected the drop, 51.6 percent and 50 percent, respectively, since their first games).

There was abundant scrambling at the GE Building. Come March, in just a few weeks, three straight Saturday-night XFL telecasts would go head-to-head against CBS's popular coverage of the NCAA basketball tournament.

Ebersol also realized that he would have to begin delivering "make-goods," or freebies, to his advertisers, as he had done when the Sydney Olympics failed to meet ratings guarantees. Ebersol and McMahon knew that falling shy of 4.5 would open the door for an advertising exodus. Ad buyers were notorious for jumping leaky ships. To this end, the league engaged in an embarrassing spin campaign. A sports-ratings chart showed up on XFL.com, and somehow the league ranked second for the week, higher than three NBA games, two days of the Nissan Open golf tournament, and two NCAA basketball games. The rankings were based on male viewers, and in all age groups, the XFL ranked second only to a Winston Cup race. This was sleight of hand. Upon closer inspection, the XFL had combined the ratings from its telecasts all three networks (NBC, TNN, and UPN) while counting the other sports as single games.

This may have tricked those wanting to be tricked, like when a wrestler miraculously wrenches his shoulder blade from the mat just before the ref counts three. Others weren't fooled so easily.

On Tuesday, February 20, Honda announced that it would permanently drop its advertising from XFL telecasts after having sat out weeks Two and Three. "We were promised this would be football, not the WWF," said Chuck Bachrach, executive vice president of Honda's ad agency, Rubin Postaer and Associates (RPA). "But really, they are merging the two. And giving us WWF on a football field." It was an odd monologue, considering how NBC had posited the league from the get-go. How could Bachrach have misunderstood the league's stated goal of combining the two? His comments sparked rumors around NBC. "They've done this before, with other clients," one NBC staffer said about RPA. "They never had any intention of staying with us in the long run. They wanted to drop out and then get all the free publicity that went with it." Honda and the agency certainly made news with their pullout, as papers were glad to cover the hit to McMahon's back pocket. Even more news came from Gerry Rubin, RPA's CEO, who recalled with nouveau-riche deportment his visit to the league's inaugural game. "The beverage of choice was not martinis with olives," he said. "And the parking lot didn't overflow with import automobiles, either." Rubin then slipped on his Bruno Maglis and beat it back to Southhampton.

McMahon flew into a rage, blaming Honda and the press for his XFL troubles. He lambasted the car company in staff meetings and plotted ways to exact revenge. *Advertising Age* would go on to report that McMahon set out a plan to blow up a Honda Accord on the field during halftime of an upcoming game. The story, like so many others about McMahon, proved more myth than matter. NBC never would have sanctioned the event, since the network pulled in millions of dollars from Honda advertising each year. Plus, McMahon was savvy enough to realize the amount of free publicity that such a stunt would generate for Honda. What did ring true about the story was the intensity of McMahon's fury, which infected everyone who drew an XFL check. From the top down, the message was clear: Honda was fair game. It wasn't long before animosity against the car manufacturer spilled over in the fraternal atmosphere that bathed the entire XFL project.

So it was that McMahon and crew looked upon February 25, 2001, with heavy hearts and involuntary sighs. When they had compiled the league schedule, this was meant to be a sure-thing telecast, New York versus Chicago, number-one and number-three TV markets in the country. Chicago's atavistic Soldier Field, where NFL cofounder George Halas and his Bears had played since long before luxury boxes and quarterback hand-warmers. Bone-chilling weather, the exact forecast that the league had used to sell itself back in the fall. The ground where Dick Butkus had played his dozen NFL seasons, and where he had filmed a gruff XFL TV ad in early winter. A game like this was perfectly positioned to amend the downward spike in the ratings.

There was just one problem. New York versus Chicago was a matchup of inveterate losers, with six losses and zero wins between them. The game-time temperature dipped below freezing, but not far enough for snow. Rain poured down, rendering the field—questionable in good weather—a soupy mess. To make matters worse, fog rolled in off Lake Michigan, a grim shroud befitting a funeral march. It may well have been, since Week Three's 3.1 rating had opened the floodgates of criticism, which, with bloodcurdling enthusiasm, began sounding the league's death knell only a quarter into its inaugural season.

"Being tops in bad football is no reason to keep the XFL," read *The New York Times*. "As NBC's XFL ship continues to take on water, it's every rat for himself," said the *New York Post*. TIME TO X OUT XFL EXPERIMENT, read a headline in *USA Today*. Business rags like *Variety, Bloomberg News,* and *The Hollywood Reporter* delineated the sobering numbers, and the sharks tightened the circle.

Crisis mode was upon Ebersol and McMahon, who began hunting for solutions that would prevent the next nine weeks (including playoffs) from killing them loudly. McMahon called on the focus groups, which told him several things: fans were lukewarm on Governor Ventura. And those who were still open to watching the XFL were looking for straight football, without all of the gimmicks. But Ebersol, swinging for the fences, still believed in blowing up the football model. While pressing each other for differing strategies, the two men managed to agree on one change for Week Four. Since the disparate components of the XFL hadn't fused organically, circumstances dictated that Ebersol and McMahon manufacture something out of the mess. With the ratings falling and the pressurized time of network TV running out, they agreed to try, for the first time, to make the hard and fast connection between football and wrestling, which until then they had hoped would magically appear from thin air.

Long ago in pro wrestling, before the days of the WWF's dominance, the "sport" was the thing. Fans attended matches to watch the men wrestle, to watch the acrobatics, even if they realized it was all fixed. Then the "angle" became the thing, and to understand the import of a WWF match was to know the history of a hundred interlaced feuds. The match wasn't about only the leaping and slamming—though they were certainly important—but also the back story, the soap opera, the row and the vendetta exacted. When McMahon witnessed his XFL head on a death spiral, he turned to his vaudeville ethic, since the game obviously wasn't the thing. He turned to Jesse Ventura.

When Ventura worked for McMahon in the 1980s, first as a wrestler and then as an announcer, the two argued constantly over money. Ventura said McMahon wasn't paying him enough. McMahon thought Ventura overestimated his importance, especially after appearing alongside Arnold Schwarzenegger in the 1986 movie *Predator*.

At the time, McMahon had a video-game deal that granted Nintendo the rights to all WWF personalities. Ventura, like everyone else in McMahon's employ, didn't see a penny from either the deal or the outside licensing opportunities that McMahon took advantage of, including the highlight videos and Topps trading cards for which McMahon had long used Ventura's likeness. Ventura thought he deserved a cut, especially when he started receiving merchandise royalty checks associated with his roles in *Predator* and *Running Man*. Ventura believed that he had played a considerable role in making the WWF what it was. He felt used. To prove his point to McMahon, Ventura signed a video-game contract of his own, with Sega-Genesis, for $40,000. In August 1990, McMahon fired him.

Ventura quickly found something to do. He ran for mayor of his hometown, Brooklyn Park, Minnesota, and won three months later. And in 1991 Ventura filed a lawsuit against McMahon, demanding a percentage of the money WWF earned from using his image on tapes, calendars, trading cards, and action figures. The case dragged on for years and, in the process, revealed that Ventura's longtime real-life enemy Hulk Hogan had been getting a 5 percent take on video sales all along. In 1994 Ventura won a judgment for roughly $900,000. He then went to work as an announcer for Ted Turner's rival WCW.

To any normal observer, this was the stuff of a lasting feud. But these weren't normal people. By design, McMahon populated his empire with stooges and cronies, last-chancers with few skills or options. Except for "The Body." Ventura made it clear time and again that his life didn't depend on McMahon's whimsy. Paradoxically, McMahon came to value his most contentious employee. Because he shot from the hip, Ventura was just about the only person in McMahon's world who he could trust.

The two men had little contact over the mid-1990s—there wasn't much reason to talk—but their relationship gained a new chapter when Ventura won the Minnesota governor's race on November 3, 1998. On *Raw Is War* the following Monday, McMahon instructed his announcers to congratulate Ventura on-air. (By contrast, Ventura's other ex-employer, WCW, inaugurated a mocking angle involving Hulk Hogan and a fictitious run for president.) McMahon's public congratulation meant a lot to Ventura, and when his old boss released a highlights tape, *Jesse "The Body" Ventura: The Mouth, The Myth, The Legend,* Ventura didn't mind so much.

Eight months after being sworn in as Minnesota's thirty-seventh governor, Ventura jumped back into the squared circle to referee a WWF SummerSlam event, held in Minneapolis's Target Center. During one match, Ventura tossed Shane McMahon out of the ring. State legislators were not pleased. "This didn't push the envelope," said Minnesota's House Majority Leader, Republican Tim Pawlenty. "It punched through it." Ventura was forging new enemies. But by inviting McMahon and his wife, Linda, to stay the night at the governor's mansion, he solidified an old alliance.

The SummerSlam appearance was another way for Ventura to challenge his quickly coalescing political opponents. At his January 1999 inauguration party, Ventura arrived riding a Harley, wearing a fringed leather jacket, a pink feather boa, skull-and-crossbones earrings, and a bandana on his head. "Let's party, Minnesota," he yelled when he took the stage. And when he learned of McMahon's plans for the XFL, he suggested that his old boss hire him as an announcer. It was another way to display his iconoclasm.

On January 23, 2001—two weeks before the start of the XFL season—Ventura submitted a Minnesota budget that contained the lowest state spending increases in fifteen years. A few days before introducing the budget, the governor disappeared in a puff of smoke, deflecting all interest in his travel plans as he walked out the door amid a hail of budget queries. Where did he go? To Las Vegas, to announce several closed XFL scrimmages. Several days later, he was back in Minnesota, where he told a group of students in Duluth where he had been all weekend. "Saturday I did two games for the XFL," he said to a round of collegiate applause. "Number one, nobody knew about it. Number two, the state's still here."

To many state legislators, Ventura had gone far enough. Was Ventura running the state or just his mouth? The *Playboy* interview. SummerSlam. And Ventura's two books, *I Ain't Got Time to Bleed* and *Do I Stand Alone?*, for which he reportedly earned a combined payout of $1 million. When he announced his intention to broadcast XFL games, a group of state representatives produced bills aimed at preventing the moonlighting. They had raised the question before. The issue was whether Ventura was technically considered a state employee. If so, then he would fall under the jurisdiction of the state ethics statute, which forbade state employees from engaging in work that they obtained specifically through their status as a state employee.

Ventura saw it coming and his attorneys prepared his XFL agreement with subsequent care. Ventura's league contract read, in part, that the "XFL shall not in any way promote or advertise Ventura's appearance in the Events, or in any Programs, by referring to Ventura as a candidate for Governor, Governor Elect or Governor of the State of Minnesota; and XFL shall not use or attempt in any way to use the prestige of the Office of the Governor of the State of Minnesota to promote or advertise Ventura's appearance in the Events, or in any programs." The XFL's explicit referral to Ventura as "Governor" would provide ammunition to those who believed that the only reason he landed the announcing job was because he was governor. "He certainly was in conflict," said Phil Krinkie, a six-term Republican representative from Shoreview, Minnesota. "He never would have gotten the XFL contract if he wasn't governor. They weren't gonna call up Jesse Ventura, former mayor of Brooklyn Park." That may have been true, but there were other reasons that Ventura fit into the original XFL template. That template was falling quickly apart. And it was obvious to even the casual observer that the XFL was damaging Ventura's political viability.

8

QUARTERBACK U.

THE WEEK FOUR TELECAST opened with play-by-play man Jim Ross in his ten-gallon hat, putting his best WWF spin on the proceedings. "Thirty thousand were expected," he said as John Gonzalez's cameras scanned the Solider Field crowd, making sure to keep the pictures tight. "But Mother Nature has flexed her muscle." The cold, hard rain kept all the fence sitters at home for the night, and the cameras were conspicuous in their unwillingness to zoom out, lest they betray section upon section of empty seats. Every fan shot consisted of just a few people, the cameras getting so close as to witness what a diet of Chicago chili cheese dogs did to a complexion.

Gonzalez was being a trooper, especially since Dick Ebersol and Ken Schanzer had dumped his favorite toy, Skycam. They didn't have the time for viewers to get acquainted with the angle, or the kind of money it took to operate Skycam, especially after the drop in ad revenue. Gone, too, were the field-long fireworks at the start of the game. The higher-ups had a different kind of fireworks display in mind.

Following Game One, Ebersol, McMahon, Schanzer, and just about everyone else involved in the preparation stages of the XFL saw red whenever Rusty Tillman's name came up. They were more than pleased to watch the developing Tillman-Ventura feud. The governor rode the coach pretty hard during the first game, and had continued whenever he could, as New York couldn't manage a win through its first three games. "He kicks a man when he's down," Tillman said. "Obviously, he's never had any adversity in his life. Like Clark Gable said: Frankly, Jesse, I don't give a damn." Tillman had taken the bait like Triple H reacting to an insult from the Undertaker. He was beginning to sound like his old self.

The first half in Chicago played out in a muddy, rainy mess. For the fourth game in a row, New York quarterback Charles Puleri displayed complete ineptitude. Jogging off the field at halftime, sideline agitator Fred Roggin asked Tillman whether he would replace Puleri with backup Wally Richardson. "That's good," Tillman snapped back. "You figured that out all by yourself?"

In the second half Tillman yanked Puleri in favor of Richardson, who drove New York to within a few yards of Chicago's end zone. The Hitmen looked like they might actually punch the ball in for a touchdown, the rain pelting the field of play. But the drive stalled at the two-yard line. Instead of trying for a touchdown on fourth down, Tillman sent in his kicker for a field goal. In a scoreless game on the road in brutal weather conditions, it was the right move. But the governor saw it as an opening. "Gutless Rusty," Ventura bellowed into the mike, before the kick went through the uprights.

Vince McMahon handled the orchestration, screaming into Fred Roggin's earpiece, ordering him after Rusty Tillman. "Rusty, Rusty, Rusty," Roggin yelped like a schnauzer. "Jesse Ventura just said you were gutless." This was how fistfights started at recess. "I don't have anything to say to Jesse Ventura," Tillman scowled. "He wouldn't know if a football was pumped or stuffed."

Gonzalez cut to a shot of Ventura standing up on the broadcast platform. He was grinning. "I'm getting under his skin," said the governor, huffing and puffing, as his Big Bad Wolf role required. This prompted Jim Ross into full WWF mode: "You got a grudge match building."

As the game lingered, like a toothache, viewers were treated to stories lifted from Hallmark's discard pile. A player's lymphoma overcome with faith. Another player, whose mother had died a few years ago during a game at the stadium, placed flowers in her vacant seat. An adoption story with an ending that warmed the cockles. The same stock storylines of an Olympics telecast. The raucous, boundary-busting league had succumbed to being the NFL's bastard brigand, complete with the piercing commentary of the governor: "There's a sack."

It was hard to blame Ventura for dull explication, since the game provided very little to inflate with his well-known brand of hot air. Instead, he cast about for more material to stoke the WWF-style angle. "I definitely think Richardson's a better quarterback," Ventura said. "I woulda found that out in training camp. Tillman couldn't figure that out." Jim Ross added his reaction, mined from the playground: "Whoa-ho." This wasn't the only tactic designed to keep viewers on board. Since the game held all the thrill of QVC, the only thing to do was hype the angle, like a steel-cage match that's previewed during the undercard. So Gonzalez ran tape of Tillman's early-season comments: "Frankly, Jesse, I don't give a damn."

Ventura lay in wait. "Rusty has issues with everybody," he said. "He's obviously an unhappy man. He had a bad childhood." Ventura displayed the bluff tactics of the bully pulpit, which he used as governor—and may attempt in an even higher office. An ad for NBC's *The West Wing* appeared on the screen. "I'm going to the West Wing tomorrow," Ventura said, bragging about an upcoming Governor's Association conference at the White House. Gonzalez's cameras cut to a fan in the Soldier Field crowd who wore a plastic Jesse Ventura mask. "That guy we saw down there, he should be president," Ventura said. Was that an official announcement? Where was the fanfare? It would have to wait for further shilling. A running back's head snapped back in a tackle, prompting Ventura to grab the bullhorn. "Great camera work here in the XFL. Really makes the fan part of the game."

Richardson led New York to a touchdown and a 10–0 lead. The fourth quarter dwindled, and as the clock ticked down, Fred Roggin located Rusty Tillman on the sideline and asked about the prospect of his first win. "The game's not over yet," Tillman said, cautious about this one ending up like the others.

"That Rusty's a smart guy," Ventura said. "If anybody's capable of blowing a ten-nothing lead with seven-fifty to go in the game, it's Rusty Tillman. He's not winning 'cause he's a good coach. He's winning 'cause he's lucky."

The game wound below one minute, and a shot of several Chicago fans graced the screen. They crowded the lens, delirious though their team was losing its fourth game in a row. They looked hooked on something very cheap. "Over thirty thousand were expected," Ross said again, stumped for anything else to say, sounding like a lonely host left with an extra keg. Was this really happening on NBC?

The clock came to its final fading digits, and Ventura reached for a crowing statement, something that would keep everyone from dozing off. He announced that he would hike down through the stands at the end of the game. He was going to interview Rusty Tillman. Ventura made a big show of unplugging himself from the broadcast booth, then walked through the empty seats toward the field. As a terrible night drew to its close, the rain still coming down in sheets, Jim Ross sounded like he was apologizing for getting sick on the new rug. "The XFL, as we all know, is a work in progress," he stammered. "But we're having fun."

Ventura made it to the field as the final whistle blew. Tillman and his Hitmen had won their first game. They just wanted to get out of the rain and on a plane back to New York. The coach jogged toward the locker room. Ventura followed in hot pursuit. He caught him at midfield, with the Bubba Cam at the governer's elbow. "Rusty," Ventura boomed into his microphone, trying to keep pace. "Ain't ya gonna talk to me?"

Tillman jogged on in silence, maintaining his composure. Finally, he couldn't resist the microphone that was right beside his jaw. "I don't wanna talk to you."

Fred Roggin was there, too, jogging along and nipping at Tillman's heel like a puppy. "Why don't you wanna talk to Jesse?" he asked.

"I'm not gonna talk to Jesse Ventura."

Tillman quickened his pace, blowing them both off, the bulldog and the Chihuahua.

This left Jesse Ventura standing in the middle of an empty field, microphone dangling at the end of his arm like a useless appendage. He looked like a wrestler in the ring playing to a depleted crowd, which obliged him by chanting "asshole" in the fading direction of Tillman. "I got him intimidated," Ventura hollered into his microphone. "He couldn't wait to get off the field. He's afraid of me."

As Tillman jogged toward the locker room, he shook his head at what had just happened. "Truth is, I would love to have given him a shot right there on the field," he would later say. "Twenty years ago, I probably would have. I didn't want to come off as Curly, Moe, and Larry. If anybody was gonna be a stooge, it was gonna be him."

The final image of the telecast left the governor of Minnesota sullied by the mud that rose above his boots. The big "C" symbol of the NFL's Chicago Bears, too long etched onto the field, showed through the XFL logo painted atop it like clown makeup. The lingering question involved McMahon's failure to adhere to a fundamental tenet of his own business—to work an angle, you need two willing participants.

John Gonzalez was forced to direct the Tillman-Ventura debacle, but he didn't like what he saw. He was friendly with Rusty Tillman and he felt awful about the way McMahon and Ventura were treating him. Gonzalez knew Tillman loved wine, so the following week, Gonzalez drove to a Hitmen practice with a bottle of Duckhorn merlot in hand. "I took it to him almost as a personal 'I'm sorry.'"

A few hours after the New York–Chicago game had come to a merciful conclusion, a poll appeared on XFL.com. "Who do you side with?" it asked. By one-thirty A.M. in the East, more than fifteen thousand votes had been cast, split evenly between Tillman and Ventura. This was going to win fans?

As the main telecast finished up, Ebersol and McMahon confronted a new headache on NBC's regional game, Birmingham versus Orlando. Matt Vasgersian was calling the game, with Jerry Lawler providing color commentary. A placekicker struggled all night, and toward the end of the game, Lawler uttered a comment that could only come from years bathed in the Us versus Them universe of McMahon's employ. After the kicker missed another field goal, Lawler said that he was "about as dependable as a Honda automobile."

The comment didn't sneak by. As Ken Schanzer later said, "Vince handled it."

In Las Vegas, Jim Criner cut loose quarterback Mike Cawley after his inept performance against L.A. He hadn't thrown the game; he was just a bad quarterback. With Ryan Clement still nursing his injured shoulder, Criner had to find someone fast.

The team claimed a quarterback off waivers, an Arena League refugee named Mark Grieb. The quarterback had spent the 1998 season with Criner in NFL Europe, and the coach believed he could trust him with the ball. "Mark is a guy we can win with," Criner said. The sentiment rumpled Clement, who realized he could lose his grip on the starting job. He needed to get back in action fast, where the NFL scouts could see him play. Clement's vague chance at the big time was crumbling before his eyes.

When Grieb showed up at the practice field behind Sam Boyd Stadium to take snaps for the first time, it was more than just Criner's anointing that filled Clement with acid. It was Grieb himself. He was well spoken and churchgoing, with a clean-cut style that would make any partyer a little uncomfortable. He was Clement's antithesis.

Clement had a goofy smile and one of those pasty, doughy bodies that come from too many nights out, too much reliance on fading resilience. The Outlaw coaches had started calling him Billy Kilmer, after the 1970s-era Washington Redskins quarterback who was as famous for his late nights as for his ability to lose an arm and a leg on the field and still toss a touchdown. Grieb studied his playbook with technical devotion, while Clement preferred to wing it, believing in his loose natural ability. Grieb went to Bible study; Clement hit the blackjack table. It was typical quarterback friction, with both players maintaining a public facade of cooperation.

A tough practice finished early in the week. The Outlaws lumbered toward the showers. Most of the guys couldn't wait to get lunch, but Grieb stayed behind. In full pads, and in full view of Coach Criner, Grieb ran the width of the field through a set of wind sprints. Clement stood and watched, laughing to himself. "Would you look at this guy," he said.

Clement left practice and soon found himself up on the Strip. He drove past the MGM Grand, with its green towers that glowed at all hours. He looked up at the marquee and saw an ad for the casino's new show, *EFX*, which starred Rick Springfield, the erstwhile teen heartthrob. Springfield hadn't been on the charts in twenty years, yet there he was up on the marquee strumming a guitar with rose petals flying from its strings, unseen money lining his pockets. Springfield had managed to resurrect a long-dead career on this end-of-the-road show. That was all Clement wanted, something approximating an old dream. "From the time I was two years old, I was gonna be a quarterback in the NFL," he said.

Growing up, Clement had split allegiances when it came to the NFL. He loved John Elway's Broncos, but he also dreamed of wearing the Raiders' silver and black. In his visions of that distant draft day when the

NFL commissioner would send his name booming over the PA, either team would do.

This was every kid's fantasy. But unlike most kids, Clement looked like he had the stuff to make it happen. As a freshman, he started as quarterback for Denver's Mullen High School varsity, beating out kids three years older for the job. He was that good, and four years later, football publications rated him at the top of the country's quarterback prospects, ahead of a high school star from Louisiana named Peyton Manning, who would go on to play for the University of Tennessee.

From a swarm of college-football programs whose famous coaches shuffled like nervous suitors around him, Clement picked the University of Miami, winner of four national championships over the previous ten years. It was a football factory that churned out NFL draft picks—eighteen first-rounders in eleven years—with a frequency unlike any other college. The real draw was Miami's quarterback lineage, which included players like Jim Kelly, Bernie Kosar, and Vinny Testaverde. The team showcased its quarterbacks as coaches took advantage of the perpetual South Florida sun, repeatedly calling plays that sent the Long Bomb deep down the field. The style was more NFL than NCAA. The previous four Miami starting quarterbacks had all won the national championship and gone on to play in the NFL. Fans called the place Quarterback U.

Clement played sparingly during his freshman season, 1994. That year, the Hurricanes lost in the national title game, the Orange Bowl, to Nebraska. Their defense boasted Ray Lewis, Warren Sapp, and Dwayne Douglas Johnson, soon to be The Rock, whose teammates often teased him about his wrestling pedigree. Clement was poised to assume the starting job of a national powerhouse. He didn't know that Miami's football program was about to suffer a monumental blow.

In 1995 the NCAA blew the whistle on a series of scandals within the program. When the sanctions came down (twenty-four precious scholarships slashed over two years), players and coaches scattered, aware of the fallow period that lay ahead. Quarterback U. fell into jeopardy just as Clement was getting the ball. To make matters worse, there was a quarterback controversy. New coach Butch Davis opened up the job before the '95 season, and it quickly became a showdown between Clement and senior Ryan Collins.

Miami booster and legendary paramour Luther Campbell, of 2 Live Crew, started mouthing off late-night at a club about a pay-for-play scheme he had devised for Miami players. Campbell mandated that Collins, who is black, be given the starting job over Clement. "If it comes down to them disrespecting a black quarterback and the black community and just black kids in general, then whatever I could do to speak out about what I know to straighten their (act), I'm going to do that. If they don't start Ryan Collins, I will tell all." The comments appeared in the *Miami Herald* the next day and created another national scandal for Clement to navigate.

A few games into the season, Clement managed to land the starting job, despite Campbell's best efforts. The team went 7–1 with Clement at the helm. The next season would be a different story. The Hurricanes dropped three straight home games and fell from the national top-twenty-five rankings for the first time in more than a decade. Clement managed to galvanize the team with his own rugged play, salvaging his junior season with a 9–3 record. Still, this wasn't how it was supposed to be. Clement and Miami were meant to play for the national title. With one season left before the NFL draft, Clement was 15–4 as Miami's starter.

Problem was, by 1997 the NCAA sanctions had so depleted the roster that Clement was throwing to four freshman wide receivers. Miami lost three straight games early that season, and the vultures started circling. Fans and media focused their anger over the sanctions and the defeats squarely on Clement, who lashed out at the criticism. "If you want to point fingers, point them at the NCAA and all those teams people loved down here. Those are the teams that had the guys who broke the rules. So if you're looking to blame, blame them." The following weekend, archrival Florida State waltzed into Miami and crushed Clement's 'Canes—*47–0*. It was Miami's fourth loss in a row, and the Orange Bowl felt like a cemetary.

Miami's last game in 1997, against Syracuse, attracted a meager Orange Bowl crowd of 25,000 fans. It rained all day. Clement broke his nose on a brutal hit early in the game, and Coach Butch Davis pulled him in the fourth quarter. It was his last college game. The Hurricanes lost 33–13, dropping their record to 5–6. It was the school's first losing season since 1979, and the first year without a bowl game since 1984. "This is the bottom," said Clement.

*   *   *

No matter the disappointments of his Miami years, Clement still knew how to operate on a football field. He worked out for NFL coaches at the obligatory predraft combine—running, jumping, and crawling like the hunk of beef that he was to the grizzled men in stretchy shorts who had million-dollar contracts stuffed into their back pockets. Clement was there in Indianapolis and couldn't believe it, watching his heroes walk by right in front of him after all these years of dreaming. There was Oakland Raiders managing partner Al Davis. Like a first-day employee in a fresh necktie, Clement couldn't resist introducing himself to the boss. "Yeah, Clement," Davis said as though in a haze, slowly relinquishing Clement's handshake. "Oh yeah, I know who you are. I keep up on you." Another day, Clement got a call from his hometown Broncos. "Look, Ryan," said Denver's offensive coordinator, Gary Kubiak. "We're looking at taking a quarterback late. And I think you might be the guy." Clement couldn't sleep as draft day drew near. His two favorite teams were taking a serious look.

On draft day, Clement had to force himself to stay awake as round after round concluded without NFL commissioner Paul Tagliabue sending his name booming out over the PA. The draft spilled into a second day, as NFL teams filled their rosters with chaff during the later rounds, when they selected players more out of hope and hunch than a belief that they would actually stick in the league. And even through all this, Clement never had cause to get off the couch. No team drafted him.

There was still hope. The only thing NFL scouts saw, Clement figured, was the 5–6 senior season record at Miami, not the NCAA sanctions that had helped create it. Clement believed he would hook on somewhere if he could just get himself in front of a coach for a few workouts. Instead, NFL teams treated Clement like the Plague. There was talk—and plenty of it—that then–Miami Dolphins head coach Jimmy Johnson, who coached the Hurricanes during part of the scandal seasons, had spread the word among his pro colleagues that Clement was bad news. People said Johnson was making Clement pay for his comments about the NCAA sanctions.

Clement's agent managed to get him face time with the Browns and the Steelers. But the teams told him before he even showed up that they had no plans of offering a contract; the workouts were the equivalent of keeping his résumé on file. Clement was at the bottom. And he couldn't escape constant news reports about the draft's number one pick, Peyton Manning, who signed a six-year, $47.9 million contract with the Indianapolis Colts—$11.6 million of it up-front. How had Clement fallen so far behind?

California's Bay Area supported two NFL teams, the 49ers and the Raiders. Even so, Pac Bell Park was just about packed for the game between Vegas and the San Francisco Demons. Crowds bunched along Willie Mays Way outside the stadium, where a droning Linkin Park song cranked out of the wall speakers. Fans were circling the entrance gates like the gulls up above. If McMahon had seven more San Franciscos, he would have done just fine.

Down on the sidelines, a square-headed reporter breathlessly explained that the turf was wet. There is no more staid convention of network football broadcasting than the cleat report. Here it was, the fourth week of the season, and fans were dealing in the same NFL inanities that just weeks before had taken such a hit from McMahon and Ebersol. It was a sign of an inner shift. "It became clearer and clearer that the football fan was our base," said Ken Schanzer. The XFL brass had come to realize that they were playing catch-up, trying to hold on to a core football audience, since the kids had long since gone away to the WB.

The teams took the field to the strains of Spinal Tap's "Hell Hole" as the stadium sound crew tried to match the foreboding atmosphere created by a crowd full of bloody scythes and horned Satan masks. This game was pitting the best offense in the XFL (the Demons averaged 315 yards per game) against the league's best defense, and Jim Criner was betting on Kelvin Kinney and crew to win the battle.

In the second quarter, the Demons scored a touchdown, the first one allowed all season by the stingy Vegas defense. Rod Smart tied the game on his first touchdown run just before halftime. The cameras gravitated toward the obligatory "We Hate He" sign in the crowd.

By the time the second half came around, Vegas quarterback Mark Grieb was looking pretty steady. He hadn't thrown an interception or committed a costly mistake. The Outlaws' offensive coordinator, Vince Alcalde, had told Ryan Clement to be ready in case Grieb faltered. When Grieb got the ball around midfield halfway through the third quarter, down 9–6 on the scoreboard, he took the snap, stepped back, and tossed a Long Bomb down the center of the field. Wideout Mike Furrey ran under the ball and hauled it in for a forty-one-yard touchdown. It was the Outlaws' longest pass play of the season. On the sideline, Ryan Clement groaned. The Outlaws took the game 16–9.

Rod Smart broke out for his best game yet, gaining 90 yards on 18 carries. Maybe now he felt like he had earned all the attention that he received at his locker stall, where he stepped back and regaled the local reporters standing before him. "I get along with everybody," Smart chuckled. He turned it up a notch when an XFL camera crew approached to tape a few comments about next week's matchup in Chicago, where he would go up against the league's top rusher, John Avery. "I had a dream last night," Smart said, stroking his chin in mock thought. "I woke up and somebody was saying 'I hate you.' I think it was John Avery." Everyone laughed.

The XFL's Week Four ratings landed with a thud on the gilded desks at NBC. The governor's version of Hatfield and McCoy, Tillman and Ventura, scored a 2.6. Not only was the XFL flirting with setting a new low in prime-time network sports ratings, but eight weeks remained in the season, including playoffs. After Week One's gargantuan 9.5, the league had plummeted in successive weeks: from 4.6 to 3.1, and now 2.6. How long could NBC sacrifice its Saturday night? "We'll stick with it, let the story lines grow, and hope for the best," Jeff Zucker told reporters on a teleconference. "I certainly hope it has bottomed out. We have to figure out the right amount of football and the right amount of show. I'm a huge football fan, but I'd love to see more show. Maybe they should give the cheerleaders poles to dance around."

The league was taking it from all sides, and the only person who was there to defend it was Jesse Ventura. "Give yourselves a hand," he told the National Press Club over a Washington luncheon on Monday, February 26. "A lot of the media dislikes Vince McMahon with a passion. The media assumed [the XFL] would be football players hitting each other with chairs. When it turned out they were fooled, then it was 'Well, it's not the NFL. The talent isn't as good.' We never said we were going to be the NFL. This league is about players who want to play the game and continue to play the game because they love it. I like to call it the *Rudy* league." With ratings this poor, comparison to a B-movie seemed about right.

*   *   *

The day after Ventura affected his defensive stance, Vince McMahon landed in Tuscon, Arizona, for a WWF telecast. Jerry Lawler was also in the Tuscon Convention Center.

Lawler was there with his twenty-nine-year-old wife of five months, Stacy Carter, who wrestled under the name "The Kat." Known as Chyna's sidekick, The Kat had spent about a year in the WWF and her biggest moment came topless in a pay-per-view.

As The King and The Kat prepared for the upcoming show, Jim Ross located Lawler in the bowels of the convention center. "Vince has decided that he doesn't want to go any further with The Kat's angle," Ross said. "And subsequently, he wants me to give her her release today."

Lawler was stunned. He stomped straight to McMahon's makeshift office in the arena and announced that he was quitting the WWF. "I'm leaving with her," Lawler said. "You had to know I would leave with her, Vince."

"I hoped you wouldn't," McMahon said coolly.

Soon after the incident, Lawler poured his heart onto his website, www.kinglawler.com: "I almost expected someone to come up to me and say with a smile, 'What a rib!' And that this would all be some kind of sick joke or something. But that didn't happen. It wasn't a joke. It was the real thing. . . . Let me say that I don't really know what is going on other than that I feel there is more to this than meets the eye. . . ." Was it so hard to connect the dots from the Honda comment to the sacking?

Two days later, McMahon asked Dick Butkus to take Lawler's place on NBC's secondary telecast. Putting Butkus in the booth was tantamount to admitting the defeat of the hybrid. What could Butkus provide besides standard football commentary in a league that originally purported to be so much more? On WWF telecasts, McMahon replaced Lawler with Paul Heyman, owner of the defunct Extreme Championship Wrestling, as he consolidated his hold on the pro wrestling empire.

9

ONE WAY OR
THE OTHER

THIS WAS JUST THE LATEST chapter in a farcical story that had been told so many times as to become fable, the story of Vince McMahon. In a public career that spanned three decades, McMahon created wrestling's brand name, its Coke; he devoured Ted Turner; and according to a good chunk of the viewing public, he stooped to conquer a new territory of sleaze TV, arm-wrestling Jerry Springer for the title of King Dirtbag. McMahon's approach had coalesced a legion of fans. It had also earned him the unanimous derision of the Establishment. What did the doyen of an ignoble age care about that? With the millennium coming to a close, the bottom line informed McMahon that he was unassailable.

In a single year, from 1998 to 1999, World Wrestling Federation revenues jumped 100 percent. The company cleared $56 million, up from $8.5 million in 1998. As recently as 1997 the WWF had posted a loss of $6.5 million, thanks to both a downturn in the wrestling business and the success of Ted Turner's rival operation, World Championship Wrestling, which chewed into McMahon's fan base. McMahon's turnaround came courtesy of a new producing approach to the WWF show. There was more sex, more violence, more everything. He took wrestling to places that Ted Turner was either unable or unwilling to go.

Once McMahon started winning the ratings war against WCW, the bankers gathered around him began talking about diversifying the business. This became the mantra at WWF headquarters in Stamford, Connecticut, where a WWF flag flapped in the wind, as though over a defended fort. Diversification was a bet against being rendered vulnerable by the collapse of a single wing of the business, as had been the case when Turner entered into wrestling. Stamping the WWF seal on a variety of products would provide a safety valve. It would also stroke the boss's ego, as he could talk about being involved in the Entertainment Business. McMahon started a record label, and his wrestling-anthem CDs pierced Billboard's Top 10. He brokered book deals for his wrestlers, who wrote best-selling memoirs. He opened his theme restaurant in Times Square. "We have what America wants," he boasted.

McMahon had tried it all before, and with near uniform failure. In 1991 he assembled the World Bodybuilding Federation, which was one letter and a few tumbles away from his bread-and-butter product. The WBF lasted eighteen months, two events, and one mention of forty-year-old Lou Ferrigno, who had planned a comeback; he had "always felt empty and unfulfilled" after giving up bodybuilding to become the Incredible Hulk. Ferrigno remained unfulfilled as McMahon lost $15 million and shuttered the WBF. Next for McMahon came Icopro, a five-day diet supplement, which promptly tanked. McMahon also tried his hand at boxing and concert promotion, experiences that only reinforced his expertise in wrestling. He bought an L.A. hotel and entertainment complex with plans to renovate it into a $100 million WWF-themed vacation spot. A short time later he quietly sold the property, proving that for the time being, he didn't have a golden touch outside the ring.

All along, McMahon believed in expansion and diversification. And in 1998 he came upon what looked like a perfect opportunity, a chance to join a group with a sterling profile. The NFL. Investors who owned the Minnesota Vikings wanted to sell. McMahon had the money. He and his family privately owned the WWF, which was worth more than the New York Yankees, the Knicks, and the Rangers combined. That wasn't the problem. The question was the NFL Board of Governors.

McMahon joined a strange group of suitors for the Vikings. There was novelist Tom Clancy, who appeared to write another deathless finale when he convened a press conference announcing that a $200 million deal for the team had been completed. It hadn't. There was a mysterious Las Vegas couple who claimed to own $2.4 billion in gold, silver, and platinum stored in a secret warehouse. The NFL discovered that the couple had gone bankrupt.

Among these inconstants, McMahon looked like a steadying influence. But when his turn came, laughter rang through NFL headquarters on Park Avenue. He didn't have a chance with the NFL Board of Governors, who pointed him toward the taxis flowing many stories below. On his way out of the experience, McMahon was heard to say of the NFL owners, "I've never met twenty-eight bigger assholes in my life."

Did McMahon really want to buy the Vikings? Was he interested in having one vote out of twenty-eight? McMahon may have found common ground on the NFL Board of Governors with the Oakland Raiders' Al Davis, but it was difficult imagining the very omnipotence of the WWF relinquishing his scepter among the oligarchic NFL. "The Minnesota Vikings stuff—that was just for press, put the WWF's name out there in a different league," said Jim Bell, who worked for five years as the WWF's senior vice president of licensing and merchandising before leaving the company in 2000. "Don't forget, he's the modern-day P. T. Barnum." Whatever his level of sincerity, McMahon wasn't finished with his NFL sideshow. He placed a few calls to Washington, D.C., asking about the Redskins, another team sitting on the block. The Redskins eventually went to Daniel Snyder for a sports-franchise record $800 million, and McMahon quickly retreated from the Entertainment Business. He spent the rest of 1998 and early 1999 amping the WWF, whipping the WCW, and solidifying his grip on pro wrestling. But he wouldn't forget the sting of his NFL foray.

It took just nine months before McMahon got a shot at rubbing balm on his wound. It was March 1999, and expressing greetings on the other end of the phone line was Carl DeMarco, president of WWF Canada. DeMarco explained that the president of the Canadian Football League, Jeff Giles, was casting about for someone with deep pockets. Labatt Breweries, which owned the CFL's Toronto Argonauts, wanted to unload the team, one of the league's most visible franchises. Giles had called DeMarco to float the idea to McMahon.

"When we met with Vince, immediately he had no interest in owning a team," Giles said. "He was more interested in owning the whole league." McMahon wanted to split the CFL into two divisions, with eight teams on each side of the border. He talked about modifying Canadian rules (among other differences, the CFL plays on a larger field and allows for three offensive downs per series instead of four), bringing the game closer to what Americans were accustomed to watching. Then he would toss in innovations of his own. "He wanted to change a lot of it," Giles said. In fact, McMahon had already composed the basic tenets of what would eventually play out on NBC. "He was using the same words to describe football at that time," Giles said, "which were 'smashmouth football,' and comparing it to the NFL, which he didn't think was that style of football. I think he looked at football as another aspect of being in the entertainment business."

The CFL talks distended through the summer of 1999. One day, Jeff Giles answered a call on his cell phone while driving through the outskirts of Toronto. It was Carl DeMarco. "Vince wants to talk to you," DeMarco said. "But he doesn't talk on cell phones. You have to find a phone booth." Giles felt like a spy as he scanned the unfamiliar territory beyond his windshield. "I was out in the middle of nowhere," he said. "So I pulled into an empty parking lot. I was in this phone booth in this big parking lot all by myself, and I'm talking with Vince McMahon on the phone."

Giles had presented McMahon's plan to the CFL Board of Governors, but the owners were skeptical. A ninety-year-old league, older than the NFL, the CFL was not about to enter lightly into the service of Vince McMahon. Canadians had witnessed the National Hockey League's Americanization, which swapped Quebecs for Colorados and robbed the game of its agrarian soul. Several CFL owners, while attracted by a payday, were reluctant to relinquish their league's autonomy to a man who presided over what some of them considered the rudest mass entertainment available. Three teams, the Edmonton Eskimos, the Saskatchewan Roughriders, and the Winnipeg Blue Bombers—all of them owned by their local communities, like the Green Bay Packers—flat-out refused to sell to McMahon. The Board of Governors would need a majority vote to approve the sale. Giles spent weeks shuttling between McMahon and his governors, repeatedly urging McMahon to reconsider buying only the Argonauts.

McMahon wasn't interested. By September 1999, it was clear that the deal wasn't going to happen. "Vince said, 'I wish the CFL well,'" said Giles. "He told us quite clearly that if we didn't want to work with him, he was going to go and start a league. It was 'I'm going to do it one way or the other. So you can either do it with me, or I'll do it separately.'"

McMahon didn't take easily to being kept from a desire. The principle of being able to have whatever you wanted—that defined power. He was determined to gain entrée to pro football, especially given what lay ahead. He planned to produce an ace from his sleeve.

It was October 19, 1999, anniversary of the 1987 stock-market crash, and a cloying Martha Stewart stood on a corner along Wall Street, handing out brioche to passersby, her smile turning several innocents to stone. Stewart's company was going public. McMahon's, too. The WWF, a family business for four generations, would soon trade on the big board. The McMahon clan, which was selling nonvoting shares purely to raise capital, would retain 97.3 percent of the company. Vince, who personally owned the majority of WWF Entertainment, was already wealthy. But now he stood to become the kind of man who shuttled castles stone by stone across the Atlantic. Yet he still couldn't win respect in many corners. "Their numbers are just fantastic," one analyst said of the WWF. "The downside is that it is a hundred percent owned by a fellow that still wrestles." Within hours of the opening bell, WWF stock doubled from its starting price of $17. It settled toward afternoon, and by close it was worth $25.25. Martha Stewart carried the day, doubling the value of her company's stock and surpassing Oprah Winfrey as the wealthiest woman in America. McMahon did just fine for himself. After the first few days of trading, WWF Entertainment was valued at $2.27 billion, the McMahons at more than $1.93 billion. It wasn't long before Vince and his minions referred to their company by a new moniker—it would be known as WWFE, its New York Stock Exchange listing. In its corporate incarnation, the wrestling circuit had finally matched in length the words that had spurred its success.

McMahon surveyed his realm. The IPO had quantified his considerable worth, and publicly. The WCW scare was a laughable memory. And the WWF's TV contract with USA Network was coming due within a year, at just the right time—WWF ratings were higher than they had ever been. The WWF machine hummed like a wrestler absorbing his steroid spike. McMahon wasn't so much restless or foolhardy as he was newly flush. What to buy?

That kind of cash augurs only larger appetites, eccentricity, the kindergarten forays that only the powerful or childlike are suffered to exhibit. Like the time when Howard Hughes arrived in Las Vegas on Thanksgiving 1966 and moved into the Desert Inn penthouse. Weeks later, when the Desert Inn owners begged him to relinquish the suite to casino high rollers, the hermitical Hughes didn't want to go. He bought the Desert Inn. And then he purchased much of everything else he saw out in the desert. If he was going to live there, locked up in his suite for years, he wanted to see his name etched on the things beyond his window.

Likewise for McMahon. Suddenly, post-IPO, it looked like he could bestow his seal on much of the world. With his fortunes and the successes they foretold, he was all of a sudden welcome in any boardroom in America—as if he needed a boost. His confidence soared. Long gone were the days of a ratings interregnum. McMahon felt like he had conquered the world, the charted portions at least, and he was ready to map the rest. He had always thought in big hunks, not little bites. That was what had enabled him to arrive at the billion-dollar payday. All that money only allowed the hunks to increase in size. Was there a bigger idea than the XFL?

"It started originally with the idea of buying the Canadian Football League," Jim Bell said. "And since they said no, Vince then had the money to consider starting it up on his own." McMahon convened a small team of his trusted lieutenants in Stamford, among them Basil DeVito, the WWF's newly appointed president of new business development. DeVito, the fourth person McMahon ever hired, had worked at the WWF from 1985 to 1994, and again from 1997 to 1998. He was a master organizer, one of McMahon's most loyal employees, and eventually rose to the position of WWF chief operating officer. DeVito briefly left the WWF for a job with the National Thoroughbred Racing Association. But McMahon lured him back to Stamford in October 1999 to head the group that would devise his new project. It was a pro football league that would incorporate the WWF attitude and stick it to the NFL. It was called Raw Football.

The boss man spelled out the concept, and everyone recognized its tenets. McMahon had long ago stopped catering to the fans in his wrestling arenas. He had transformed the WWF from a live experience into a spectacle for TV, with fans little more than atmosphere, like a studio audience at a talk-show taping. The NFL still did things the old-fashioned way, putting on games for a live audience. Commercial breaks were short, play was constant, and the stadium show differed little from what fans watched from the couch. When it came to football, McMahon wanted to reverse the NFL philosophy. He wanted to get closer to the action, and to the character of the game—all of it orchestrated for the benefit of the viewer, rather than the spectator.

Jim Bell attended the strategy sessions. "Vince was trying to go back to football when he remembered it being more enjoyable to watch. The days of Dick Butkus, the days when the quarterback wasn't an endangered species. And then blend in some new rules that would make it a more exciting game." At first Bell didn't have much enthusiasm. As a marketing veteran, he knew full well the dominance of the NFL, how difficult it would be to establish a rival league. Nonetheless, Bell shopped a marketing plan to licensees, gauging interest.

At the same time, McMahon was trying to find a TV outlet for his hypothetical brand of football. On this front, several factors were converging. The McMahons invoked a clause that allowed the WWF to opt out of its TV contract with Barry Diller's USA Network. They didn't necessarily want to leave USA; they wanted a better deal than the one they signed in early 1998, when WWF ratings were slim. Plus, they wanted to include an important clause in any new contract—that USA broadcast their new football league as a condition of landing the WWF deal. USA execs, however, weren't so sure. Was the burden of an unproven football league—which existed only on paper—outweighed by the proven asset of the WWF? *Raw Is War* was the number one regularly scheduled cable program in the world. The longer USA dragged its feet, the more McMahon seethed.

Meanwhile, Jim Bell, fresh from his foray to companies such as Nike and Spalding, had undergone a sweeping change of opinion. Every company that Bell approached wanted in on McMahon's new project. "We were beating them off with a stick," Bell said. The results confirmed McMahon's hunch, not only in his football concept but also in his juice within the Entertainment Business. As long as McMahon's name was attached, any project could find interested parties. Now he just needed a broadcast partner.

Basil DeVito, Jim Bell, and the rest of the Stamford brass figured that the league would best be served by appearing on a second-tier broadcast network (like UPN or WB) in conjunction with a cable channel (such as TNT or

TNN). This wasn't the NFL. It would take time for fans to get their heads around the product, which had been rechristened as XFL. McMahon had to start small. "We wanted to hit singles and doubles with the property—not home runs," Bell says. "The original plan was to push on Sunday, where football viewership was already established. The idea was you had a spring league at a time when sports was at a wane on TV. And you had an opportunity to build a league. There was no doubt that this was a long-term proposition."

Launching the league without a TV contract would have been insane. But a certain kind of willful insanity was the norm on the heels of the WWF's IPO. McMahon felt invincible. And the feedback he received from Bell's marketing report buoyed him even further. The millennium turned without definitive word from USA. McMahon was more than antsy. He felt insulted.

Under a spell of rage and hubris, McMahon hurriedly called a press conference for February 3, 2000, at the WWF Restaurant in Times Square. He knew that the USA execs would be watching.

McMahon strode calmly into the restaurant wearing his standard sharkskin suit with an open collar. Basil De Vito was there. So was ex–Dallas Cowboy great Drew Pearson, who lent the proceedings a measure of dignity. Pearson ran a successful licensing business in Addison, Texas, and McMahon had tapped him as much for his football reputation as for his business acumen. The press conference was such a rush job that McMahon had called Pearson only a few days before. Also on the dais was Mike Keller, an ex-NFL and USFL front-office man who would be the XFL's vice president of operations.

The room was packed with reporters as McMahon laid out his plans for the football revolution. "The NFL has become known as the 'No Fun League,'" he said. "But this will be an extra-fun league. It will be exciting and it will be extreme." McMahon spoke softly, almost inaudibly. This wasn't the stock, declarative Mister McMahon figure from the ring, a facade he routinely assumed whenever he faced a media phalanx. This time it was different. Perhaps it had dawned on him, the risk he was taking. Not only did McMahon not have a broadcast partner, he didn't have a single team, a single coach, a single player.

But he recovered his bravado, lashing out at the league that had spurned him. "In the NFL you can't celebrate a touchdown," he said. "That's un-

American." He made his infamous remark about pantywaists and sissies. He wasn't talking so much about the style of play but—his memory never short—to the style of owner. This was wrestling's old prematch bully tactic, and as in wrestling, the best feuds occurred when the two combatants held a genuine dislike for each other. "We will go where the NFL has never gone, where the NFL is afraid to go, because we are afraid of nothing."

A reporter brought up the failure of the World Bodybuilding Federation. "I don't look at the past," McMahon said.

Asked if he was concerned about WWFE's stock price, which had recently dropped, he replied, "Wall Street can kiss my ass."

When another reporter asked if getting into real competition meant he was "going legit," McMahon answered, "May I never, ever be thought of as fucking legit."

All of this sounded well and good, but there was little substance behind McMahon's bluster. Without any teams or a broadcast partner, the only thing tangible about the XFL was its red and black logo, which had been printed up a few days before the press conference.

McMahon slid out of his restaurant and into a waiting limousine, where he collapsed into the car's soft leather. He grinned on his ride back toward Stamford, unsure of what the future held. He had taken a huge gamble. Like Bugsy Siegel opening his Flamingo Hotel when it was only half finished, McMahon couldn't wait to get out of the gate.

In Week Four of the XFL season, the Tillman-Ventura farce overshadowed the meager accomplishment of the New York/New Jersey Hitmen's first win. As Rusty Tillman pulled into the Giants Stadium parking lot for the season's fifth game, he was trying to figure out how to put together a few more victories. Tillman saw a man standing in the parking lot up ahead. He was waving something in his hand. Tillman slowed his car. The man in the road wore a long, dark overcoat. He was gesturing as though he wanted to talk. Tillman glided to a stop in front of the stranger and rolled down his window.

"You Rusty Tillman?" the man asked. Tillman nodded. He looked at the object that the man had been waving. It was a badge. "I'm with the Minnesota Secret Service," he said.

Tillman didn't know what the guy was talking about. Was this a joke? He looked closely at the badge. It looked like the real thing. The stranger was sizing up Tillman. "Governor Ventura thinks you might do something tonight."

Tillman laughed. It had been a long week. He had two young kids, and they kept asking their dad why the governor yelled at him on TV. He had just switched starting quarterbacks. And the Hitmen still didn't have any office furniture; they were holding meetings on card tables and folding chairs. When an old friend, Leonard Shapiro of *The Washington Post*, called Tillman earlier in the week, the coach let loose with all his frustrations. His comments landed in the February 28 edition of the paper.

"I told them when I signed on to coach this team, I'm not going to do this WWF garbage," Tillman said. "I'm a football coach." Tillman blasted the quality of the telecast. "I think their TV announcers are awful. Jesse is terrible. [UPN color commentator] Brian Bosworth isn't any good. People would be better off tuning out the sound and listening to the radio, if there is radio. They don't know what they're talking about. I don't think they get it, and the ratings are being halved every week."

This was the spirit that Ebersol and McMahon had been looking for during Game One, yet not in the form they had hoped to encounter it. McMahon read the article, and he called up Tillman. "Well, I can't take it back, Vince," Tillman told his boss. "You told me to be myself." McMahon may have been irked by the editorial, but it did play into his hands. NBC had scheduled a game between Birmingham and San Francisco on its national XFL telecast. But when the Tillman-Ventura battle took center stage, the network switched the national game to Los Angeles versus New York. All week long, NBC ran ads highlighting the so-called Blood Feud between Tillman and Ventura, rather than pushing the game itself. Ebersol and McMahon believed this would attract some semblance of an audience.

In a pregame interview that was broadcast over the PA to twenty-seven thousand fans in Giants Stadium, sideline reporter Fred Roggin asked Rusty Tillman a simple question: "Are you afraid of Jesse Ventura?" The coach just laughed, turning away to his assistants. Up in the booth, Ventura provided commentary. "He's speechless. He didn't talk last week, and he won't talk this week." During the game, when the Hitmen called a time-out because they had the wrong personnel on the field, Ventura sounded off again. "It's the responsibility of the head coach to keep things running smoothly. Why does he pass the buck?" At halftime, Roggin grabbed Tillman and asked his opinion of Ventura's on-air criticism. "Good for him," the coach said. "I really don't care."

Tillman wasn't providing anything to keep the controversy going. "When I got into the league, I knew that there was going to be a certain amount of this atmosphere," Tillman would say later. "So it wasn't a surprise to me. But I told my players before the first game in Las Vegas that I wasn't going to embarrass them on national TV. I wasn't going to make it a soap opera."

L.A.'s Tommy Maddox threw two touchdown passes, Jose Cortez kicked three field goals, and the Xtreme handed Tillman's Hitmen their fourth loss, 22–7. The highlight of the night, however, occurred during the Burger King All-Access halftime camera. Finally, the XFL transmitted truly groundbreaking video from inside the locker room. As a camera pushed its way through a Giants Stadium locker room door, it caught an assistant coach relieving himself into a urinal. Jim Ross had to fill the dead air. "That's somebody going to the bathroom," he said.

With the Tillman-Ventura feud fizzling out, Ebersol and McMahon moved on to their next project to rekindle interest in the XFL. It was another gem from the WWF vault. As Saturday's game at Giants Stadium ended, Jim Ross hyped the following week's gimmick, harrumphing into the microphone: "It's a blatant attempt to increase ratings."

The XFL needed something. Earlier in the week, on a teleconference, a reporter asked NBC West Coast president Scott Sassa why the ratings had declined so sharply. "I don't know why," Sassa said. "If you have the answer . . ." His voice trailed off into the hiss of the phone line.

Coming off their decisive victory in San Francisco, the Las Vegas Outlaws traveled to Chicago to play the Enforcers, who had yet to win a game. Ryan Clement felt like he was ready to go. Short of surgery, his shoulder was as healed as it was going to be. He practiced all week, and offensive coordinator Vince Alcalde told him he would see playing time against Chicago. Jim Criner said very little of anything. Clement and Mark Grieb shared a hotel room in Chicago, and Clement overheard his rival telling his mother on the phone that the starting job was his. The Outlaws weren't too worried about playing with a backup QB. Their defense continued to dominate, and Chicago had displayed an aversion to the end zone. The Vegas defense was the best in the XFL. Kelvin Kinney continued to lead the league in sacks.

Not many people knew what Kinney had gone through to get there. He didn't talk about it much. Besides, everybody had their sob stories, otherwise they'd be in the NFL.

Kinney was never supposed to make the Washington Redskins, who drafted him in the sixth round of the 1996 NFL draft, out of Division IAA Virginia State. The Redskins coaches referred to him as a "fun" pick, a player chosen deep in the draft on the slim chance that he would pan out. At six-foot-seven, 230 pounds, Kinney was too light to play defensive line and too tall to play linebacker. He entered training camp determined, as the ninth of ten West Virginian children would have to be, and he was still with the Redskins heading into the team's first 1996 preseason game, against the Bills.

Kinney ran onto the field at Buffalo's Rich Stadium in the first half. He lined up across from John Fina, the Bills 300-pound All-Pro guard. At the instant the ball left the center's hand, Kinney darted around Fina. The Bills guard then exhibited the quickness that had earned him such universal praise. It all happened in an instant. Fina's monumental shoe crashed down on his opponent's left foot, and when Kinney continued his stride, jerking his foot upward . . . it cracked. It was like a shingle of water-damaged wood splitting in half as the bone in Kinney's left foot splintered the length of its outer edge. But this was the NFL. Kinney was a rookie. He played the rest of the game.

"This is it right here," Kinney said, slipping his foot out of the flip-flop that he wore at all times. The foot looked a little like his but more like a cadaver's, lumpy and swollen and malformed. Kinney sat at the bar inside Sunset Station casino in Henderson, Nevada, the slot machines pinging behind him. He ordered a steak.

Kinney couldn't sustain his charade for long that year, especially when he had trouble stumbling across the locker room floor. He needed surgery. Doctors inserted a three-inch screw into his foot to hold it together; rookie season was over before it began. The Redskins liked the little they had seen of

Kinney and they kept him around. He spent the fall in the weight room, where he bulked up to 265 pounds, impressing coaches with his ability to eat seven meals a day. Four months after the injury, when he was supposed to resume walking, a physician noticed that the screw in his foot was misaligned. The first doctor had botched the job.

Another surgery, this one to graft bone from his hip. After a prolonged rehab, Kinney finally recovered, at least well enough to suit up for the Redskins in the fall of 1997. He suffered another foot injury during training camp, an avulsion fracture to his ankle, when a ligament ripped from the bone. Kinney was getting paid to inflict pain on others, and he was falling apart. But this was the NFL, where drawing a paycheck means playing with busted parts. Kinney made it into four games in 1997. In 1998, he started twelve of sixteen games at right end.

He tore into his steak, his eyes glazing over at the memory of his NFL career. "I think I played in the greatest era of Hall of Famers ever," he said. "Joe Montana, Steve Young, Terrell Davis, Troy Aikman, Emmitt Smith, Thurman Thomas, Barry Sanders." It would be wrong to say that anyone except a guy married to the owner's daughter could feel secure about his position in the NFL. But after starting twelve games, Kinney felt some measure of comfort as he geared up for his third active season in the NFL. There was good news at home, too. His girlfriend, Gloriann, soon to be his wife, was pregnant with their first child. When he and the Redskins took the field at Foxborough Stadium for an exhibition game against the New England Patriots in the summer of 1999, Kinney had little reason to fear the evening's outcome. Preseason games didn't mean much, anyway. But everything changed that night, around the time the referee called Kinney on a fifteen-yard roughing-the-passer penalty.

Gloriann, then six months pregnant, was steering her Mercedes toward the couple's home in Columbus, Ohio. She never saw the car that rear-ended her and then kept going. She fell hard against the steering wheel. By the time Kinney made it to Columbus, a miscarriage was complete. They had lost a son.

When Kinney called Redskins coaches and requested a few days with Gloriann, head coach Norv Turner demanded that Kinney return to training camp immediately. This was the NFL. When Kinney failed to return the next day, the Redskins cut him. Turner didn't have it in him to deliver the news personally, nor did player personnel director Vinny Cerrato. But Cerrato could talk to the papers. "We've raised our level of expectations, set high standards and goals," he said. "You either jump on board or you don't. This ship is headed in one direction."

Maybe Kinney had it coming it to him. In all his time with the Redskins, he recorded just one sack. But even if Washington was looking for an excuse to cut him, Norv Turner couldn't have displayed less class.

Kinney caught on with the Detroit Lions, then with the Oakland Raiders. But teams were reluctant to put faith in his bum foot. By the 2000 training camp, Kinney was a five-year NFL vet and was required by the league's union rules to earn at least $ 525,000 per year. "I'm high-risk," he said. "I got five years in the league. They have to pay me the minimum when they can pay a rookie $150,000. And they know he'll finish the season. My chances of going back to the NFL are slim and none." Kinney eventually found himself back in Detroit, this time playing for the Arena League's Fury.

Kinney earned $864,000 in his last NFL season, $45,000 for a year in the XFL. "That's not a lot of money. That much you could spend around here." He waved a huge hand at the gaming tables behind him, at the frizzy-haired grandmas and their buckets of nickels. "That much is not enough to keep me coming to Vegas away from my wife."

Kinney talked about football all night, talked like a first-timer at an AA meeting. He wasn't in the XFL for the money. And he knew he had exhausted his chances in the NFL. He exacerbated the constant pain of his various ailments for another reason entirely.

"Do you know what it's like to have your name announced on Saturday?" he said. "You can remember when you were twelve or thirteen and you had Betty Sue in the corner and you stuck your Johnson in her and wondered what happened. That's the feeling you reach. And multiply it by ten."

The Soldier Field crowd was dotted with plenty of anti–HE HATE ME signs. As the players prepared for the game's first snap, a Chicago defensive lineman bashed Smart on the big screen: "It's catchy if you're illiterate." There weren't many laughs. There weren't many people, maybe ten thousand. Music scorched the air. Several fans wore bags over their heads in shame of the 0–4 Enforcers. The field was comprised of yellow weeds, which XFL workers had painted green.

The game lumbered along, with grunting and tackling sounds reverberating over the PA. The Outlaws built a 13–0 first-half lead against a porous Chicago defense, with Mark Grieb throwing two touchdown passes, both to new acquisition Yo Murphy. Rod Smart ran well (116 yards on 21 carries for the day), outshining Chicago's John Avery, the former NFL first-round pick.

Near the end of the third quarter, the Vegas defense allowed a touchdown, only its second of the season, to which the Enforcers quickly added a field goal. By the time the fourth quarter rolled around, Grieb and the offense had been stuck in the mud for some time, unable to pad their four-point lead. The score stood at 13–9.

The game was winding down, with less than two minutes on the clock, when Chicago quarterback Kevin McDougal, a former starter at Notre Dame, got the ball at his own seventeen-yard line. He connected on a few short passes before sending a Long Bomb down the right sidelines. The ball fell harmlessly to the painted turf. Then an official let loose with the laundry. Pass interference on the Outlaws. There was little time left, and the meager lot of fans still in the stadium rose to their feet, their team within striking distance on the Vegas end of the field. The Outlaws defense caved, allowing McDougal to thread a strike between two defensive backs. Kelvin Kinney and his mates couldn't get to McDougal in time. With the clock running out, Enforcer tailback LeShon Johnson rumbled into the end zone from the two-yard line. Chicago had its first win. A fat guy in the thirty-seventh row ripped off his shirt in jubilation, his skin reddened by the searing winter air.

The Vegas offense had sputtered when the team needed it most in the second half. All Ryan Clement could do was watch from the sidelines. Criner wouldn't put him in the game. Clement shuffled with the rest of the team to the cramped Soldier Field locker room. The place was built eons ago, for men half the size of current players. Clement and Grieb dressed in abutting stalls, which meant that they practically sat in each other's laps. Clement turned to grab his Right Guard, and Grieb whispered into his shirt, "We did all right. We moved the ball well. Next week we'll get a little better." Grieb shuffled to the middle of the locker room for a stick of Juicy Fruit, and Clement bent down to tie his shoe, muttering into the floor, "I'm ready to go. He's *gotta* put me in there. Man, I coulda done better than *that.*"

Jim Criner had finished dressing in his coach's room, sweat pouring from his forehead. He looked like someone had just emptied his bank account. The last thing he needed was the bought-and-sold Las Vegas TV sports reporter, who entered in his brand-new XFL varsity jacket, his cameraman's bright light shining into Criner's eyes. "Are you gonna start Ryan next game?" asked the cheery TV man. Criner glared. "Now, look, don't you go getting me into any quarterback controversy!" Criner yelled. The blood rose to his face. "Why do you always focus on the negative?" The TV guy fidgeted in his new coat. His leather sleeves squeaked. He motioned to his cameraman to shut down the equipment. "Geez, Coach," he said, his voice reaching a soprano's pitch, "I'm your biggest fan. We always give you lots of coverage, and we're always positive. I wanna see the league succeed more than anybody. I love this team. I—"

Criner cut him off, grown weary of the sorry display. "All right, all right," he said. "It's okay." By this date, the only media types supporting the XFL were guys like this, homers stuck in the purgatory of TV market number three hundred and five. TV man waddled through the exit. Criner cinched his belt and grabbed a bottle of gel, squishing a gob of the stuff the size of an ice-cream scoop into his hand and then running it through his damp hair.

Things weren't much better for Ebersol and McMahon. During Week Five of NBC's national telecast, John Gonzalez's cameras again had to skirt the issue of empty seats, this time in Giants Stadium. When the Nielsen numbers came in, there was no more skirting. The rating: 2.4, a new bottom for the league. The XFL was flirting with the all-time record for the lowest rating in prime-time-network sports: Game Three of the 2000 Stanley Cup finals, which drew a 2.3 rating on ABC on June 3. Five weeks remained in the XFL regular season. Three of those Saturday nights would see the XFL go head-to-head with the NCAA basketball tournament on CBS, essential sports viewing that could seriously deplete the XFL's retreating audience.

The 2.4 only solidified the XFL's status as an institutionalized joke. The XFL was such a target that even men beholden to Scott Sassa and Jeff Zucker joined in on the fun. "Apparently the ratings for the XFL football are so bad," Jay Leno said during his *Tonight Show* monologue, "the executives said, 'Just burn the network for the insurance money.'" Conan O'Brien was right behind him. "I have to put the right spin on this because I'm also on NBC," O'Brien said, commenting on the league's ratings. "Apparently, they went through the toilet."

The relationship between Ebersol and McMahon wasn't immune to the creeping infection. During the fifth week, McMahon ended a conference call with several XFL licensing and marketing reps with a somber declaration. He exhaled into the speakerphone: "I think my fifteen-year relationship with Dick Ebersol is done."

It was hard to tell if he was sincere or merely winking at the doomsayers. If McMahon was being genuine, there were reasons for the split beyond the grave ratings decline. The two old friends had begun to disagree on a strategy for reviving the league. "They argued all the time about the programming," said a high-level WWF employee. McMahon scanned focus group information and realized that there were, in fact, viewers still open to watching the XFL. They were diehard sports fans, there to see traditional football during the NFL's offseason.

Ebersol still held on to the belief that the XFL could be a big splash. "In many ways," said the WWF source, "Ebersol wanted more wrestling gimmicks and Vince wanted it to be pure football." In the limited time they had to regenerate the league's ratings, Ebersol and McMahon drifted apart over the target audience. The confusion obscured the scope of the original XFL model.

10

A GRAND ILLUSION

IN THE BEGINNING, there was a memo.

"Heretofore, television has done a remarkable job bringing the game to the viewer—now we are going to take the viewer to the game!! We will utilize every production technique . . . to heighten the viewer's feeling of actually sitting in the stands and participating personally in the excitement and color. . . . We will have cameras mounted in jeeps, on mike booms, in risers or helicopters, or anything necessary to get the complete story of the game. We will use a 'creepy-peepy' camera to get the impact shots that we cannot get from a fixed camera—a coach's face as a man drops a pass in the clear—a pretty cheerleader just after her hero has scored a touchdown. . . . In short—we are going to add show business to sports! . . . We will be setting the standards that everyone will be talking about and that others will spend years trying to equal."

The year was 1960, when Roone Arledge, a young TV producer vying for the top job on ABC's college football telecast, delivered the above note to his bosses. He got the job. And he then proceeded to reinvent televised sports with programs such as *Wide World of Sports, Monday Night Football,* and the Olympic Games. Before Roone Arledge, sports TV was a snooze, meant merely as an advertisement to lure fans down to the stadium. Arledge wanted to produce TV that entertained the slob at home on the couch. That's what the producer ended up doing, creating an industrial complex populated by Domino's, DIRECTV, and the King of Beers. His programs earned monumental ratings, while Arledge himself gained untouchable status at ABC, where he fostered a cult of personality that infected the talent flocking to his sports division. It was a culture of scrolling expense accounts—limos, helicopters, floozies—draped in an air of entitlement that inflamed competitors who weren't having as much fun. It was just the place for eager young talent like Dick Ebersol, who became Arledge's assistant.

Ebersol spent nine years under Arledge and learned from his boss the value of the big score that went against conventional wisdom yet dictated future thinking. In 1974, Ebersol moved to NBC, where he shepherded the creation of *Saturday Night Live*. With the success of the show, Ebersol became the youngest vice president in NBC history at twenty-eight. He was a tireless worker, and he had an ego that matched his six-foot-five frame. Every facet of Ebersol's life reflected his inner pace. He met actress Susan Saint James on the *SNL* set in 1981 and married her just six weeks later.

After ten years at NBC, Ebersol resigned to form his own company, No Sleep Productions, where he developed such shows as *Friday Night Videos* and *Later with Bob Costas*. He continually cast about for a different way to approach TV, as he had learned from Arledge. He was willing to listen to anything. Almost anything.

When his agent called up one day in 1985, Ebersol had to laugh. The agent suggested he meet a guy named Vince McMahon, the head of the World Wrestling Federation, who was interested in developing a TV show. Pro wrestling? Roone Arledge wouldn't have touched it. Ebersol hung up the phone and called his friend Brandon Tartikoff, who was then NBC's chief programmer. "You won't believe my agent," Ebersol said, and the two men had a big laugh.

At NBC headquarters a few days later, Ebersol ran into David Letterman, who was represented by the same agent. "You won't believe what our agent tried to sell me the other day," Ebersol said. "He tried to sell me this wrestling thing with Vince McMahon." Letterman could offer only a bemused smile. In 1985 Letterman was a decade away from going corporate comedy. He was still counterculture. He had seen the WWF, and he thought it was pretty funny. Letterman had given pro wrestling one of its greatest pop-culture crossover moments when Jerry Lawler slapped the neck-braced Andy Kaufman on his show three years before. He told Ebersol to think seriously about it. Letterman said that he had been watching the WWF on the USA Network. It was a wild show called *TNT*—fights would break out, wrestlers would get married, anything could happen.

Ebersol went ahead and arranged a meeting with Vince McMahon. In the space of twenty minutes, McMahon brokered a deal to produce his first network wrestling show.

Together, Ebersol and McMahon developed *Saturday Night's Main Event,* which NBC bought as a monthly replacement for *SNL* reruns. The show was an instant success, often earning better ratings than *SNL. Main Event* ran on NBC for six years and proved that the WWF was something a surprising number of people wanted to watch. Ebersol and McMahon became close friends; they took trips to Atlantic City together. Their relationship marked the beginning of McMahon's ascendance. When Ebersol rejoined NBC in 1989 as sports president, he divested himself of his WWF stake and watched his former partner's till spill over.

McMahon went on to conquer TV's underbelly, while Ebersol continued to display an equally unconventional approach to the business, winning increasing rein with his sports department and kudos from his bosses at NBC's parent company, General Electric. He added a title, senior vice president of NBC News, and as his career progressed, Ebersol's greatest talent, the art of the deal, began to show itself. Ebersol landed the rights to anything he wanted—the NFL, NBA, Major League Baseball, tennis, golf, horse racing—making his division the only profitable sports department among the networks. Whispering sweet nothings into the ear of a potential partner, he became famous for treating negotiations like seductions . . . or like black ops.

In 1995 Ebersol secretly flew to the World Track and Field Championships in Göteborg, Sweden, for the negotiation that would forge his legacy. Carefully avoiding notice by the ABC crew that broadcast the championships, Ebersol holed up in a back room of the Sheraton and then rode the hotel's service elevators to meet with International Olympic Committee chairman Juan Antonio Samaranch. Ebersol acquired the rights to telecast the 2000 and 2002 Olympics; six weeks later, he locked up the 2004, 2006, and 2008 Olympics. Competing networks hadn't considered the possibility for such an audacious plan. They figured there would be a traditional round of bidding for 2000 in Sydney. Fox chief Rupert Murdoch, an Australian, took the news like a death in the family. "He's lapped the field," said Roone Arledge. Ebersol knew the worth of the masterstroke, like when he enlisted Muhammad Ali to light the Olympics torch at the 1996 Atlanta Summer Games. The Olympics coup further endeared him to the GE bosses, who created a special title just for him—chairman of NBC Sports and NBC Olympics. He was riding high. But this was TV, and Ebersol's golden age didn't last long.

As it was for his old partner Vince McMahon, pro football was Ebersol's undoing, the itch that he couldn't scratch. When bidding opened for a new NFL rights package in early January 1998, NBC, which had broadcast NFL games for twenty-eight straight years, faced a dilemma. NBC had been paying $217 million a year for the right to air AFC games. CBS, which still smarted from losing out during the last round of negotiations, in 1994, was determined to pay whatever it took for any available slate of games. "When we found out what CBS bid, we told the commissioner in five or ten seconds, 'Count us out. Don't even send us the piece of paper to sign,'" Ebersol told reporters. CBS agreed to pay $4 billion over eight years, more than twice the amount that NBC had paid under its previous contract. NBC viewed the deal as a losing proposition.

Ebersol made a halfhearted attempt to steal the *Monday Night Football* franchise from ABC. He bid $500 million a year for the NFL's most valuable property, but ABC retained it for $550 million. The negotiations made everyone in the TV-sports world reevaluate the way business was being done. "That crystalized in our mind that if you were going to be renting rights, which essentially is what any rights deal is, if it went well, you would be enhancing the value of that property," said Ken Schanzer, NBC Sports president. "And when you came to renew it, if you made some money, the league would take all of that money and then want you to pay more. So you pay an increase equivalent to your profitability, plus some premium beyond it. You might or might not catch up with it. And then if you got to the place where you were dealing with someone like the NFL, the NFL said, [Dallas Cowboys owner] Jerry Jones in fact said it, 'We don't care if you lose a quarter of a billion dollars. You can afford it.' Well, we made the decision that we couldn't afford it."

The entire NFL package, split among four networks (ABC, CBS, ESPN, and Fox), totalled $17.6 billion over eight years. With a value of roughly

$2.25 billion a season, the NFL contract dwarfed all other sports-TV deals. The next highest package, a four-year NBA deal that NBC shared with Turner Sports, was worth $660 million a season. "The NFL is a great sports property, but there is no property we would go after that would lose at least $150 million a year," Ebersol said once the dealing was done. "We see this as reckless. We're paid a salary to make money, and there was no chance of making money in this deal. You don't work for a GE company and come home at the end of the day to tell [GE CEO] Jack Welch you just lost $150 million."

It wasn't the first time Ebersol had taken a stand. In 1990 he spoke out against CBS's four-year $1.06 billion deal for Major League Baseball. Critics said Ebersol was bitter, but as CBS drowned in baseball's red ink, the NBC sports boss came off like a sage.

This time, though, his rant was little more than yelling into a stiff wind as competitors eagerly opened their wallets. For Ebersol, there was another price potentially steeper than the $500 million that CBS would pay the NFL every season. In a network TV climate with an increasing inventory of low-rated shows, the NFL was a proven ratings earner that theoretically drove audiences to a network's other programs, through the constant ads that bombarded fans during games. Football left NBC—the broadcaster of the first Super Bowl—and a large measure of prestige with it. NBC knew what to expect. In 1994 Fox wrestled the NFC package away from CBS by bidding more than $100 million more per season. It was a price that revealed Rupert Murdoch's belief in the importance of the NFL, which he chose over a national newscast as a vehicle of legitimization for his young network. After losing the NFL in 1994, CBS's sports division atrophied, and its overall ratings tanked. The network even went on the block. "We know better than anyone else what it's like to have the NFL," said Mel Karmazin, the chairman of the CBS station group, upon regaining the football contract in 1998. "And what it's like not to have the NFL." Signs reading NFL ON CBS hung on walls at Black Rock, CBS's headquarters in New York, the day the network regained pro football. Elevator operators wore celebratory caps. This was Ebersol's future—years of ratings decline, a dulling of the peacock's plume, a longing for the day he could distribute Dutch Masters to the clean-up crew.

What did the future of sports TV hold? Surely NFL rights would only cost more at the next round of negotiations, no easier to swallow at that later date. Ebersol's mind got spinning. There had to be a better way. There had to be some middle ground where a network sports department could broadcast pro football from a location other than the poorhouse. Why should NFL commissioner Paul Tagliabue get to walk through the house and pocket all your silver—while you helped him to it? Sitting in the captain's chair and watching the NFL fade to black hurt Ebersol. And it made him think, and think hard, lest his name be lumped in with the losers. Roone Arledge's world never teetered like this, and it was because he managed to rewrite all the rules; he was always a step ahead of the competition. Ebersol wondered about his own legacy. Would he stand in the shadow of his old boss or on a marble block of his own?

Never mind that Ebersol had locked up the Olympic Games. The praise he earned for his forward thinking was a hazy memory. The Olympics are no NFL. Marion Jones is no Marshall Faulk. There's no substitute for the two-minute drill on American TV. Without the NFL, NBC Sports—and, by extension, the network as a whole—couldn't help but seem withered and by a considerable degree.

NBC did have other problems. *Survivor* would soon hit the air, spurring every squawking producer, agent, and adman on either coast to profess an undying passion for reality programs. ("I am *so* into the reality genre" was usually how it went, with the cheap enthusiasm that passed for sincerity in these circles.) Soon everyone would be scrambling to devise a show that mimicked *Survivor*, both in design and in the bottom-line results it generated for CBS—an estimated $1 billion profit over its first eighteen months. Along came a tidal wave of similar programs: *Big Brother, Temptation Island, The Mole,* and many, too many, others. NBC, accepting this second dose of reality, was outmaneuvered again, without an "It" show of its own. GE execs scolded NBC president Bob Wright for missing the biggest wave to hit TV in many years. NBC was in a bind: no football, no reality TV.

Dick Ebersol wasn't about to watch his dominion shrink without massing an offensive. "Our feeling was that if there were a way to own something, we could be in a position to have an asset that over time could be worth something," said Ken Schanzer. In May 1998, five months after NBC demurred in the NFL bidding war, Ebersol met with Turner Broadcasting, the cable group that had lost its portion of NFL rights to ESPN in the same talks. Ebersol proposed a football partnership with Turner Sports, which was riding high at the time from its pro wrestling success with WCW. The two parties devised a league of spring football, played during prime time. But the numbers were troublesome. "Neither Turner nor we were prepared to absorb all of the cost," Schanzer said. "We were trying to find people to invest in it who weren't necessarily going to take dollars out, who weren't going to be owners."

The league's price tag was considerable: Along with production costs, there would be the expense of outfitting twelve teams and paying each player a planned $100,000 salary (which the XFL eventually chopped in half). After a year and a half of talks and calculations, the deal was kaput, dubbed "too ambitious" by one negotiator. The announcement of the venture's failure came on December 1, 1999, just three weeks before NBC unveiled a six-year $1.2 billion contract with NASCAR, which Ebersol had acquired to fill the Sunday afternoons vacated by the NFL. Turner Sports, whose WCW was by that time hemorrhaging from its nefarious battle with the WWF, no longer had the optimism that would have encouraged it to sink funds into a fragile football league.

Again Ebersol was left empty-handed, frustrated. He looked at his calendar and realized that NBC's deal with the NBA, which still turned a profit, had just two years remaining. If Ebersol lost pro basketball when negotiations reopened in late 2001, NBC Sports might as well close up shop and sell off its remaining programming to the Golf Channel. Ebersol found himself at his desk casting about for something, anything, when his assistant poked her head into his office on the fifteenth floor of the GE Building. Aimee Leone went back a long way with her boss. She had worked for him during the days of *Saturday Night's Main Event* fifteen years before. Leone suggested Ebersol take a look at one of the many live feeds that funneled into the building every day. Ebersol switched on his TV.

There was Vince McMahon, going on about something or other, as he always did, with those swollen cheeks, that preternatural tan, that wolf's bearing. And just what was he talking about? Ebersol had to turn up the set to hear McMahon's mumbles.

Could it be? His old friend was talking about football. Yes, yes, he *was* talking about football. There was McMahon in his WWF Restaurant at Times Square, launching his first salvo at football's monolith, insulting the NFL. Ebersol liked what he heard. TV, specifically Arledge's *Monday Night Football*, made the NFL what it had become—a TV property more than a football league. And the NFL turned around and gouged the networks. This did sound good. No matter that this—what did McMahon call it?—this XFL was a larva of a flea on the deck of the *Titanic*, McMahon was talking about a brand-new pro football league. Ebersol listened as his old friend slipped into his Mister McMahon role and pronounced the dawn of a new football epoch. Ebersol had found the answer to all of his troubles.

McMahon's eyes may have fluttered toward sleep as his limo edged its way north. It had been a long day, and he would need his rest if the XFL was going to work. He was interrupted by the bothersome twitter of a cell phone. God, did he hate cell phones.

It was one of those calls you shouldn't take, an unwanted dinnertime solicitation. Have a look at the caller ID and walk away. Or if you answer it by accident, just say no thank you, I'm not interested. Click . . . Instead, giddiness washed over McMahon, and he pressed the talk button. Instantly, he recognized the voice on the end of the line. "Vince," said Ebersol. "Don't do anything else yet."

This was just the thing Ebersol had been looking for. How much risk could there be? If he and his old friend could forge a deal, putting football back on the network would cost a sliver of what the NFL charged, and producing each game could cost less than three hours of regular prime-time programming. By the end of the phone call, a structural plank of the original XFL business model was on its way to becoming a withering memory, modest goals exchanged for the greater dream of instant world domination.

Shortly thereafter, McMahon rode the elevator to the fifteenth floor of the GE Building. His meeting with Ebersol was less business and more bull session. The men had made each other a lot of money during their relationship. Besides, the two parties had been down this road before, NBC with Turner, the WWF with the CFL. They knew the jargon and most of the numbers. Ebersol and McMahon weren't looking to establish a TV-rights deal. That was too simple. In NBC, McMahon would get a fifty-fifty partner who would not only absorb half of the roughly $100 million first-season costs but also buy $30 million of WWFE stock as a sign of good faith. There were so many upsides to a handshake with NBC as to obscure the fundamental importance of the downsides. The shimmering brilliance of the combination proved blinding.

"Vince went for the deal because of friendship, Ebersol," said Jim Bell, the former WWF senior vice president of licensing and merchandising. "And there was the fact that now you had a joint-venture partner who was going to absorb fifty percent of the bill. But I think inherent in that are some real problems. You're starting to go away from a basic plan of going it alone and building it. It's much easier to hit singles and doubles than it is to hit home runs. The moment NBC enters the picture, now you have to hit a home run." Expectations were higher on a major network like NBC than they would have been if McMahon aired his games on a lower-tier network. Plus, NBC's weekend afternoons were spoken for, especially since Ebersol inked the NASCAR deal. The only place to go was prime time—the biggest pressure cooker in TV. By slotting the league on Saturday night, NBC would try to invigorate what had become worthless territory. "Vince never should have let XFL programming be used as a guinea pig for NBC to play with on Saturday night," Bell said. "Men eighteen to thirty-four are not home then, and if they are home, they sure as hell are not watching TV. That hurt. The whole NBC partnership hurt. Vince let a friendship of fifteen years with Dick Ebersol supersede good business."

For NBC, the XFL looked like the answer to the sleeper hold with which the NFL held the networks. "It was a logical extension of rights fees going to a place in which they were so untenable and potentially so damaging to the company that the natural conclusion of that was to look elsewhere, to look for a different business model," said Ken Schanzer. "And that's what we were doing. I mean, essentially this was all about a different business model."

Teaming with McMahon was another selling point for NBC. Everything McMahon did seemed to attract scores of young viewers. For the just concluded 1999 season, *Raw Is War* had drawn 47 percent more male viewers aged 12 to 24 than *Monday Night Football* in head-to-head broadcasts. McMahon produced nine hours of weekly wrestling programming across two networks. He would use one empire to flog another.

The establishment of the XFL would mark the first ownership by a network of a substantial sports league. To Ebersol, who had once declared sports leagues unnecessary middlemen, this was the juiciest part of the deal. Paradoxically, in owning the league, NBC would take a lower financial risk than it would in merely paying for the privilege of airing games. Disney, which owned ABC and ESPN, would pay $9.2 billion in NFL rights through 2005, Fox $4.4 billion, and CBS $4 billion. By comparison, it looked like NBC was getting free programming. "We did some economic modeling, took it to GE, and Jack Welch was immediately supportive of it; Bob Wright was very supportive of it," said Schanzer. "It was a fifty-million-dollar swing of the bat. If it worked, it would have worked in spades and it would have really thrown off something valuable. And if it didn't work, it was a good try. It was large enough to have been big in success, but small enough in a company like GE in which the loss was manageable." Football was back on the network; never mind that it was an unproven brand.

On March 29, 2000, NBC and the WWF announced their XFL partnership. "Vince clearly is the person in America who is able to speak to the eighteen-to-thirty-four audience," Dick Ebersol said. "We'd like to ignite the imagination of the male audience." To those on the inside, it was easy to fall in love with the match: NBC's football know-how, WWF's wrestling burlesque, with both entities versed in the vagaries of star making. The union gave the league unprecedented muscle for a start-up. The WWF predicted that the XFL would pull in $85 million in revenues during its first season, while Wall Street analysts projected that the league would become profitable by its third year.

Once the deal was final, Ebersol and Schanzer called John Gonzalez onto the carpet to devise the look and feel of the broadcast. "It's our league," Schanzer told the director. "Cooperation will be a hundred percent."

During his years as NBC's coordinating producer for NFL telecasts, Gonzalez had presented dozens of access-predicated technical proposals to the league. The NFL, slow-pawed sloth, was loath to tinker with a machine that ran too smoothly. Plus, coaches and players nixed anything that could compromise their competitive edge.

But the XFL was founded on the ethos of a Peeping Tom. With this in mind, Gonzalez proposed an on-field cameraman, microphones clipped to dozens of players and coaches, cameras in the locker room and on the bench. "I requested all of that stuff of the NFL for decades," Gonzalez said.

There was no bigger wish on the list than the riddle that had puzzled Gonzalez for fifteen years.

It was the device called Skycam, and it hovered above the field on wires fastened to the four corners of a stadium. Skycam debuted in 1985, and Gonzalez included it in NBC's coverage of the Orange Bowl that year. He utilized it in small doses, mostly for replays, but by the end of the game, he was convinced he had seen the future of televised football. The camera dropped viewers right on top of the players, instead of placing them halfway across the stadium, where the game's speed and violence were difficult to grasp. Skycam let fans feel the snap of the tailback's neck as he got hammered by a linebacker. But it was a tricky product, and Gonzalez could never figure out how to use it properly. Nobody could. Skycam had trouble picking up passes downfield. The play often darted wide of the screen. Still, Gonzalez believed in the technology. "I thought Skycam had never been used properly." This was more than a personal crusade or a meaningless search for a different way of doing things—Gonzalez had a theory.

He reported to WWF headquarters in Stamford, where McMahon would invariably greet his updates with skepticism: "This *is* going to work, isn't it?" This time Gonzalez yanked down a screen at the end of the conference room. He flipped a switch, and an image of a football field projected onto the screen. "The young viewers that we're after tend to shy away from *Monday Night Football,*" Gonzalez told his bosses. "Because they're probably on their computers playing video games." Gonzalez gestured to the projection, an image taken from Madden 2000, the ubiquitous football video game. Madden 2000 had become one of the most successful video games ever made because it felt so realistic. Those who played the game sensed what it was like being the quarterback squatting under center. A big reason was the on-screen viewpoint: the same one that Skycam afforded, just off the quarterback's shoulder. Looking at the image on the screen, Ebersol and McMahon immediately realized the potential of unspoken communication to the coveted demographic. (Once the XFL telecast faltered, Ken Schanzer considered the Skycam a blunder. "Gonzalez said, 'This is how your kids watch football,'" Schanzer would say later. "And it is. But football fans don't watch football that way.")

The bosses agreed to the Skycam. But Gonzalez was having trouble with his on-field camera. He couldn't find anyone to operate it. NBC's regular crew of freelance cameramen liked the idea but balked at the network's standard pay rate. The work was too hazardous. They would be risking serious injury. "No problem," McMahon boomed in a meeting. "I got guys. I got a guy named Bubba who will do this in a minute." The conference room burst with laughter. "Yeah, Bubba Cam," said Ken Schanzer. "We'll call him Bubba Cam." When Gonzalez phoned Bubba, a WWF cameraman, he didn't want anything to do with getting mixed up with 300-pound linemen. NBC finally raised the pay and found a few cameramen willing to venture into harm's way. Bubba wasn't one of them, but the name stuck.

While NBC's telecast took shape, McMahon hammered out the remainder of the XFL TV deal. His XFL press conference did little to spur the USA Network into action. So McMahon met with Viacom, which owned CBS, MTV, UPN, and TNN, among other properties. McMahon and Viacom execs hammered out a deal that shifted four weekly WWF shows from USA to TNN. A fifth show would air on MTV. There were many riders to the deal, including an agreement for TNN and UPN to air one XFL game each on Sunday afternoons. Viacom considered the XFL a negligible expense of acquiring the WWF.

So much of the XFL partnership was personal, hinging on McMahon's showmanship, Ebersol's unconventionality, and their own zealot's belief in each other's abilities. This wasn't just a simple business transaction. Both men held grudges against the NFL. This was their revenge. And it was just the kind of thing that Arledge would have loved, although the old man wasn't so taken with the idea of NBC teaming up with the WWF's evil empire. He made a few rare remarks to the *New York Times:* "At some point you have to decide how classy you wanna be." But there were elements of the XFL that Arledge had always championed. It was a potential leap forward, and it dealt largely in intangibles. "We thought if we could find a way to capture some of the magic that Vince had captured in wrestling, that that would be a very, very potent combination," Ken Schanzer said. "That was the core idea. This was blowing up the product. This was saying we're just going to start over."

There were other considerations as well. Dick Ebersol suffered a heart attack in 1995. He quit eating meat and cut down on his two-hundred-day annual travel schedule. He started running twenty-five miles a week. He lost thirty pounds. He was fifty-two when he heard McMahon's plan for the XFL. How many more big splashes were left to him? The XFL—if it worked—could have reshaped television and recast Ebersol.

For all his accomplishments, Ebersol could not outstrip Arledge, to whom he owed a dubious debt, since a man whose achievements rank very near his mentor's often remains a footnote.

11

AN AUTOGRAPH
RESTORED

SHAMED BY THEIR LOSS to Chicago, the Las Vegas Outlaws
boarded a plane at O'Hare, the cocky swagger precipitated by two
dominant, season-opening wins absent from their shamble down the concourse. Vegas had lost two of three games. Week Six presented an opportunity to reverse the prevailing trend.

In the Orlando Rage, the XFL's only undefeated team at 5–0, the Outlaws
would have their Goliath, and on his home turf, the Citrus Bowl. A win in
Orlando would propel Vegas toward its final four games with a sense of purpose. A loss would leave it at break-even, with little time to plug the leaks.
The last thing the Outlaws wanted was a battle for a playoff spot, but that's
what it looked like they were in for, since they were tied with L.A. and San
Francisco in the Western Division, from which two teams would qualify for
the postseason.

Jim Criner flew his team to Orlando directly after the loss in Chicago,
rather than lose a travel day during what was already a shortened practice
week. There was no time for distraction. Yet that was all Ryan Clement and
Mark Grieb had coming to them when they arrived in Orlando.

Criner had watched Mark Grieb's Long Bomb touchdown in San Francisco. He had also witnessed the backup's inability to move the ball during
the second half of the game at Soldier Field. Ryan Clement was chirping
away about being ready for action. Criner wasn't sure, and instead of tapping
his starter at the beginning of the week, he chose to let the quarterbacks battle it out in practices leading up to the Saturday-night game in Orlando. It

was the biggest game of the season, and the Outlaws didn't know who would play the most important position.

The team practiced on a high school field out in suburban Orlando as nervous teenage girls huddled in book-clutching groups behind the end zone on their way to PE class. Kelvin Kinney stood on the sidelines in khaki pants, forlorn and displaced, watching his teammates practice. He had aggravated an old ankle injury against Chicago, and he moved gingerly along the fading chalk, saving himself for the real action Saturday night. Would he be able to play against Orlando? "Hell yeah," he barked in his deep voice, revealing the Scrabble tiles of his teeth, the single gold square catching the sun. "This is the biggest game of the year against the so-called best team in the league. You think I'm not gonna play?" Ryan Clement clutched his ribs in laughter as Mark Grieb once again ran his conspicuous wind sprints after Coach Criner's final whistle.

Rod Smart had a jump in his step, knifing untouched through the defensive line during half-speed plays without pads. As usual, he found a way to stand out, wearing the only pair of black socks on the field. After practice and a shower, Smart hopped in his rental car and took off for Lakeland, his hometown, twenty minutes away. His mother still lived there, and for reasons all too familiar to both Smart and the parole board, she couldn't come to him.

In a season with two fistfuls of games, the Outlaws were about to play their second hand. NFL scouts would be at the game or watching on NBC, examining the dominating Vegas defense and the unbeaten Orlando offense for talent they may have missed. They would be watching the other side of the ball, too. The Outlaws didn't need any more motivation than that. But for Clement and Smart, the game managed to assume even greater proportions.

With a few teammates piled into his rental car, Rod Smart pulled up outside his mother's house. As if it had an ear for narrative, the house sat across the tracks from Disney World. It was located on a dead-end road that looked like it may have been carved by a backhoe peeling out of a K-turn. A dozen bunkerlike dwellings roosted next to one another. Valerie Smart's house hunched halfway up on the right, a sagging, whitewashed one-story home with a window facing the street, its blind pulled low. A tired old sedan stretched as though for a final nap on the front lawn, flattening what was left of the grass. Dusk ratcheted down, and HE HATE ME stepped from his car.

The front door of the house swung open to reveal Valerie Smart, who stood there in pink slippers. "My baby," she said, revealing a few gold teeth and wrapping her son in her arms. Rod scooted into the house, and everyone settled into the cramped front room, spilling onto the sofa and the worn carpeting. A few bedrooms cast off a small hallway in the back. Tootsie Rolls and Smarties were scattered on a coffee table. A painting of Mary J. Blige hung like a deity's portrait above the entertainment center, where *Laverne & Shirley* played on the TV.

Valerie marched into the kitchen, which filled the house with a thousand aromas: collard greens with pigtails and ham hocks, candied yams, broccoli and cheese, ham with pineapples, and sweet-potato pie. Valerie stirred the contents of a pot, and her smile wiped away every gray molecule. In the next room, Rod breathed the familiar smells, which he couldn't separate from a history like the darkening sky outside. This was the real genesis of HE HATE ME, a concept well beyond the grasp of Fred Roggin's sideline queries.

Valerie Smart, whom everybody called Val, had known Rod's father for just a few weeks. This was in Miami, where the courts had dispatched her for passing out pot in Lakeland. She couldn't stand life in the Miami halfway house, and she busted out homesick. She was lost in Miami, asking anyone for a ride back home. She ended up at a guy's apartment. They got high. They sneaked into a drive-in theater. She braided his hair. When Val made it back to Lakeland, she discovered she was pregnant. She was thirteen years old.

"Had a C-section, 'cause Rod's feet was coming out first." Val laughed. "He wanted to run out." She scooped piles of food onto a plate with an arm covered in the bubbled skin of a vicious burn. "It snowed the day we left the hospital, January 18, 1977. I ain't never seen no snow before. I called Grandma and said, 'The world is fitting to end.'"

Another son, George, came along two years after Rod. With no dad around, the boys played with their mother all the time. Val raced the boys. She had run track in school. "I remember the first time Rod beat me," she said. "I fell down in the road." Val shook her head. "My mama came outside and beat me with a shoe. She said, 'You know you weren't straight. You got no business racing.'" By that time, Val had moved on to harder drugs.

She delivered heaping plates of food to the boys in the next room, briefly obscuring everyone's vision of the *Def Comedy Jam* tape now playing on the TV. Val went to prison in 1986 for dealing cocaine. When Rod visited her for the first time, she could think of only one way to handle the uneasiness. She challenged him to a race, just like old times. They took off across the prison exercise yard, running from something they couldn't see. "Cocaine," Val said now, her smile disappearing for the first time since Rod had walked through the door. "You can't use it successfully. You lose your life. Period."

Rod had never seen his father, not even in a picture. When Val got out of prison, she decided to do something about it. She took Rod to Miami, and they searched for his dad. With nothing more than a name to go on, they came up empty. Spent and frustrated, Val walked down to the beach with Rod. They had a picnic. They swam in the Atlantic. Rod sensed his mother's despair and he grabbed her hand. "Mama, I ain't got no daddy," he said. "You my daddy."

Val smiled at the memory. "Those waves'll knock you down," she said.

As a kid, Rod spent a lot of time doing all the wrong things. Just like his mother. "Trouble was second nature to me growing up. I was always getting into something—fights, stealing, breaking into stuff. It didn't matter. But as I matured, I understood that there was an end to that, because of the consequences. I always wanted to get away from home, 'cause that's where the center of trouble was, in Lakeland. I saw that football could get me out of Lakeland by giving me a college scholarship. So I started doing better in school. People started trying to help me, where, before, everyone was against me."

Rod went on to star on Lakeland High School's football team and earn a scholarship to Western Kentucky University. Through football, he lifted himself from his circumstances. His mother wasn't as fortunate. In June 1996, Val was burned on 30 percent of her body, and she spent a month in the hospital. When she recovered, prosecutors charged her with arson, claiming that she had singed herself while setting fire to a police substation. Her alibi: she claimed to have been smoking crack with a man who lit her on fire. Health officials judged Val unfit for trial and committed her to a state mental facility. When Val got out in 1999, officials placed her on house arrest for two years.

"My baby's in the Outlaws and his mama's an outlaw," Val joked, watching Rod plow through his dinner. The conditions of her house arrest prevented her from attending Saturday's game at the Citrus Bowl. She claimed to be in the process of putting everything in order. "The whole thing with Rod and the XFL, it keeps me going, watching him on TV," she said. "His mama's doing better. We're both proud of each other."

Val ran her hands through Rod's hair. She was stuck in a dream far away from Disney World. She talked of visiting Rod in Las Vegas and she thought less about the cards and dice than about the endless stretch of desert. "I can't wait till I come out there," she said. "I'm gonna get in a car and drive. Oh Lord, I'm gonna drive. And then I'm gonna come up over that mountain, and when I get over that mountain, I'm gonna look down into the little valley . . ." She trailed off, her hands working through Rod's hair.

In this was the real meaning of HE HATE ME, not any invective launched across the field of play, or an insolence derived from a life of abundance. HE HATE ME was born of humility, the broken-down bringing up that was the essence of cliché. A network crew would follow Smart around one night the week of the Orlando game, capturing the standard against-all-odds story that producers planned to broadcast during a time-out on Saturday's telecast. It would be the typical uplifting tale of "circumstances overcome," but it would have no life to it. Unlike the letters of the league that had commandeered Smart's riff as an unofficial slogan, HE HATE ME really did have a deeper meaning. But those in charge of the XFL's reality concept weren't interested in unearthing it. Unfortunately, on NBC, only the cliché came through.

"You've got to turn up the dial," said Jim Criner, red-faced, mustering every bit of cajoling, come-with-me juice in his small frame. "More intensity every quarter. More in the fourth than in the first." The Outlaws squeezed into a tiny conference room on the second floor of a downtown Orlando hotel. Video of the Orlando Rage clicked forward and backward on the big screen at the front of the room, the miniature players high-stepping then comically backpedaling as the coaches explained and reiterated particular tendencies they had discovered in their opponent's game. Criner let one clip play all the way through. It was a long touchdown pass against the Rage from a game a few weeks before. "You see this receiver here? Watch what happens now. Their safeties like to hit you, but they're not the fastest." Criner nodded toward the center of the room at Ryan Clement, who leaned back in his chair like a belligerent ninth-grader. Criner decided that he had seen all that he wanted from Mark Grieb during the second half in Chicago. He left the decision to the night before the big game, but he chose Clement to start at quarterback.

It was a chance for Clement, maybe a last chance at ever seeing the inside of an NFL jersey. Even if it was just a practice jersey or a call from his agent to say that the Broncos liked his stuff. Something, anything, so he could stop thinking about the NFL and why he had never gotten a chance. Sitting in that strategy session the night before the Orlando game, Clement knew he would have to perform or Grieb might take over for good.

The meeting continued, with Criner drilling his key points one last time. "Number ninety-nine—he's the hardest guy for us to block. He's no Superman, but he's their best player. Number twenty-three—he's a gambler and a guesser. He loves to get picks." It felt like a pre-mission run-through for the Dirty Dozen. So many huge dudes had never sat so still for so long. Flesh spilled in every direction, like dough bursting from the seams of a Pillsbury canister. Between Criner's comments, the position coaches leaned in and whispered asides to certain players. "That's exactly what we talked about in practice, remember?" "Right there—you gotta hit that gap with speed." Strange vocabulary filled the air: Sally, Outlaw, Nevada, Puma, Adidas, play-calling code words—as did snorts, coughs, and the stirring sound of mucus cultivation.

The meeting concluded with sage instruction from Criner. "We wanna do what they think we're gonna do. But with a different look." The coach likely confused more than a few of his charges with his Maxwell Smart elliptical mantra. The players dutifully stood and converged in the center of the hotel conference-room carpet, which was a dizzying array of checks, diamonds, triangles, and stripes in aqua, tan, black, brown, and yellow. It was enough to make them forget everything they had heard. But there were no jokes, no chatter. The players stood in the middle of the room, raising their hands in the air, their limbs coming together in the shape of a pep-rally bonfire. Criner counted up one, two, three, and the room exploded: "Outlaws!"

The players spilled out into the hallway, the chant still ringing in their ears. Everyone was subdued, their minds on the upcoming game. Most of the players wandered toward the elevator bank clutching playbooks. There was a prayer meeting going on in the conference room across the hall, and a few players stopped at a merchandise table to flip through books with titles like *Discovering the Lord* and *Jesus Is My Friend*, looking for a final bit of inspiration that would carry over into the big game. Then they moved along, took the elevator up for bed. In a few minutes, the garish carpet stood devoid of Outlaws, and the hotel resumed its lonely hum. A phone rang at the front desk, a basketball game played on a TV down at the bar, a bellman hustled past in his brocade coat, his polyester pants zipping at the inner thigh.

It wasn't long before movement renewed in the hotel at the ding of an elevator, which then coughed its cargo into the lobby. Ryan Clement had lead feet on the field, but he was pretty sneaky otherwise. While his teammates underwent the meditative steps doled out by a sports psychologist, or skimmed the vagaries of a friendship with the Almighty, or did whatever they did to get ready for the biggest game of the year, Clement glided calmly through the lobby, past the bellman and his epaulettes, and made quick tracks for the valet stand. He hopped in his rented SUV and took off down the road, driving into a light Florida drizzle, the black mirrored street the only witness to Clement's car. Not until he was out of sight of the wound-up coaches losing sleep over game film did Clement slip out of 007 mode. He popped a CD into the stereo and steered onto the highway. Eminem's nasally rhymes filled the car's vaulted interior.

This hadn't always been Clement's pregame routine. He used to be the guy cooped up with the playbook, leaving nothing to chance, clearing his mind of all thought but football days before kickoff. It was the same pattern that had prepared him for what was meant to be a sterling future. As his car chewed up lane dividers, it was clear that his patterns had changed.

The SUV wound up at the Exchange, a gussied-up roach motel of stores and restaurants that serves as a local hangout in Disney land. Clement walked by the trinket shops at a brisk clip, in contrast to the Friday-night crowd trolling lazily past, without purpose and drunk enough. Wherever he was, whatever he was doing, the game was never far from his mind. "For me, football has always been so important, number one," Clement said. "Everything depended on it." He made a few knowing turns down an alleyway, up a set of back stairs, and across the threshold of a bar. Ybor's was the name, a little place crowded with meatheads in plaid shirts who ordered theme martinis and sawdust cigars from a neglected humidor behind the bar. A barmaid in a cat suit poured the drinks. A magician turned facile card tricks in the corner.

Clement winked at the barmaid like he knew her. A few guys recognized Clement, and he didn't spend much time on his bar stool before some drunk tumbled forward, saying, "Hey, aren't you . . . ?" Clement just nodded and turned away, his face curling into a grimace as he grabbed a bottle from the barmaid, their fingers momentarily overlapping. Clement once had the power of the BMOC, though by his own account, he rarely wielded it. He was still with the same woman he had dated since junior high back in Denver. He was the football star. And her last name was Sachs, as in Goldman, Sachs & Co. During the XFL season, she was the oft-calling type. Six calls in twenty minutes to his cell phone, which he had somehow misplaced on his way to Ybor's. Ms. Sachs could get to be a little much, with her designs on Clement's future, all of her plans of being the wife of an NFL quarterback or the wife of a senator or the wife of *somebody*. But she was back in Denver, and Clement wasn't. The barmaid neglected her work.

After the 1998 NFL draft had come and gone, Clement realized that he had to find something to do with himself. He hooked on with the Arena Football League team in Orlando, the Predators. Then he joined the Scottish Claymores of NFL Europe, where Jim Criner coached. A month later, he found himself with the Saskatchewan Roughriders of the CFL, his third league in the same season, and he hadn't played much in any of them. His confidence was shot. And without confidence, a quarterback might as well take a seat in the stands, grab a beer, and get wasted. Which is just what Clement did, still scorched by the hell of his last season at Miami. "There's nothing like going to a place that's Quarterback U. when you get there and when you leave it's not."

Clement peered at his image in the glass behind the bar and sank back on his stool. He didn't have the girth of personality to follow Dwayne Douglas Johnson down the road to show business. All Clement could come up with was law school, which would have provided solid footing for the family business. A great-grandfather had served as governor of Wyoming, and there were judges and lawyers in the rest of the family. Mostly, Clement unhinged himself from any planning after having spent so much time preparing for only one thing.

Without the prospect of playing in the NFL, Clement's life began to crumble. "It's not just me but my family, friends, my girlfriend—everyone's affected by this," he said. "It got to the point where my parents' relationship depended on how well I played." He had tired of being the embodiment of everyone else's dreams. By the winter of 1999, Peyton Manning was cashing huge paychecks, taping TV commercials, and having his physical genius dissected on SportsCenter; Clement was back in Miami, sleeping on a friend's floor and working the door at a couple of bars. He partied all night, every night, drowning one headache with the fruits of another.

Along the way, something happened besides numbing the past and paying for it in the morning. Clement found a measure of humility. And he changed into somebody people wanted to associate with on equal terms. In college, Clement had served as his own personal tribunal. In one typical instance, he questioned the leg injury that kept Miami's top rusher out of practice for a few weeks. Clement called the player "the milkman" in the papers, claiming that he milked all the R&R he could out of the injury. "I was real sanctimonious," Clement said. "Telling people what to do, how to act."

He caught the barmaid's eye as she poured a shot of Goldschlager for a red-faced guy in a striped Hilfiger shirt. A cheer rose from the corner of the bar, where the magician had completed a trick. "Man, I was so uptight. And I had this routine before games. I had this tape I would listen to on my Walkman at my locker. It started out with the Eagles' 'Take It Easy,' then 'Southern Cross,' by Crosby Stills & Nash. Then some Phil Collins, 'In the Air Tonight.' Then I'd end up with AC/DC, 'Back in Black.' When I went on the field, I was ready to kill a guy. I was so wound up, some of my passes just had too much on them. I'd overthrow guys, toss it into the dirt, just be out of control."

In early 2000, Clement's research into humility continued. He took a job with Reebok selling cleats to college football teams. The pay was $30,000 a year. "I was like a poor man's Al Bundy," he said. When Jim Criner called about the XFL job, Clement was just starting to get over football. "Football delays real life. That's all this shit does. Don't go get a job. Don't go try and move yourself up in the world by committing to something like graduate school. Because you gotta commit yourself to this football thing. God, I respect guys who're banging away. But I also respect guys who take a look at it and say, 'No, I gotta go do something else.'" Clement couldn't figure out which description he fit. It didn't take long for the old hopes to revive. "I don't think I was ever given a fair shake with the NFL. The more I think about it, the more it haunts me." The Miami Hurricanes had just completed their first eleven-win season in eight years, and Clement had something to prove to all the people who identified him with the school's now-completed dark period. He took the field that first night in Las Vegas determined to answer all the scouts and coaches, all the detractors down in South Florida, all the family and friends who couldn't hide their disappointment. "When I threw that touchdown to Nakia Jenkins that first game, I had tears when I came off the field."

He was the prodigal assuming the old skin one last time. But he wasn't the old pedant. He was Billy Kilmer, playing it fast and loose, especially since the old patterns never worked. Forget the sanctimony and the classic-rock mix tape. What did he do to prepare for the game against Orlando, the biggest game of the year? He went out and got hammered. "I find that when I do this stuff, I play better," he said, taking a sip of whiskey and then biting at the air. "I play better when I'm relaxed, when I'm not so uptight."

The magician from the corner of the bar approached Clement and asked him to draw a card. Clement pulled the king of clubs. "Now sign your name on the face of the card," instructed the magician, handing over a Sharpie. Clement shook out his wrist and signed his name with a flourish. He had done this before. "There's just something about football that you can't get from anywhere else," he said, tilting his head as though it would help him see his point better. "It's hard to explain." Clement flattened his palms in front of him. "The field is fifty yards wide. When you walk to the line of scrimmage, you can't see all the way laterally, but pretty close to it. You're calling the play, you have all this stuff flying around in your head, the crowd is going off. All your senses are heightened to this fine point."

The magician took Clement's king of clubs between his fingers and slowly tore it in half, then into quarters. He did this deliberately, and as he tore, Clement's perfect signature went to pieces before his own eyes. Clement watched carefully, as though attentiveness would produce a clue to what would happen. The magician placed the card's four pieces in his palm and made a fist. When he opened his hand, the remnants were gone. Then he shuffled his deck of cards. They flashed in and out of the light, the bar lamps dancing off the laminate. Clement gazed at the magician's hands, which blurred into a single image.

"Let me tell you something," Clement said, struggling to continue his football explication. "I remember my junior year, we're playing Florida State in the Orange Bowl. Number three against number six. We're both four and oh." His hands did plenty of talking. "We're down early, like ten minutes in, we're down seventeen—nothing. We gave 'em a couple easy ones, turned the ball over, and they scored off the turnovers. But then we came back." Clement repositioned himself on his bar stool. The magician stopped shuffling. "It's third and twenty, and I hit Yatil Green for forty yards. We go eighty yards for a touchdown, and the place is going crazy. We get the ball back. And we drive down the field again. And I throw another touchdown pass to Yatil Green."

"All right," exclaimed the magician.

"Seventy-five thousand people are going absolutely nuts," Clement said, indulging himself on the memory. The bar was flooded with chatter, crowd noise in miniature. Clement's eyes telescoped. "Your head just pops off." He grabbed his beer and looked at the liquid swishing around in the bottle. "If you've ever done a line of blow . . ." There was a pause.

The magician broke the silence. "Pick a card, any card," he said, spreading out the pack. Clement did as he was told. "Now turn it over," ordered the magician. Clement looked at the card in his hand, the bar lights catching its sheen. It was the king of clubs, reconstituted. Clement's flourished autograph faced him, miraculously restored.

12

A REAL BUST

BY WEEK SIX, THE XFL had assumed the form of a comatose relative, its wilting, machine-induced breaths begging the question: Pull the plug or have the doctor try a miracle cure? "We knew we were in trouble," said Ken Schanzer. "We could just sense it. We hadn't given up. But we knew we had a real bust. 'Cause it just didn't fly, and you're now trying to figure out how to repair it. You're trying to save it. You're trying to keep it afloat."

Out of this desperation came the league's "blatant attempt to increase ratings," the scheme that announcer Jim Ross had introduced during the finale of the Los Angeles–New York contest a week before. NBC ran ads all week selling the bit, which would occur during the upcoming Orlando–Las Vegas game. The commercials featured a honey-haired woman in soft focus. They looked like Hef could have shot them. "Krissy Carlson, Actual XFL Cheerleader," the bottom of the screen read. The tummy-baring Carlson sashayed toward the camera, flanked by two hulking guys in black jerseys whose heads disappeared above the frame. "A lot of you tuned in to the XFL the first week," Carlson said. "Unfortunately, most of you never came back. Well, we listened to you. And we've made the rule changes to give you what you really want. So come back. At halftime, we'll take you into the cheerleaders' locker room."

Finally, McMahon planned to deliver on the promise of prurience, adhering to his mantra that "there is never enough sex." He hadn't found a way to incorporate sex seamlessly into the overall XFL broadcast—at least in a way that sustained the drool through the commercial break—so he turned to this stunt out of desperation. The upcoming game was the league's last opportunity to grab the attention of a supposedly captive sports audience. The following week, CBS would broadcast the first of three consecutive Saturday nights of the NCAA basketball tournament. The monthlong lull between the Super Bowl and March Madness was just about over. Few people involved with the XFL believed that the cheerleader cam would win huge ratings. But it could at least help the league stave off a questionable achievement: the lowest TV ratings ever in network prime time.

McMahon's WWF writers drew up plans for the halftime gig. This, it seemed, was where NBC drew the line. The network aired the segment, though it had little to do with preparing it. John Gonzalez still had to oversee the production, and he adopted the mind-set of an employee simply drawing a paycheck, instead of someone who had poured himself into the league over a period of many months. "I thought, 'Well, whatever they've decided, let's do it better than it's ever been done.'"

By the time Week Six arrived, most media outlets had given up on poking at the XFL, or even nudging it like a jellyfish washed ashore, gelatinous and wasted. The league managed to issue a statement that kept it in the news anyway, and in the doghouse of reporterly opinion.

The press release said that beginning with the league's second season, the XFL would broaden its talent pool by signing players as young as eighteen. Presumably, these would be players fresh out of high school who were ineligible to play in college due to poor scholastic performance. For years, the NFL signed players who left college early, and though the league had never allowed anyone as young as eighteen to play, the other major leagues—the NBA, NHL, and Major League Baseball—did. While hockey produced major physical collisions, none of the three sports was as violent as pro football, where serious injury was all but guaranteed—especially for the inexperienced. The media took its cuts, blasting McMahon and the XFL for exploiting the underaged (a similar charge levied at the WWF).

Eighteen did happen to fall into a certain age group. The XFL was in such dire need of male viewers in the "coveted demo" that hiring them onto the teams was at least one way of guaranteeing their involvement.

Around the time of the announcement, Linda McMahon ascended a podium at a Bear Stearns investment conference in Boca Raton, Florida. She was there to discuss the business of the WWF, but someone in the crowd asked about the future of the XFL. Stuck between the differing roles of XFL comastermind and oracle of a publicly traded company, McMahon paid heed to the latter. The WWF was "committed through this first season," she said of the XFL, "[but we're] taking a look at it on a week-by-week basis. I think we have to evaluate the viability of the product in the marketplace." Her comments marked the first shiver in the company line. Not even NBC, many voiced behemoth that it was, had allowed a slip regarding the questionable future of the Saturday-evening eyesore. Within hours, speculation began to flutter that Vince McMahon would pull out of his partnership with NBC, hanging his XFL albatross around the neck of his friend Ebersol. On Wednesday, March 7, a terse missive fired from Stamford, signed by Linda McMahon herself. "While World Wrestling Federation Entertainment continues to evaluate the XFL on a weekly basis," read the press release, "we stand committed to our long-term goal of making the XFL a viable brand of alternative football."

Linda McMahon was confused. For those familiar with the gospel of the WWF, it didn't come as a surprise. Over the years, Vince McMahon had succeeded in folding his family into the WWF's stage play. Linda and the couple's children, Shane and Stephanie, joined Vince as characters in the ring. By offering up his family for ridicule, McMahon played to the disposition of his audience, which enjoyed watching the boss get his comeupance.

Linda McMahon's mix-up in Boca Raton fit into a recent WWF subplot. According to the story line, Linda had started swallowing pills, and Vince was catting around. Near Valentine's Day, a scene played out in which Linda, woozy and nearly comatose from her medication, sat helpless and bleary-eyed, pills spread out on a table before her and a blanket covering her lap. Vince handed her a box of Valentine's chocolates, but when his wife kept staring blankly into space, Trish Stratus, one of Vince's "concubines," appeared.

Given the strain, it was remarkable that Linda McMahon even made it to the Bear Sterns conference. Nonetheless, her words inevitably intensified speculation about the future of the league. Would NBC continue with it? *Could* NBC continue with it? And if not, would Vince McMahon, his ego bruised, scrap the whole league after a single year?

Ryan Clement led his team out of the tunnel at the Citrus Bowl on Saturday night, showing no indication that he had gone to sleep well past four A.M., a puddle of hundred-proof drool collecting on his hotel pillow. He looked as ready to go as any other player. The cheerleaders sauntered onto the field past their drill sergeant, Jay Howarth, who screeched into the PA in cloying fishwife chirps. "Hey Orlando, meet your Rage cheerleaderrrrrrrssssss." The Man in the Orange Gloves was there, too, though now his arm wound with the excitement of a roller-coaster operator pulling the lever one more time. There wasn't much riding on the briskness of the production.

For this game, McMahon demoted announcer Jim Ross, reinstated Matt Vasgersian, and elevated sideline reporter Mike Adamle to a new three-man upstairs mix. The Almighty Focus Group suggested that viewers wanted announcers who could dissect and analyze plays, providing more than just a persona. Adamle, a seven-season NFL veteran with the right kind of hair, had spent several years engaging in apocalyptic pronouncements on *American Gladiators*. He got the task of classing up the telecast. Some maître d'. Standing ready for a run-through before the telecast, Adamle shrank beside Jesse Ventura, who earned the attention of the fans continuing to stream into the stadium. All eyes were trained on the baseball hat that cloaked a state-capitol head.

Ventura clutched a microphone in his fist, ready to deliver what he considered the Fan's perspective. He believed that football announcers were too dull, too safe. When he announced a game, he wanted to say the same things he would yell if he was sitting at home. Ventura wanted to tell it like it was. Dick Ebersol knew full well the power of such an arrangement, having worked with the original agitator decades ago on *Monday Night Football*.

Beyond alopecia, Jesse Ventura shared precious little with Howard Cosell. Their joint membership in the society of provocation was the important thing here. Cosell clicked as a host of *MNF* because when the show premiered in 1970, there was no bombast in the sports booth. The networks broadcast NFL games in the hushed, reverential tones of an evensong. For a time, Cosell changed all that with his irascible approach. Many fans hated Cosell, but they tuned in *Monday Night Football* to exorcise the demon.

Ebersol had been counting on a similar fan reaction with the governor. Ventura was eminently more likable than Cosell, but the governor did manage to polarize people all the same. He had the ability to charm and irritate at the same time, a combination that made it difficult for even detractors to turn away from his antics. Ventura's act worked in politics for much the same reason that Cosell's had worked in sports broadcasting. He said what he thought. This was just the thing that Ebersol and McMahon had purchased—Ventura's overactive mouth, which emitted equal parts insight, venom, and (calculated) buffoonery.

There was just one problem—1970 was a long time ago. In the present day, booming voices and thunderous declamations are all you hear in the sports booth. That's what it takes to be heard. Ventura had the volume, but he lacked the substantive commentary of Cosell or even someone like Fox's John Madden, whose shtick has long since grown stale but who still manages to engage viewers through the sheer force of his knowledge. Jesse was just Jesse, very direct, very loud. That was enough in the political arena of the compromisers, but not in sports TV, especially when Ventura didn't prepare adequately for the games and couldn't communicate much of anything in the way of football acumen.

It wasn't as though Ventura didn't give it a solid try. And he stood behind the product when he had very little to gain by doing so. Any other politician, adept as the breed is at the grinning backward shuffle, would have distanced himself from the flailing endeavor after Week Two. Ventura remained, not only fulfilling his contract but doing his share to defend the league's collapse.

"I don't know why the ratings fell," he said, grabbing a seat on a crate on the Orlando broadcast platform minutes before air time. The headsetted NBC technophiles looked at each other in panic, wondering what Ventura was doing taking a breather. "I think Vince really has his hands tied by NBC. See, there's a difference between cable and the network. Vince can be much more risqué on cable. The wrestling is on cable, and he can do all sorts of things that he couldn't do if it was on NBC. Look at *The Man Show.* They couldn't do what they do on the network." Ventura chomped on a cigar. "I love that show, *The Man Show.*"

This was no small feat: a sitting governor announcing enthusiastic support for a TV program that included up-skirt shots of women named the Juggies jumping on trampolines. But this was Jesse Ventura, he of the VIET-NAM—WE WERE WINNING WHEN I LEFT baseball hat and the election-clinching party of mosh pits and body surfing. That's what made him "The Body," an unwillingness to bend to convention.

It was what sustained his relationship with McMahon. It was what drew the segmented hordes into an electoral force. Like the twenty-something white guys in rumpled T-shirts who walked down from Row Z of the Citrus Bowl to a railing beyond which security said they couldn't venture. The fans didn't seem too fussed, and they whispered to one another in a huddle. When they broke, it was to yell: "One, two, three—Jessseeeeeeeee." The governor turned his head and acknowledged the fans with a wink. The guys high-fived one another and wiggled back to their seats, carrying a story that would earn ragged edges through exhaustive telling. This pattern repeated itself several times throughout the game. A group of drunks would yell the governor's name in unison, hoping that their collective voice would be heard. Usually it was, and in midbroadcast Ventura would turn slightly, just enough to recognize the gesture. He would wink or wave and return to the game, sending the fans atwitter.

This was the entire point of McMahon's seating his commentators among the fans, which meshed with Ventura's own populist views. McMahon claimed that his announcers wouldn't "dine on quiche and sip champagne" like the pampered media up in the press box. In advance of the setup, it was easy to picture Ventura passing hot dogs down the aisle and making side bets with Joey from the Jiffy Lube. The plan demonstrated once again McMahon's supposed desire to obscure the line between those who ran the show and those who enjoyed it.

McMahon loved the people, they said, though the theory emanated from little proof. Here was evidence that McMahon's love fell in line with a Perón style of affection, a billionaire's detached head-patting of the proletariat. The bit about the announcers sitting in the cheap seats didn't turn out as pledged. Ventura and Vasgersian didn't sit in the stands. There were no hot dogs passing down the aisle. The announcers were located in the regular seats, sure, and not behind glass in a heated room. That part was true. But in Orlando that night, as every night, the XFL broadcasters rubbed elbows only with their producers and spotters. The XFL production crew had constructed an entire platform in the middle of the stands, roping off access to the announcers.

Granted, the technical problems of seating announcers—not to mention a governor—among an unpredictable crowd would have been insurmountable. But that's what McMahon had promised. What he delivered was another shell game. He clearly identified the XFL in opposition to the Establishment. But McMahon's announcers did not grow closer to the crowd. They only consumed a good portion of low-level fifty-yard-line seats, forcing many paying fans farther toward the nosebleeds.

Another group of fans yelled for Ventura. "Jessseeeeeee!" They didn't seem to care that they couldn't speak directly to "The Body." This was the type of popularity that caused Ventura's name to be bandied about as a running mate for Al Gore in the 2000 election. There was even talk that Ventura would run for president himself in 2004. In Orlando, there was no Secret Service following him around, just his standard-issue Minnesota troopers in black trench coats, both of whom were stressed by their lack of control over the open-air location. "Am I gonna run for president?" Ventura asked, smoothing down his salt-and-pepper mustache. "I'm very humbled and honored that there's any consideration of myself to be the most powerful man in the free world. To even be considered is beyond any expectation I ever had in my life, ever. But we have a president, and we should give him a fair chance and see what he does. He'll have four years. And at the end of his four years, at that point in time, we'll see how he's done and what the situation is with the country—and whether he's beatable. I mean, if you're going to run for the office, I run to win, and it's very difficult to unseat an incumbent. Also, do you ever notice how much these guys age? I mean, they come in young and virile and full of energy, and four years later a fifty-year-old looks seventy. I want to stay as good-looking as I am for as long as I can."

That is not a no. Would the country elect someone who chased a football coach across a muddy field, begging him for a punch-up on live TV? Sometimes it's best to check your charm at the door. That was the difficulty with Ventura. Charm had gotten him this far. It had also caused him all kinds of headaches in Minnesota, where a determined faction of state senators were trying to rein it in, complaining that his weekend XFL job was adversely affecting the one for which he had been elected. Ventura carted around his freedom of will like a medal, like a cause. "If I took off flying around the country every weekend raising a war chest, then I'd be considered honorable," he said, his voice tugging at each syllable. "That would be honorable?"

The XFL hadn't hired Ventura to supply expert analysis. He was meant to stand for something. He was a symbol, not an employee. He was emblematic of the ability to reinvent, of McMahon's vision to change the way people watched sports. As the XFL formula fell apart, Ventura was revealed as one of its most glaring incompatible pieces. But was this his fault? He undoubtedly would have found more success in the booth if he had something interesting to talk about, instead of what McMahon cobbled together.

Ventura took his post off Matt Vasgersian's left shoulder. Their backs were to the field as the XFL's video intro of wet babes and big hits played on the monitors in front of them. Vasgersian welcomed the TV audience to Orlando by running down the matchup between the league's best defense and the only undefeated team. Then the reinstated host happily hoisted the company line. "Well, those of you who might have thought we sold out a few weeks ago and hit rock bottom were wrong." He grinned into the camera. "To help us get there completely, let's check in with Fred Roggin."

Down on the field, Roggin planted himself amid a huddle of Orlando Rage cheerleaders who wore red bottoms and tops piped with orange flames, their Abs of Steel spanning the gap. Roggin looked like a dad ogling his daughter's friends at a pool party. "Some have called it an unprecedented television event," he said. "Others have called it a desperate ploy to increase sagging ratings. In any event, XFL founder, chairman, and noted racketeer"—Roggin paused to raise a glib eyebrow. "Noted *raconteur* . . . Vince McMahon has ordered a camera into the locker room of the Orlando cheerleaders at halftime to capture the essence of whatever it is they do." Roggin leaned toward the cheerleader to his right. "Bev, how do you feel about a camera being in your locker room?"

"I think it's great," said Bev, a gung ho type with a purchased tan. "They bring the cameras into the players' locker room. It's time they brought them into the cheerleader's locker room. We get in there, we just get comfortable, and we wanna take off some . . ."

A gangly blonde standing behind Bev cut her off. "Don't tell them about that," she yelled in a manner that revealed the ellipses on the script.

Bev turned back to Roggin with a big grin. "Well, I guess you'll have to see."

Roggin peered into the camera: "An anxious nation awaits."

The segment felt like it had ended. But as with all things WWF, it went beyond its natural allotment in search of the thousandth deus ex machina. Vince McMahon swooped into the scene—out of nowhere.

"Hey Fred, hang on a second here," he said in his Voice, which sounded artificially baritone, like a ten-year-old on a prank call. He ambled artificially into the picture bow-legged, like an actor playing a cowboy. He was as one big empty cloud. "What I would like is, I would like to introduce all of you ladies to the one man that's gonna be privileged enough to walk into your locker room with a camera. And here he is." McMahon corralled the Bubba Cam operator standing behind him, a pudgy guy in a black getup and a hockey helmet. "His name is Bruno. Say hi to the girls, Bruno."

The meekest voice emitted from behind the chicken wire of Bruno's hockey mask: "Hi, girls."

The cheerleaders made a grand show of enveloping him. "Hi, Bruno," they squealed in unison. They glanced around to see if they had been convincing.

Ryan Clement marched the Outlaws down the field on their opening drive. He looked sharp, zipping passes to receivers, notably the new standout, Yo Murphy. Rod Smart looked just as solid, pounding the ball up the middle and then turning the corner outside. With Clement at something less than full strength, Jim Criner was depending on Smart to carry a bigger load than usual. In the Outlaws' previous two games, HE HATE ME had gained 210 yards on 40 carries after averaging just 46 yards in the first two weeks of the season. He had found his rhythm.

John Gonzalez punched up the segment that producers had taped with Rod Smart earlier in the week. It was a nighttime video of Smart walking the Lakeland streets. "Growing up in the projects, all the bad stuff around you, you grow to feel that you don't want that in life," Smart said. The segment barely scratched the surface before play continued on the field. There was a bigger story here. It wasn't a pretty one, but it had the details to lift it from the purgatory of platitude. Over several prime-time Saturdays, NBC had spent an inordinate amount of time pointing its cameras on the back of Smart's jersey, holding him up as a character worth getting to know. When it came to uncovering Smart's character—and the genesis of HE HATE ME— the XFL failed. This was the difference between real and "reality." NBC offered the gloss, not the grit and missed out on the story behind the league's biggest name.

The Outlaws' drive stalled, forcing a punt, but Clement jogged off the field feeling good about his arm and his timing. After the Rage fumbled, Clement ran back onto the field. A few plays later, he found fullback Ben Snell in the end zone on a four-yard touchdown pass. The crowd went silent.

During Orlando's next possession, on third down, Kelvin Kinney swooped in and knocked the ball from the hands of quarterback Jeff Brohm. Kinney pounded his chest for the cameras.

Everything was going the Outlaws' way. On their next possession, Clement handed the ball to Smart, who ended up in a pile near the line of scrimmage. Everyone peeled away, but Smart remained on the turf. He ripped off his helmet and covered his face with his hands. A replay showed that Smart had taken the shoulder of an Orlando defender on his right knee just as he planted his foot to make a cut. On the telecast, Smart could be heard yelling, "My knee!" A Bubba Cam closed in on the scene, but a glove suctioned over the lens. Just as in Week Three, the players themselves acted as censors.

NBC cut to a commercial as Smart and the trainers headed for the Vegas sideline. During the time-out, a team of trainers hovered over Smart on a metal bench. They pushed and pulled at his leg. He sat up a little straighter. He got to his feet. He took a few steps. By the time the telecast resumed, Smart was jogging up and down the sideline. It was only a scare. Two plays later, Smart was jogging toward the huddle.

When Orlando got the ball back, the Rage offense finally got on track and Jeff Brohm took his team in for a score. Vegas then kicked a field goal. Orlando answered with a second touchdown. At the half, the score stood at 14–9, with Orlando in the lead.

*   *   *

Before NBC dropped out for a commercial, John Gonzalez cut to a shot of Vince McMahon, who held a water bottle in his fist, pacing outside a door that read ORLANDO RAGE CHEERLEADERS, AUTHORIZED PERSONNEL ONLY. He projected anger. Bruno, the Bubba Cam operator, hustled up.

"Where the hell have you been?" McMahon yelled, his nose an inch from the wire mesh of Bruno's hockey mask.

"I got here as quick as I could," Bruno squealed.

McMahon exploded. "As quick as you could . . . Do you realize this moment? Do you realize how big this moment is? Do you realize this is our blatant attempt to increase television ratings tonight?"

McMahon ordered Bruno into a folding chair. The cameraman slipped off the helmet, which revealed a fat, bald head. Encumbered by all of his black equipment, he looked like Darth Vader, when he finally reveals his face at the end of *Return of the Jedi.* "You're sweating like a pig," said a disgusted McMahon.

After the commercial break, the cameras depicted the inner workings of the players' locker rooms. There was no audio. Only the speculation of Vasgersian and Ventura. NBC had abandoned the all-access cameras. Nothing had ever come from them. Life is comprised of small moments, but they aren't what people want to watch. NBC should have hammered out this problem before it offered up a couple players sucking on orange peels. The locker room camera ultimately resembled Andy Warhol's *Sleep,* a five-hour film of a man's extended nap. Very real. And very boring.

NBC instead cut to the scene outside the Rage cheerleaders' locker room. All John Gonzalez did was press "Play." The cheerleader cam wasn't going to be the live massage-fest that viewers were expecting. It wasn't live at all. A WWF crew shot the segment earlier in the week.

"Are you ready?" McMahon asked Bruno.

Bruno's head bounced like a bobble-head doll's.

McMahon gathered Bruno from the folding chair. He slung an arm across his shoulders and spun him around to face the locker room. "On the other side of that door is sheer paradise. Now then, I want you to get in there, and I want you to go get me some ratings." McMahon shoved Bruno toward the locker room. The cameraman slammed his Uncle Fester forehead into the door, then dropped to the floor in mock concussion.

McMahon lost it in C-actor form, screaming like a housewife who had lost her Valium. He bent over the fallen Bruno.

"Hey! You idiot! You idiot! Get up! Get up! Get up! You idiot! Hey! [sotto voce] He's unconscious. Hey, wake up! Wake up! Hey, wake up! Wake up!"

McMahon slapped Bruno in the face. The picture blurred. The sound muffled. Female voices could be heard begging Bruno to arise. The picture sharpened to reveal a huddle of Orlando Rage cheerleaders.

The following segment would have won the Emmy for Best Non Sequitur, had there been such an award. The hyped cheerleader cam, the blatant attempt at ratings, was not a cheerleader cam at all. It was, instead, a peek into the WWF imagination that created the league. It was the strangest thing that NBC had ever broadcast.

Music kicked in—"You Are So Beautiful," by Joe Cocker—along with a shot of the cheerleaders in a row, wearing flowing Cleopatra gowns, grooming one another's hair. This was Bruno's steamy dream sequence. It began tamely, but switched quickly to the bizarre. The screen wiped to a shot of several cheerleaders contorting over a Twister board. They played the game with two men dressed in gorilla suits. The next scene depicted a couple of cheerleaders in towels lathering up a man who wore a Rage helmet and a jersey that read, SHE LOVE ME.

In what followed, NBC finally achieved its goal of airing something that no one had ever seen on prime time. The screen wiped to a shot of two women sitting in leather armchairs. They stroked squealing piglets, with their feet propped on the backs of two men who wore hog masks. The next shot depicted a cheerleader dressed in dominatrix gear, waving a riding crop at a man in a rabbit suit. Next was a shot of a card table around which three cheerleaders played strip poker with the devil. "Satan" had just won a hand, prompting the woman seated to his left to unhook her bra. Before viewers could catch a peek, the dream sequence whisked to the showers. This was the steamy setting of the first XFL TV ads, which had generated much free publicity for the league in the form of moral scorn. Finally, here it was, to the point: nudity, or something approximating it. Silhouettes wiggled behind frosted glass. McMahon had shown bare breasts on his WWF pay-per-views. How much skin would he show now? How much would NBC allow him to show? A shower door opened. And out stepped Rodney Dangerfield with a towel stretched tight around his sagging physique. He shrugged. "When I played football I always fell in love with the center."

The screen blurred again, and the scene returned to the hallway, where an overflow of hair and breasts tried to rouse Bruno "in real time." McMahon descended on the cheerleaders in mock anger. He ordered them onto the field. Halftime was over.

"You ruined this whole damn thing for me," McMahon screamed at Bruno, kicking him in the gut. "Look at you. Wake up! Wake up! Wake up!" He emptied his water bottle on the cameraman's pudgy face, yanked him to his feet, and shoved him toward the door that led to the field. McMahon threw Bruno's helmet against the wall. He seethed into the lens.

The bossman's acting left much to be desired. This was nothing new. In the ring, his character hadn't wanted for purpose and definition. Beyond it, this new Mister McMahon, though equally lecherous and single-minded, was too amorphous for McMahon to grasp. In the XFL, he had no evil empire to represent, no white knight to attack. Without such marked sides to which an audience could grant allegiance, Mister McMahon fell flat. Instead of rooting for his comeuppance, viewers were left to wonder at the very point of him. His mischief was cheap, adolescent. Robbed of the WWF's grandiose opera, with its buttress of subplots and demons, McMahon became a cable-access infomerchant wasting everyone's time.

As for the cheerleader cam, it was a bizarre gag—and another empty XFL promise.

Orlando couldn't do much with the ball in the third quarter. Though the Las Vegas defensive backs gave up a few big pass plays, the front seven were starting to turn the game in their favor. Ryan Clement still looked sharp, but his offensive line had trouble containing the Rage defensive push. Vegas kicked a field goal, narrowing the score to 14–12 by the end of the third quarter.

The pressure was on Clement and Smart to perform, and in their own backyards. If they ever wanted a tryout, this was it, in prime time with the scouts watching from upstairs. Clement handed the ball to Smart, who tip-toed toward right end as the Orlando defense strung itself out. It looked like the Rage had Smart wrapped up. But when Smart reached the corner of the defensive front, he turned on the juice. He reeled off a thirty-one-yard run before being knocked out of bounds at Orlando's twenty-two-yard line. The Outlaws offense was rolling. The NFL scouts up in the press box took note, muttering to one another under their breath. Smart again got the call, and he ran right once more. Rage defenders had Smart in their grasp, but he shed them and kept on chugging. Orlando knocked him out of bounds at the three-yard line. The scouts leaned in again. "You gonna let him put 'hate' on the back of his jersey?" one scout asked another. "Yeah, Cough'll love that" was the answer, referring to Tom Coughlin, coach of the Jacksonville Jaguars.

It was first and goal for Vegas. Smart got the handoff, but the Rage stuffed him. On second down, he got the carry again, with the same result. On third down, from the two-yard line, Jim Criner didn't try anything fancy. Smart had taken the team down the field. Clement handed the ball to the tailback. The Rage turned Smart back. Three plays. Three runs. Three stuffs. Vegas settled for a field goal, retaking the lead, 15–14. A giant opportunity had gone by the board.

The Outlaws had taken considerable time off the clock with their drive. When Orlando got the ball, there were fewer than eight minutes left in the game. Vegas held Brohm and his offense to limited yardage on their first two downs. On third down, the Rage had six yards to go. Brohm scrambled, then heaved the ball deep. His receiver hauled in the pass at the Vegas eighteen-yard line. The Vegas defensive backs couldn't stick with Orlando's receivers. John Gonzalez cut to Jim Criner, who sucked on his lips. As the clock ticked under five minutes, Brohm fired a touchdown pass from sixteen yards out. Criner sniffled. The score was 21–15.

The Outlaws regained the ball at their twenty-eight-yard line. On first down, Orlando dropped Rod Smart for a loss. On second down, he caught a pass for six yards. On third down, Clement put the ball in the turf. With 3:15 on the clock and fourth down coming up, Criner called a time-out. Six points down, would he punt the ball and bet on his defense? Or would he gamble and go for the first down? The telecast recorded it all as Clement, Criner, and the assistant coaches huddled on the sideline.

"We can kick it and play defense," Criner said, his gaze focused on the grass as he listened to suggestions on his headset. All eyes were on Criner. He pursed his lips. He rocked from side to side. "Okay," he said. "Let's go for it."

When Clement took the fourth-down snap, he immediately shuffled to his left. The play was a screen pass. Clement delivered the ball. The Rage sniffed it out, and they dropped Vegas for a three-yard loss. Criner ripped off his headset and yelled loudly and directly into a nearby microphone, "Fuck me! Fuck!"

But the game wasn't over. The Outlaws defense held. The Rage stared at fourth down and four yards to go on the Vegas twenty-nine-yard line. Orlando punted, burying Vegas at its own ten-yard line.

Ryan Clement had one last chance. The clock read 1:43. The score was 21–15. It was ninety yards for a touchdown. If the Outlaws were going to pull out the win, they would have to do it on Clement's arm. There just wasn't time for anything else.

"Green eighty-five Hawk," Clement yelled to the huddle. The Outlaws broke and lined up for the play. Clement took the snap and backpedaled four steps. He stood on his own goal line. He scanned downfield for a receiver. Then the pocket began to close in on him. A defensive lineman hit Clement low. Another lineman hit him in the midsection. Two more swarmed over top. As Clement collapsed, the football squirted out of his hands and onto the painted grass of the end zone. A Rage lineman fell on the ball like it was a hunk of gold. Orlando touchdown. Final score: 27–15.

At the finish, Clement lay facedown on the field, red field chalk caked onto his eye-black. Like a vulnerable island, he remained on the grass as opponents circumnavigated him, engaged in a victory dance. The stadium buzz faded away and Clement occupied his own head, blades of grass tickling his nose. This was how it was going to be, then . . . He picked himself up and dusted the detritus of the night from his black pants. Walking toward the sideline, weighted to one side like a car with a busted headlight, he wore a smirk. It was a battle shield.

It was all done, all but the clean-up crew. Most of the players jogged off the field under the lights, heading to the showers before the hot water ran out. A few lingered on the field talking to old college friends on the opposing team, accepting victory and defeat in equal smiles so long as the paychecks arrived on time.

Except, Kelvin Kinney. Back in Chicago a week earlier, in the pin-drop locker room of a different bitter defeat, other Outlaws had explained how the XFL was their chance at returning to the big money, talking with the zeal of those who try to subdue themselves into being lone believers. But when a reporter asked Kinney why he took the XFL job, his answer came as a bark: "A championship," he said before turning with a wince on his busted foot and heading for the trainer's room, where he shivered not so much at the pain as the bad news.

"How long will it take to heal?" he asked, nodding at the softball pulsating on his left ankle. "Six weeks," said the trainer, who twisted and prodded the foot with little regard for the electricity that scorched the body to which it was attached. *"Six weeks?"* asked Kinney, incredulous, his voice rising, his nostrils flaring. The trainer winked. "We tape you up, protect you, give you a shot," he said in the clipped manner of a busy mechanic. "You can play." Kinney sat back against the wall and closed his eyes, a mountain of a man in all sorts of discomfort, volunteering for more.

After the Orlando game, Kinney stood alone at the forty-yard line, a solitary figure on a field of the departed. He struggled with his shoulder pads, his uniform jersey still covering them, wrestling the contraption over his bullet-shaped head. Finally, he managed to rip off the pads. He stood in a drenched white T-shirt with ripped sleeves, his naked arms resembling the legs of a sculpture. He stared into the ground at nothing, his jaw come undone, his shoulder pads dangling from his right hand. Slowly, his legs took him off the field.

Up on the broadcast platform, Team Ventura prepared for its own departure, through a sea of drunken admirers. The governor descended the stadium steps like an oaf, one shiver per footfall quivering through his entire body. Fans leaped at Ventura like German shepherds on link chains, reaching an arc in the air, snapping their jaws just before him, emboldened in their approach by the knowledge of its fruitlessness. Ventura's bodyguards surrounded him. They never knew when that one would appear, the one who is linked to no chain, who, in his sobriety, is drunker than the rest.

"Jesse!" yelled a fan, sloshing a beer against his Orlando Rage T-shirt. "Jesse, you should run for governor of Florida." Ventura kept his eyes on the stairs, feeling purposefully with his giant hands for the shoulders of the men encircling him. He was careful not to lose his balance on the half-steps of the stadium, those steps that every stadium has, which are the right size for no one over the age of seven. "Jesse, you rock," shouted another one of the crowd, which attempted in unvoiced consensus to follow en masse through a tunnel leading toward the concourse that was built for three abreast. "Show us your chrome dome," said another onlooker, who made a halfhearted attempt to grab the governor's baseball hat.

The crowd pushed through the tunnel. Ventura's eyes glazed over. No longer was he the jovial, riffing governor, Schwarzenegger's alien-fighting buddy. This was a crush. This was an English football match. It needed to be over.

The crowd refused to release its grip. Ventura wouldn't halt and give the fans their due, render a colorful pronouncement. So the crowd turned against him. A man in a camouflage hat had tried in vain throughout the entire game to get the governor's autograph. Now he was angry. "You piece of shit," he yelled. "Nice job signing autographs, you piece of shit." Clutching his Coors, the man led the charge after Ventura. The royal entourage ignored him. The spittle that had spent an entire four quarters collecting at the corners of his thick mouth found its purpose, hurling in a rope and landing squarely on the XFL logo of the governor's jacket. "Nice job you piece of shit," the man said again, working the words out of his acidic hole.

Finally the governor arrived on the concourse, a few hundred paces from his limousine. There was more of the unsettled public. A frenzied, sweaty man jumped in front of the procession. He wore a black T-shirt with Ventura's cartoon likeness silk-screened on the front. JESSE THE BODY, JESSE THE MIND, it read. In his right hand, the man held an electric-pink yard glass. In his left hand, he held a disposable camera. "Hey Jesse, lemme get a picture," he yelled, backpedaling with dexterity. "The two of us. I wore this T-shirt for you." The governor had space to raise his eyes. He chuckled at the T-shirt, at the unsolicited homage. His steps only got bigger. "Aw, come on," whined the fan. "Come on, just one picture." As the governor passed him by, the man in the T-shirt yelled to the rafters. Then he tilted his head for a swallow from the hot-pink yard glass.

Ventura had almost arrived at his car, but not before a half-dozen more people registered the clamor on the concourse and joined the fast-travelling procession. Ventura reached his limo, into which he was shoved by his protectors, whose faces betrayed relief at having escaped the scene without incident. One bodyguard remained outside the limo and its two warming escort vehicles as a wavering man in a concert shirt and XFL baseball hat hovered around the scene. "Hey" was what the man seemed to be saying, the carbonation of the moment having overtaken him. "Hey, Jesse," he said. The bodyguard moved toward the fan and whispered something in his ear. "Hey, Jesse," said the man, unperturbed. "You suck. You fucking suck. You're a fucking . . ." He slurred the noun that would have explained it all. It stuck in his throat, and in his effort to extract it, he engaged in physical exertion that left him off balance and vulnerable to the bodyguard's shove, which deposited him on the blacktop. The governor's caravan took off for the airstrip, enveloping the drunken man in a blue-white cloud of exhaust. This was the remainder of the XFL fan base. So much for sitting in the stands.

Within an hour, once a teary-eyed Jim Criner had highlighted the need to be "more consistent on offense, better under center," Ryan Clement found himself back at the bar Ybor's. "I'm gonna take the heat for this one," he said, his cheeks still flushed from the game. "Fuck, fuck, fuck," he yelled in crescendo, his shouts competing with the mall rock that filled the room. He pounded his good fist into the bar, holding his splinted hand at his side. Clement had completed twenty of thirty passes against the Rage. The aggressive Orlando rush did him in. He was sacked four times. He busted a finger. In the gloom of the defeat, Clement let off some steam. "Criner tells me I'm a pretty boy," he said. "He fucks with my head. And Grieb, he likes to coach me from the sidelines. He went to Stanford, so he thinks he's smart. I guess he is, but I don't wanna hear it."

Clement was about to step on an early-morning plane filled with silence back home to Vegas. Till then he lifted another beer.

13

HE HATE BOB COSTAS

VINCE MCMAHON LOOKED SPENT and haggard when TNN announcer Bob Golic approached him outside San Francisco's Pac Bell Park before Sunday's telecast. Golic asked his boss how he was doing. "Not so good," McMahon said, projecting storm clouds. "Last night didn't go the way I had hoped."

What did the cheerleader cam do for XFL ratings? The game pulled in a 2.4. It was the identical dismal number that the previous week's game had earned. It wasn't a dip, marking the first week of the season where ratings didn't fall from the previous game. But it was another dim sign, as the promise of gratis flesh failed to coax a rise from an audience that was supposedly prone to priapism.

And so McMahon wallowed in the hollow feeling of a man who realizes that his last-ditch effort has fallen flat. It didn't help that the WWF's stock price had just hit an all-time low at $11.81. Not quite in tatters, McMahon's world teetered, while facing the very real prospect of crumbling in the coming tumult of the NCAA Final Four. Including playoffs, six weeks of XFL games remained. For McMahon, that meant another month and a half of being reminded that his grand vision was becoming a humiliating failure. In the twisting plunge, he found a scapegoat.

Larry Stewart was sitting at his desk in the expansive, bustling newsroom of the *Los Angeles Times*. Reporters in crisp white shirts hustled up the cubicle aisles. The monotone drone of typing and talking filled the air like wings buzzing against one another in a hive. Stewart's phone rang. The paper's TV-sports columnist, Stewart was assigned to the XFL. He would admit that it wasn't a tough job, since his boss, Bill Dwyre, didn't believe that the XFL warranted more than passing coverage in the back of the sports section, beneath the small print of the horse-racing results. Bill Dwyre had graduated from Notre Dame in the same class as *Monday Night Football* producer Don Ohlmeyer, whose son, Drew, worked as the L.A. Xtreme director of communications. But nothing could convince Dwyre that the XFL was something people really wanted to read about. Dwyre had given the league solid play on its opening weekends, and coverage had dwindled along with the ratings.

When Larry Stewart picked up his phone and listened to the booming voice on the other end of the line, he knew Dwyre would run this story ahead of the ponies. It was Vince McMahon calling.

McMahon had been upset about Bill Plaschke's column in the paper after the league's second game. Of all the negative publicity, that piece stuck out. To McMahon, it was prime evidence of the media's predisposition against him—and, by extension, against the XFL. Instead of pointing out the thrill of a close game, Plaschke had focused on the hot tub behind the end zone and the man who got tossed from his wheelchair. McMahon was upset with the *Los Angeles Times,* but not so angry that he wouldn't use the paper as a publicity tool. He was adept as anyone at working the game.

What McMahon said, exactly, and what Bill Dwyre ran on page three of the Thursday, March 15 edition of the *Times* under Larry Stewart's byline, was that Jesse Ventura was on "thin ice" as an XFL announcer. "We've made mistakes," McMahon said. "And I think our biggest one was our selection of announcers. We need football announcers, not WWF announcers. Our research shows people don't like [Ventura] on the XFL. He's too over the top. Hyperbole turns people off. They know when you're not telling the truth."

McMahon's billion was predicated on hyperbole. He was swathed in hyperbole. Practically everything he said was gauged toward maximum exaggeration. Now the ruler of all falsity was claiming higher ground. This was like Ron Jeremy preaching abstinence.

It sounded like another wrestling ploy. Just like the Rusty Tillman episode.

Reporters caught up with Ventura in St. Paul on Thursday morning and asked him about McMahon's comments. "I'm not getting into that," the governor said, stopping the conversation before it started. He didn't mention McMahon's name; this was no angle. Suddenly roles shifted, and Ventura was playing the part of Rusty Tillman, exasperated by a surprise attack, craving its evaporation. Privately, Ventura fumed, but he wasn't about to start sniping. On his weekly radio program, Ventura went on to say that he wasn't "a quitter," dashing any hope for the spectacle of bickering. "I made a commitment," he sniffed. "I will fulfill that commitment." Shortly thereafter, Ventura stopped talking about the XFL altogether, declining any and all interviews on the subject.

It was another sign of the difference between McMahon and Ventura, though many Americans couldn't be bothered to distinguish between them. They were both wrestling characters, after all, full of rhetoric and embellishment. But when Ventura simmered down, he had a glimmer of propriety about him. When the XFL tubed, Ventura didn't break ranks. He remained the team player, the one with repose. McMahon snubbed him from within.

The McMahon camp claimed that the boss was merely reiterating a set of facts. "[His comments in the *Los Angeles Times*] were based on a research project that had been fielded by the XFL and NBC," said Jim Bell, the former WWF vice president of marketing. "It came back with Jesse not scoring high marks and Jim Ross not scoring high marks. Vince just repeated what was in the research document." McMahon's central point was correct—Ventura didn't work well on the broadcasts. But claiming that Ventura was one of the XFL's "biggest" mistakes was like blaming a forty-five-point loss on the place-kicker. McMahon singled out Ventura because the governor was big enough to single out. He was the huge target, the diversion that McMahon needed at a time when he was taking so much personal heat for the league's failure.

But was there more to this than the simple assigning of blame? McMahon had always believed that Ventura overvalued himself. Ventura had never known his place in the rigid caste system of the WWF, where, Hulk Hogan once said, McMahon would "ride the horse until it drops. Shoot it. Then eat the horse."

When Ventura won the gubernatorial election in 1998, he vaulted over McMahon in national prominence. He was on the cover of every newsmagazine. He was a guest on every network. He gained the seal of societal approval that McMahon could never attain. McMahon burned with the belief that Ventura owed his very existence to the WWF. With his public denunciation, McMahon could remind the governor that he was still the boss.

McMahon played his own game and lost, forgetting that it takes only one match to turn a hero into a heel.

By this time, NBC's support for the league itself had long since evaporated, especially among the rank and file. "Most of us are embarrassed by it," said a producer in NBC's Olympics division. "Sports telecasts have degrees of integrity and worth, and this is taking it pretty low. There is concern. But we're not losing sleep over it. No one is rallying behind it. No one watches it here as far as being a loyal NBC employee. The real thing is how this reflects on the network as a whole. It's like watching a train wreck. You watch the halftime show and see Vince McMahon throw the cameraman into the locker room door of the Orlando Rage cheerleaders. Do I see that and say, 'Jesus Christ, I'm embarrassed to be associated with that'? Yes. All of us, to some degree, feel a little dirty."

There was more to it than guilt by association. As layoffs and budget chops continued to plague the network, the XFL stuck out like a Porsche in a recession. "Everyone talks around NBC about how we could use a big show," said a producer for *Dateline*. "In terms of *Millionaire* or *Survivor*, we haven't come up with anything like that. There's a lot of resentment to Sports for getting huge amounts of money and getting budgets we only dream of. The Olympics were viewed as a failure. And we have to take the blame. Everyone's losing jobs. They're firing people across the board. We're not spared."

Stores of harsh sentiment projected toward the XFL, even from within the GE Building. No longer was there vague frustration about the NFL's escalating price tag. NBC employees could now direct their anger toward the tangible embarrassment of the XFL. Everyone forgot Dick Ebersol's reason for buying in to the league in the first place. People went by what they saw— not by how it came to be in front of them—and what they saw was a loss of prestige. "NBC's involvement is a disgrace for the network—disgraceful and disgusting," said Chet Simmons, the network's first Sports president. "If being angry at the NFL because they didn't get a piece of the NFL in the last contract forced them to do that, then they're crazy. That should never be a motivation. Anybody who I had been with at NBC—there are a bunch of us left around—we talked, and we all felt the same way. We were very disappointed. A lot of the guys I worked with who have passed on must have been flipping. To put the peacock in front of any event that we did was a very prideful moment. NBC, take it back twenty years and what did you think about? World Series, Wimbledon, Major League Baseball, professional football, being part of the first Super Bowl. How much better does that get? And you can't even put that in the same breath with the XFL. It turns your stomach."

Simmons wasn't the only distinguished member of the NBC enclave who grieved at the XFL's tarnish. It became a company pastime, as people were quick to point out that they had had nothing to do with it. Ebersol had spared his top on-air talent, such as Marv Albert and Bob Costas, from engaging in pronouncements on HE HATE ME and the rest. And generally, they returned the favor with editorial silence. Costas, who joined NBC in 1980, owed Ebersol that much. During the late 1980s, Ebersol, whom Costas once called "the czar of my universe," developed his free-form late-night interview program, *Later with Bob Costas*. Costas built a career on his silken tongue (he loved to hear the sounds it made) and had a willingness to denounce whatever he considered unrefined. Eventually, he couldn't resist taking a shot at the XFL. "It has to be at least a decade since I mused out loud, 'Why doesn't somebody combine mediocre high school football with a tawdry strip club?'" he said. "Finally, somebody takes my idea and runs with it."

In addition to his duties at NBC, Bob Costas hosted a live program on HBO, *On the Record with Bob Costas*. He interviewed relevant sports figures, usually in a probing style that was hard to find elsewhere on TV. In advance of the March 14 edition of Costas's program, the press drummed up plenty of hype. Costas had invited two controversial guests, both of whom placed interviewers somewhere between roach and dung beetle on the roster of animated existence.

Bobby Knight would appear. He was the college basketball coach whom Indiana University had recently fired for physically abusing his players. The author of legendary tirades, Knight physically intimidated reporters into asking silly questions, which he then hurled back at them as evidence of their sorrowful time on Earth. Six months before, just after Indiana let him go, Knight engaged in a verbal scrap with an ESPN reporter that made headlines—even after the firing, he was still biting heads off. Costas was going to have his hands full.

The other guest on the show was no greater pushover. It would be Vince McMahon.

In Bob Costas, Vince McMahon would come face-to-face with the sports-media establishment. Costas had worked the World Series, the Super Bowl, the NBA Finals, and the Olympics. He had won eleven Sports Emmy Awards. This wouldn't be a press conference where McMahon could orchestrate the flow of conversation from behind the only microphone. McMahon would enter Costas's bully pulpit, beneath the disorienting lights of a live telecast.

Costas and McMahon sat opposite each other in deep library chairs, with a raised kidney-shaped console between them. Their knees almost touched. A digital tapestry of Manhattan scenery served as a backdrop on the set, which resembled a metallic hangar. It was easy to see that Costas, sitting so close to his guest, gave away a half a foot and fifty pounds to the bulging McMahon.

Costas began the interview by asking McMahon about the future of the XFL; McMahon said he was in for the long haul. The interview settled into its opening moments, devoid of barbs, until Costas said that TV people considered the XFL "a low-rent form of television." McMahon smirked when he heard the words. He hunched forward in his chair, as though preparing to lunge at Costas. The outline of a vein flashed along his neck. To McMahon, Costas's claim that the XFL was low-rent was another sign of the attribute he hated most about WWF critics. "We are going to have to convince the media to cover this for the event that it is, not the perceptions you as an elitist, which you are in my opinion. . . ."

McMahon had begun to cast the interview in a familiar light—the populist versus the snob. Having done so, he was willing to delineate several reasons for the league's failing. It actually sounded like McMahon was owning up to his shortcomings. Then he took another shot at Ventura. "We also had the wrong announcers out there."

Costas seized the opportunity to highlight the aversion that most established announcers had to working under McMahon's dominion. "And this is not necessarily from people who wish you ill, but within the business—"

"Why would anyone want to wish me ill?" McMahon asked, his face a mask of solicitude.

"The show is only an hour long," Costas answered. "We will get to that in a minute."

Instead, Costas cued a video. It was a recent WWF episode in which McMahon berated Trish Stratus, his "concubine," inside the ring. As the clip played, McMahon goaded Stratus into stripping to her underwear in front of a packed arena in Washington, D.C. A WWF voice squealed over the action: "I came to Washington, D.C., and I'm gonna get to see bush."

The show returned to the studio, with Costas pointing out that McMahon ended up draping his jacket over Stratus. McMahon deadpanned. "I am the consummate gentlemen. I would never want to do anything in bad taste."

Costas sharpened his voice as though scolding a small child for a lapse in judgment. "What is the possible justification of what we just saw?"

McMahon reddened as he realized the ambush set for him. He'd had no prior knowledge that Costas was going to run the clip. He thought he was going to talk about the XFL. He lost his train of thought. "Let's find the most salacious, out-of-character thing you could find. Let's edit it and put it right up here." Costas countered in his clipped, diligent delivery, claiming the Stratus scene as a general example of WWF fare.

McMahon shimmied in his library chair. He would take only so much. His voice dropped in octave. He assumed a verbal swagger. He slipped noticeably into Mister McMahon. "Don't make me raise my voice. I don't want to do that with you. Even though you're doing it with me. But you wanna play that way, boy, I can play." McMahon strung out the word "boy," pronouncing it in a vaguely southern manner as though he were going to show this city slicker a thing or two. McMahon was losing his cool, and the interview was about to assume a deeper energy.

"These things don't happen, haven't happened?" Costas asked.

"You want to let me finish here for a second, pal?!" Mister McMahon belted it out like he was doing a bit with "Stone Cold" Steve Austin, instead of the seven-time Sportscaster of the Year.

Costas pressed his point, with a tranquillity that only enraged his guest further.

McMahon scooted to the edge of his seat. The chair's back legs lifted off the floor, and smacked down with a thud on the metallic set. McMahon yelled. He stabbed a finger within inches of Costas's nose. "Then shut your mouth!" McMahon looked like he was going to punch his much smaller host, or maybe just slap him for being so fastidious, so self-righteous. Even without a studio audience, Mr. McMahon was still playing to the crowd.

Costas didn't budge. He was enjoying the spectacle. How could viewers turn this off?

But McMahon has no dummy. He realized he had to change his tactic. There were at least fifteen minutes remaining in the segment, and he couldn't scream until the end.

Instead, he sought to divert the argument from wrestling, likening the WWF's brand of entertainment to the risque content that two HBO programs, *The Sopranos* and *Sex in the City,* included in Emmy-winning episodes. It was an old argument. "Why are you on your high seat here, your high chair?" he asked.

Costas countered by redirecting the discussion. He brought up an item of news regarding the WWF. A court in Miami, Florida, had only days before convicted a fourteen-year-old boy, Lionel Tate, of first-degree murder in the beating death of his six-year-old playmate, Tiffany Eunick. Tate body-slammed Eunick to death in 1999, fracturing her skull and pulverizing her liver. Tate's attorney argued that his client had learned such punishing physical maneuvers from watching pro wrestling. In a post-trial statement, the judge in the case said that it was "inconceivable that Tiffany's injuries could have been caused by . . . replicating professional wrestling moves." The attorney's tactic backfired, but McMahon had to face questions about the case as though he had been complicit in the killing.

"Bob, you're disappointing me," McMahon said. "You were supposed to come here and know your stuff, okay." He leaned in for emphasis. "But if you're gonna jump me and jump all over me, then you should have watched some of this. You should really know your facts."

This was a worn ploy of McMahon's, floating a fib or a jab, then moving on before anyone could challenge it. This was standard practice in the WWF. But Costas stood his ground. "I've seen some of it," he interjected.

McMahon reddened. This wasn't how his interviews usually played out. Like Bobby Knight, he intimidated reporters into submission. But Costas wasn't backing down. McMahon adjusted his seat and leaned in toward his host again, the padded shoulders of his shiny suit nearly blocking Costas's face from the camera lens. When he opened his mouth, the force of his breath appeared to ruffle Costas's hair. "Would. You. Let. Me. Finish." He yelled. He was almost nose to nose with the host.

Costas just smiled. "Absolutely," he said.

". . . What I'm gonna say here, pal," McMahon continued, though the look on Costas's face unnerved him. "With a big smile," he said, mimicking Costas's grin with one of his own. He shook his head.

"This is amusing me," Costas said.

"It's amusing you?" McMahon asked. "You're amusing me."

"Okay, good. We're both amused."

They both sounded like Joe Pesci.

McMahon had succeeded in diverting the discussion of a serious issue, chewing up time with silly patter. It was humorous, but it wasn't substantive. And it spurred the question: Was McMahon a genuine polemic, as he claimed to be? To this point, his interview had been more performance than appearance—a familiar equation. He managed to obfuscate a weakness in actual debate as he spewed WWF-style spite all over HBO's pristine hangar.

Again, the two men went back and forth. McMahon said that pro wrestling had nothing to do with the girl's death. Costas needled him with exactitude.

"Would you please let me finish?" McMahon begged.

"Absolutely," said Costas.

"You're sure? You're not gonna interrupt me? You're gonna let me finish?"

This time McMahon looked like he had lost all control. He must have sensed the acid buildup because he took a long, silent sip from the blue coffee mug that sat before him. It was a dramatic pause.

The interview continued.

Costas grilled McMahon about the WWF's treatment of women, hinting at the video he had played earlier. McMahon huffed, saying that Costas had used the segment to smear him. "It's a real class move on your part."

McMahon's insult ate at Costas, who interrupted his guest once more. "It's interesting to see you lecturing somebody about class."

The color drained from McMahon's face. He screwed his eyes on Costas. "I don't have class?" he asked.

"I'm saying you're a strange one to be delivering that lecture."

"So now you're interrupting me again," McMahon bellowed.

"Proceed."

But the arm wrestling wasn't finished. McMahon wagged his head from side to side. "Ya know what? This is the Bob Costas Interrupt Program, right?"

"That's a characterization I think few would share. But it might work for you in this instance."

"It works for me. I mean, take a look at the tape when you play it back. How many times does Bob Costas interrupt Vince McMahon before he let him answer the question?"

Before long, time was up. "Vince, we gotta go," Costas said.

"Oh, it's too bad," said McMahon, in pantomime of the gracious guest. "This is *such* a delightful show, Bob. Thank you *so* much for having me on."

"I appreciate your coming on," said Costas, wearing a smirk of his own.

"It's a delight," said McMahon. The two men shook hands.

After a short break in the program, Bobby Knight scowled from the deep library chair. But there was no fire from Knight. In contrast to the person who had warmed his seat, Knight came off as a cuddly grandpa shot in Barbara Walters soft focus. He was the one who had a demonstrated capability for violence, having been caught on tape choking one of his players. Yet it was Knight who got the free ride with Costas in an interview that bordered on celebrity journalism.

How much of McMahon's performance was real, and how much of it emanated from the practiced character of Mister McMahon? "There were times when I thought he would pick up Bob and throw him across the room," said a producer for *On the Record with Bob Costas*. "But it's not like

McMahon went into the green room after the interview and started kicking things around. How close was he genuinely to that and how much was shtick? I don't know. The play between Bob and Vince was minimal. They shook hands and he left. But then he goes around talking it up. He needs the publicity."

Indeed he did, and he trumpeted the appearance as another sign of his virility, championing himself as the indemnifier of lost causes. Viewers could interpret the guest shot either way, and a great many did, falling along predictable lines. "Score a takedown for Bob Costas," stated the *USA Today;* while Mike Francesa, a host on the influential New York sports-talk radio station WFAN, on which McMahon had recently given an extended interview, said that the WWF boss "ate Costas alive." The show was such a hit that the *New York Times* went to the effort of calculating the number of times each man had interrupted the other: McMahon twenty-seven, Costas twenty-two. Both came off in ways that served their particular purpose, just like the Andy Kaufman–Jerry Lawler feud in the early 1980s. It felt like it could have been fixed, worked, as they say in pro wrestling, as though managed in order to engender a particular crowd reaction.

However people judged it, the appearance had further revealed the tactics and thought processes of the man who had created the XFL in his own image. The show had also given McMahon the chance to lash out after taking six weeks' worth of heat on the league. It must have been liberating for him to recover his ability to dictate a spectacle.

At dusk, a sea of kids wearing droopy NBA jerseys, bikers in beards, and teenagers with hideous acne made its way toward the Staples Center in downtown Los Angeles. Swerving car headlights bounced off a thousand scissoring legs. Against the parking lot blacktop, they had the flickering effect of a movie projector. There was a steady hum of chatter and the clip-clop of shoes as the crowd flooded in the direction of the white dome up ahead.

The face of pro football materialized from the mass of bodies. Dick Butkus was there to see what all the noise was about. He was there for WWF *Raw Is War,* Vince McMahon's showpiece, the spectacle that augured the XFL. While he didn't know much about pro wrestling, Dick Butkus understood plenty about the value of theatrics. He used to spit gobs on the football between plays, a little gift to the terrified quarterback on the other side of the line.

Butkus had taken the free tickets gladly, though he was becoming increasingly dissatisfied with the way that his bosses were running things. He was still handling his duties as XFL director of competition while also filling in for Jerry Lawler on NBC's backup game, the regional telecast that almost no one saw. Rumors had circulated that Vince McMahon was trying to hire former New York Giants linebacker Lawrence Taylor for the permanent announcing spot. Until then, Butkus was happy to help. That wasn't the problem. What bothered him was NBC's weekly hedging. With every decision critical to staving off ratings decline, the network would wait until midweek to decide which game it would televise nationally, which game had the best chance of getting the biggest audience. Butkus never knew where NBC needed him until the last minute. That kept him from traveling in his RV from his home in Malibu. Butkus was forced to head to the airport. And he'd rather drive cross-country than endure the hassles of flying.

Butkus didn't know much about Vince McMahon or pro wrestling before he signed on with the XFL. He met McMahon for the first time only when they discussed his job. Butkus went off of his instincts with people, as though still playing linebacker and judging tendencies in a split second. He liked McMahon. He understood his businesslike approach. And he also liked McMahon's bravado. The guy's got some balls, he thought. But Butkus had no concept of McMahon's place in the world. "I didn't realize how much the press really hated the guy." As he watched the media reaction to the league's first few weeks, Butkus began to understand what he had gotten himself into. "After the second game, I was literally shocked. L.A. loses on a last-minute field goal, and I get home and watch the sports shows and they're literally ripping the shit out of everything, and I was like 'What the hell?' You couldn't have had a more exciting game, and the *L.A. Times* had an article about the hot tub in the end zone. Then the next weekend with Vegas was a great game, and I said to myself, 'The press can't duck this one.' But they did. I started to think it was a goddamn conspiracy." It was time for Butkus to see what inspired the hatred.

Inside, the Staples Center was packed with fans. This was the colossal

cookie-cutter arena that had recently replaced the sagging L.A. Forum out in
Inglewood. The Forum was dank and cramped, but that was part of its
charm. It had character. The Forum represented a lost era of pro sport, before
it went from no money to big money to ridiculous money. Before it got its
own TV station (ESPN) and its own congressional lobby. Before the food
got better and everything else went stale. Before the WWF started stealing
viewers from *Monday Night Football.*

Lakers forward Robert Horry sat behind Dick Butkus in the arena's lower
bowl. Dennis Hopper wasn't far away. Signs dotted the crowd in fluorescent
yellow, orange, and red. A security guard waded through the fans at ringside.
The message on the back of his yellow staff T-shirt read COME GET SOME,
but he wasn't looking for a fight. He was the house censor, checking for pro-
fane scribblings, which the WWF prohibited from its telecasts. One fan
playfully kept an offending sign out of the reach of the guard, who eventually grabbed it and folded it under his arm. The sign didn't have a cuss word
on it. WHERE IS LAWLER, it read. After that, the security man confiscated
another sign, this one containing the word "fuck," held by a boy who looked
like he had just learned the word. Butkus took it all in.

A menacing structure that looked like a huge spiderweb hung in one corner of the arena. It was draped in white fabric, lit blue and red. It looked like
a ghostly medieval lair. From this web, the wrestlers would run down a metal
ramp toward the ring. The PA announcer revved up the crowd. *Raw Is War*
was about to begin.

Everything started on the big TV screen in the corner, just off the spiderweb. A video commenced, updating the fans on previous matches and
reminding everyone who had a vendetta, who could get caught in the
upcoming crossfire. So many story lines moved across the screen in thirty
seconds, it was hard for Butkus to keep pace, since he lacked the year's worth
of back story. The screen split, showing the crowd who was scheduled to face
off throughout the night. Dedicated fans knew the lineage of the disputes,
the wrinkles and nuances of episodic hatred. As with an old NBC radio
serial, you had to stay tuned to grasp it all.

As quickly as the reel began, the explication concluded and the pictures
on the screen picked up their pace, zapping from one aggressive millisecond
image to another. It was a series of WWF aggro-lights. Blood spurted, bod-

ies slammed, torsos whipped around like rotors. There were easily fifty shots in ten seconds—*boom-boom-boom-boom-boom-boom-boom*. It was impossible to process it all, yet simple to recognize commonalities with the XFL.

The big screen went black, and the house lights cut. The arena became a vacuum. All sound and light sucked into the spiderweb. White-hot fireworks sizzled like popping corn along the underside of the scoreboard, cracking like a thousand flashbulbs. Then the explosions progressed along wires toward the spiderweb. *Crack-crack-crackle*. The popped corn reached the spiderweb. Then something terrible happened. It was more implosion than explosion. *Kaaaaa-kaaaaaa-kaaaaaa-POW!!!!!* Towering fireworks rocked the spiderweb, shooting high into the air. The Staples Center waffled. It felt like the building leaned to one side, then pulled itself right. Dozen of red spots dotted the field of vision. No one said much. Everyone had lost the ability to hear in the assault. "Jeez," yelled Butkus, giving off a laugh.

Several matches opened the action. The audience knew the drill. Fans conserved their energy for later, except a few die-hards who screamed incessantly and indiscriminately throughout the evening.

It was time for a commercial. There were plenty of extended breaks between the matches, as McMahon paid the bills. The big screen filled the time with constant motion, playing, replaying, foreshadowing any number of past and future matches. There was always something on. It was a shell game. Look that way while something—or, invariably, nothing—happened over here. The tactic mimicked the standard wrestling ploy of distracting the referee while a guy smuggles a razor into the ring.

The telecast returned, and the screen filled with Dennis Hopper's smirk. The crowd roared. After a few matches, Vince McMahon hopped into the ring. Butkus grinned, curious as to what would happen to the guy who signed his paychecks. McMahon had brought along Trish Stratus. Still photos projected on the big screen as McMahon mentioned Stratus's "humbling" turn in Washington, D.C., a week earlier. This was the clip that Costas had used on his HBO show. The fans booed. Shane McMahon sprinted out of the spiderweb. He leaped into the ring and decked his father, avenging his mother's bruised dignity.

Butkus chuckled to himself. "The guy's an actor," he said. He was getting a handle on the genre that had produced the Orlando cheerleader cam.

Butkus's face appeared on the big screen. The crowd roared its approval. McMahon used the occasion to segue into an XFL highlight package rolling out on the big screen. The cheering quickly ceased. One man on the far side of the arena stood up and waved an L.A. Xtreme banner. Everyone around him sat with their homemade signs resting on the laps. As the XFL tape played on, a guy wearing a skull-and-crossbones bandana cupped his hands over his mouth and yelled in the direction of the empty ring, "Let's see some wrestling!"

When the music kicked in again, the place got off its feet. The fans recognized the tune. It meant that The Rock was about to enter the ring. It meant that finally, the night's big match was about to go down. The Rock raised his oiled figure between the ropes and stood on the mat as the crowd roared around him, everyone on their feet. Lights blasted the wrestler from every angle, and the fluorescent signs in the crowd rocked up and down like fake ocean waves from an old theater production. A spindly teenage boy in a black WWF T-shirt jumped from his seat. His dark silhouette encased itself in the lit figure of The Rock, who lifted his trademark eyebrow. This was what they had come to see.

The Rock opened the match with a double-leg takedown on Kurt Angle. He pinned Angle to the mat, but only for a two-count. Debra, "Stone Cold" Steve Austin's wife, who was "managing" The Rock, exhorted from his corner. Angle ducked under the ropes, and The Rock clotheslined him from behind. "Kill that motherfucker!" yelled a grandmother sitting near Butkus. The Rock threw Angle into a barricade. Angle picked up a folding chair and slammed The Rock in the gut. Angle clasped The Rock in a bear hug. But as the crowd chanted for him, The Rock started fighting back. He caught Angle in a spine buster, then hit him with his famous People's Elbow.

The fans were as loud as the opening fireworks, as frothy as the wrestlers. The Rock pinned Angle, but the ref was slow to start the count. Angle escaped, grabbed The Rock's ankle, and started twisting. Fans toppled over one another for better views. Women shrieked. "Noooo!" "Let him go!" "No, no! Don't do it!" The ref yelled at Angle, but he refused to let go, twisting the foot even further. The ref disqualified Angle, and the match was over in a hail of shouts and clanging bells.

Debra hopped into the ring. With the announcer reporting the results, Kurt Angle slammed Debra to the mat and put an ankle lock on her. Stone Cold flew out of the spiderweb. The crowd saw him coming. Pandemonium broke out. Stone Cold started beating Angle. Then he took out The Rock. More bells rang, nachos flew in the air, half the house went hoarse.

Here was McMahon's genius. In a single show, he was able to combine explication of an old grudge, promotion of a developing story line, and the promise of action into a seamless ballet that strung out the violence just as long as an audience could possibly stand it. The ad breaks had gone on forever. He was a master of milking the product. But this wasn't without a guarantee.

Fans couldn't pull away because they knew that even though they would have to sit through incessant replays and interminable commercial breaks, McMahon would ultimately give them what they wanted. There would always be a payoff. That was just one way pro wrestling differed from pro football, where the only guarantee involved uncertainty. You never know who's going to win. HE HATE ME wasn't going to run for a touchdown every week, and not every game would end on the last play.

As *Raw Is War* came to a close, Butkus headed for the door. He was so beefy, he looked like he should have been a pro wrestler. But this wasn't Butkus's world. Not that he held anything against what he had seen. "It's like a soap opera," he said. "It's entertainment."

With the loss in Orlando, the Outlaws dropped to .500, though with four games remaining, the playoffs remained a very real prospect. They would play both L.A. (who owned a 4–2 record) and San Francisco (3–3) once more each. If they won those two games, it was hard to imagine they would miss out on one of the Western Division's two postseason spots. On Saturday, for NBC's main telecast, Vegas was to play a home game against the Birmingham Bolts, a struggling 2–4 team in the Eastern Division. There was no hiding the bruised looks on the Outlaws' faces when they disembarked at McCarran Airport. They would have to ramp it up if they wanted to make the playoffs.

During practice that week, the model planes kept buzzing. It was all the players could hear, as opposed to early-season practices when their bragging had drowned out all other sound. There were other airplanes in the sky, too. The practice field sat along the westerly approach to the airport. Every few minutes, another hundred high rollers enlarged from a distant speck as a 737 downshifted, ripping the air along a dotted-line descent. Those planes were so far away, untouchable, and the Outlaws were left to associate with the miniature versions, as though the true stature of this XFL had been revealed to them.

Against Birmingham, Ryan Clement played his best game of the season. He threw three touchdown passes. The Vegas defense regained its dominant form. The unit scored two touchdowns of its own and recorded seven sacks.

In the third quarter, with the Outlaws deep in Birmingham territory, Vegas tight end Rickey Brady fired off the line of scrimmage near the right hash marks. After a few steps, he turned to face Clement, who delivered the ball perfectly. Brady chugged for the goal line, where an undersize Birmingham defensive back rushed to tackle him. Brady lowered his shoulder into the defender's chest. The smaller man performed a cartwheel, spinning nose-first into the turf. Brady whirled and spiked the ball in his face. The Outlaws won easily, 34–12.

It should be noted that during the game, the XFL finally took a first tentative step at marketing Rod Smart. Stadium ushers provided fans with white hand towels emblazoned with HE HATE ME. The marketing scheme appeared to work. NBC included numerous shots of the crowd waving the towels throughout the Outlaws' romp. There was just one problem. Rod Smart didn't appear in the game. His scare in Orlando turned out to be a knee sprain, and Jim Criner kept him on the sidelines so he would be fully healed for the critical L.A. game the following week. The blunder in timing summed up everything perfectly.

None of that mattered to the fans in the stands. One man hoisted a sign. It read, HE HATE BOB COSTAS.

14

HOLDING ON

THE OUTLAWS RIGHTED THE SHIP just in time for the critical weeks that lay ahead. Saturday, March 24, they would face the first-place team in the Western Division, the 5–2 Los Angeles Xtreme, on the road at the L.A. Coliseum. This was the team that handed Vegas its first loss, in Week Three, when an injured Ryan Clement could only watch from the sidelines as a fourth-quarter interception decided the game. As practices rolled out in Henderson, the team was mindful of Jim Criner's comments from a month earlier: "We'll get 'em when it counts." Saturday's game was going to count in a big way. If L.A. quarterback Tommy Maddox and his team won, they would clinch a playoff spot. If the Outlaws won, they would pull even with the Xtreme for the Western Division lead, putting them in line not just to make the playoffs but to host a first-round game.

Criner and his assistants spent the three-hour practice sessions yelling and swearing. The players lacked their usual chumminess, and the plastic jet fighters that wound through continual loops above the field didn't seem to register. At the end of one crisp practice, Criner gathered his team at mid-field. "With all the noise and damn stuff that's going on around us, you did a good job of knowing what the hell was going on," he said. The Outlaws had looked unbeatable against Birmingham, and the performance had lifted their spirits. Saturday would be their redemption, and they couldn't wait to get it on.

Practice ended, and the players wandered off toward the showers. PR man Trey FitzGerald caught up to number 74, offensive tackle Jon Blackman. "Hey, Jon," said FitzGerald. "NBC wants to talk to you."

"They do?" Blackman asked.

"Yeah."

Blackman kept on walking. "Tell 'em to fuck off."

It was an altogether different story in Manhattan. In Rockefeller Center, the flags of dozens of different countries flapped in the breeze around the perimeter of the famous ice-skating rink, which was still open despite climbing temperatures. Nearby, midwestern tourists jostled for camera time outside the *Today* show studio. Up on the fifteenth floor of the GE Building, NBC execs absorbed some very sobering numbers. With XFL games rating a 2.4 for two straight weeks, Dick Ebersol and Ken Schanzer figured that the league had leveled off. It was a terrible number, nearly half of what they had promised advertisers. They had wondered for weeks when the bleeding would stop, how big their true audience was. Although they would have chosen something greater than a 2.4, at least the hemorrhaging had been stanched. Or so they thought.

On March 17, for the Birmingham–Las Vegas game, XFL ratings dropped another 33 percent. It would have been fashionable to call the new number slender. It was a 1.6. The second round of the NCAA basketball tournament had taken its toll. Ebersol, Schanzer, and the few men above them in the company realized that the 1.6 had broken the record for the lowest-rated prime-time sports programming in network TV history. The 1.6 shattered the old mark by a third. But was there even more hurt to come? The XFL had fallen so far, the latest number was so minuscule, that it prompted the question: Had any program, of any genre, ever rated lower in all the years of prime-time network TV?

Nielsen Media Research refused to comb its archives, which extended to the 1950s. All the firm would say was that according to its figures, the Las Vegas–Birmingham XFL telecast represented the lowest-rated night on ABC, CBS, NBC, or Fox in the thirteen-year history of Nielsen's people-meter sample, which provided detailed demographics. That was informative, but it wasn't conclusive. What about all-time TV history?

Rival network researchers quickly went to work, tackling the task as though a Christmas bonus depended on it. They found one show, an August 30, 1997, ABC News special about drug policy. The program also aired on

Saturday night, and it also rated a 1.6. This data provided some context. If the XFL rested on the bottom, at least it had a companion. Then researchers managed to find a program that had actually scored lower than the drugs and the football. It was an old Fox sitcom called *Mr. President,* starring George C. Scott. The Friday, February 13, 1988, airing had earned a 1.5.

The XFL had managed to avoid ignominy after all, and by the slimmest of margins—one tenth of one rating point. Or, to put it into actual numbers, out of the more than 100 million national households with a TV set, roughly 100,000 fewer homes tuned in Patton than watched HE HATE ME. It wasn't the 2000 Florida ballot, but it was still a squeaker. And though this wasn't necessarily cause to celebrate up in the GE Building, it was cause to sigh. They weren't the worst.

There was just one hitch. When the offending episode of *Mr. President* aired in 1988, Fox had been on the air for less than a year. *The Simpsons* was nearly two years away. Fox hardly qualified as a major network. Then–NBC entertainment president Brandon Tartikoff said as much at the time, taking countless opportunities to ridicule "the fourth network." He said in a 1988 interview that it was "nice to have a Fox network to make a few jokes about." In 2001 NBC was providing gag material.

There was the XFL, which seemed to take it on the chin nightly on the network's own talk shows. And then there was a new sitcom that Jeff Zucker unveiled on Monday, March 19. He had convened a group of media reporters and advertising executives on the set of *The West Wing* on the Warner Bros. Burbank, California, lot for a standard early look at what was in the works for the coming season. Zucker said that he would take "calculated risks" in programming, stressing the word "calculated" as though delineating a forthcoming gamble from the one that had caused him to crap out on Saturday nights.

Zucker introduced his latest calculated risk. On the dais stood Bob Newhart, the drowsy seventy-one-year-old comedian and former accountant whose witticisms were so subtle that days were often required to process them. By his side slumped Sisqo, the twenty-two-year-old singer who was famous for recording "Thong Song," an ode to the female buttocks. Many of the lyrics were difficult to decipher. The chorus, however, was clear, and it earned Sisqo unending praise on MTV's *TRL.* It went simply, "Tha-thong-tha-thong-thong-thong." Sisqo, whose head was painted silver, and Newhart, whose was not, shuffled nervously as Jeff Zucker explained that NBC had teamed the men in an as yet untitled program that the network hoped would reverse its long string of sitcom failures. The show never got to a pilot.

On Thursday, March 22, Vince McMahon walked a few blocks from his Times Square WWF restaurant. When he crossed the threshold of the New York Times Building, security guards instantly recognized him and practically bowed before the impresario. McMahon made his way upstairs, where he and XFL president Basil DeVito met for two hours with the paper's sports editor, Neil Andur, and the sports media columnist, Richard Sandomir. McMahon wasn't combative; nor was he conciliatory. He had assumed his businessman cloak—even though he was dressed entirely in leather. Sandomir then wrote a story for the paper in which McMahon dampened NBC's future involvement. "I hope NBC steps up with us, but if they can't, they can't," McMahon said. "We won't hold their feet to the fire."

A day later on the opposite end of the continent, McMahon sat down to lunch in a downtown Los Angeles restaurant. Bill Dwyre, the *Los Angeles Times* sports editor, and Larry Stewart, the sports media reporter, sat across the table. "We should have done this sooner," McMahon told his companions. His visits in L.A. and New York proved that McMahon finally understood the price that the XFL paid when he alienated the mainstream press. With the WWF, it never mattered what the sportswriters thought. McMahon didn't have to be diplomatic when faced with their uninspired questions. He could even lash out at them. It didn't really matter. Most of them ignored pro wrestling anyway, since it wasn't a sport. And if they did denigrate the spectacle in print, their judgments only reinforced McMahon's antiestablishment credentials among WWF fans.

McMahon discovered that real sport presented a different landscape, where the intricate web of India-ink opinion makers actually did make opinions. Fans of real sports trusted the people who wrote about real sports. With Jeff Zucker declining comment on the future of the XFL and the season's critical final weeks approaching, McMahon had come to L.A. to break bread. "Just give us a chance," he was saying to Dwyre and Stewart in between bites. The Xtreme were in first place. L.A. was a huge market. "Just give us a chance." The newspapermen had never met McMahon, and they found him charming and self-effacing. They enjoyed his company so much, in fact, that when they finished lunch, they walked across the street and gave McMahon a tour of the *Times* newsroom. McMahon kept saying, "We should have done this sooner." In the space of one week, he was trying to undo all the publicity damage he had done to his league since he first announced it.

And his company had another announcement. On that very day, all media outlets registered the alert to stand by for an important message from the WWF. Linda McMahon was about to open a conference call. Was this an announcement on the fate of the XFL?

As reporters listened, they quickly learned that the WWF had purchased World Championship Wrestling, its only rival. While WCW ratings had fallen sharply in the previous couple of seasons, its programs remained highly visible, seen in 94 percent of the country. Linda McMahon claimed that with the acquisition, the WWF could quickly double its revenues. Plans were set in motion to formulate story lines pitting wrestlers from the leagues against one another. The WWF had just become a monopoly. For all the people piling on the XFL, McMahon could now point to what may have been his most impressive achievement—he had beaten Ted Turner. For a moment, everyone forgot about the XFL.

The Los Angeles Coliseum was never any good for football. Only a college team with bloodletting alumni could consistently sell out ninety thousand seats. The stadium was decrepit and outdated, with cramped locker rooms and crumbling walls. It was more sinking relic than charming heirloom. The Olympic track that surrounded the field distanced the fans from the action. It felt like you were watching a game from a seat beyond the walls of the real stadium. The place was so awful that the NFL's Raiders had returned to a stadium in Oakland that they had whined about a decade earlier.

A Samoan rent-a-cop patrolled a terrace in the upper reaches of the Coliseum. There were a few minutes until kickoff of the L.A.–Las Vegas game, and as he looked down at the meager crowd seeming miles below him, he let out a *pfft*. "We got fifteen thousand for a Garfield High School game in November," he said. "That's just for a regular game, not a playoff game or nothing." He gestured toward the field, and his hand covered half of the pay-ing crowd. "But this, I've never seen this small number of people." There were maybe eight thousand in the Coliseum. And this for the Xtreme's biggest game of the season so far.

There were plenty of things to keep the crowds away. It was a sunny day. The USC men's basketball team was playing on TV in the NCAA tourna-ment. The L.A. Kings were in the middle of an NHL playoff game, in front of eighteen thousand fans at the Staples Center just up the road. And there was the fact that this was the XFL and not the NFL, which had discovered that even it couldn't support a team in the country's second-largest city.

A local radio DJ broadcast live from beneath a white tent in the Coliseum parking lot. Something by Creed played, while a few people milled around the tent, collecting credit-card pamphlets from the radio station's card table. The song finished and the DJ took the microphone. His voice boomed across the parking lot, which was as empty as the dwindling hours of a trade show. "Yo, all right," he yelled. "Let's hear it for the Trojans." Even at its own game, the XFL was being overshadowed.

Rod Smart stretched out on the Coliseum's pockmarked field. He reached for his toes. His knee felt about perfect. Ryan Clement practiced his three-step drop. Kelvin Kinney head-butted another lineman, revving himself up. Music blared through the empty stadium, standing in for genuine atmos-phere, as in a tourist bar. Jay Howarth grabbed the PA microphone and began squawking to the vacant seats, hyping the Xtreme cheerleaders. The downtown L.A. skyline was shrouded in smog.

At 6–2, the Xtreme entered the game having just handed Orlando its first loss of the season. L.A. was the hottest team in the XFL. But Vegas still had the league's top defense. The Outlaws also had a league-high thirty-one sacks, led by Kelvin Kinney, who had registered an XFL-best nine. L.A.'s Tommy Maddox led the league in passing and touchdown throws, but Vegas had held him to small numbers in their first game. There was one intangible. The Outlaws led the league in turnovers and giveaways. L.A. was second in both categories. This may have seemed inconsequential, except for the fact that the teams' first meeting had turned on an interception.

L.A. kicked off to begin the game. Chrys Chukwuma waited deep in his own end to field the kick. He caught the ball. Then he laid it on the turf. The Xtreme recovered the fumble on the Vegas seventeen-yard line. Two plays later, Maddox found his favorite receiver, Jermaine Copeland, for a ten-yard touchdown pass. It was just a minute into the game, and the Outlaws were in a six-point hole.

They recovered quickly. Rod Smart took a handoff and scampered twenty-one yards outside right tackle for a score. He then converted the extra point. After a dubious beginning, Vegas had the lead, 7–6.

Maddox and Clement then traded touchdown passes. Las Vegas led, 14–12. Midway through the second quarter, Maddox threw another touchdown pass and L.A. retook the lead, 18–14. The rest of the half was all Xtreme. L.A. took a 26–14 lead into the intermission. The vaunted Vegas defense had come unhinged.

Down 12 points on the road, Vegas couldn't come all the way back. The Outlaws scored two more touchdowns, but they couldn't keep Maddox off the field. L.A. won the game, 35–26, clinching a playoff berth. At the end, the Outlaws walked off the field like extras from a Vietnam movie, shocked to a crawl.

The Vegas locker room was silent except for the hiss of the showers and the words that several Outlaws mumbled into reporters' cassette recorders. Players stalked the tight quarters of the old stadium's locker room, tiny hotel towels tucked at the waist, one hand eating double-decker slices of pizza, the other slurping a can of beer. The windowless accommodations trapped the smells of the evening: sweat, dirt, grass, pizza, and beer.

Word came in that San Francisco had broken a two-game losing streak with a 21–12 win over Memphis. The Demons and Outlaws had identical 4–4 records. They were scheduled to meet at Sam Boyd Stadium in a week's time.

Ryan Clement looked like he'd gone fifteen rounds with a meat tenderizer. He grimaced and toweled his damp hair. "They're still paying me more than I'd make anywhere else. I'm just tired of taking too many painkillers."

Kelvin Kinney grabbed his shoes from the top of his stall. In so doing, he

ripped down a good portion of the locker, inadvertently slamming a teammate in the head with an old two-by-four. Everything was falling apart. Kinney lumbered to a common alleyway, where whoops and hollers echoed from
the Xtreme locker room twenty yards away. He ran a palm across his face.
"Horrible," he said. "It's tough when you lose 'em like that. The plane ride'll
be like a funeral." He exhaled deeply. He had lost all his humor. "I wish I
didn't care so much. 'Cause then it wouldn't hurt so much."

When Ryan Clement piled onto the bus, the coaches just stared straight
ahead, unwilling to look at the guy some felt just couldn't get the job done.
Miami had been just the same, with everyone blaming him. Clement
couldn't wait to get back to Vegas. There were good times waiting for him
there, a friend's bachelor party.

The bus pulled out for LAX.

She wore only yellow hot pants. She slid headfirst from the ceiling to the
floor, cradling a brass pole between her shoulder and chin as though it were
one long telephone. This was Crazy Horse Too, the Las Vegas strip club
located a long block west of the Strip, from where Circus Circus casino was
a blurry blob of overlapping light. In the back room, fields of women swayed
like grain stalks in the wind, with the practiced head flip of insincere laughter. They patrolled the vast darkened space in bikinis, heels, and tiny clutch
purses packed tight with dirty, crumpled bills. It was three girls for every guy.
And a lot of the guys were Denver Broncos. Ryan Clement walked through
the front door and joined the Broncos' bachelor party.

The strippers that night, as ever, realized this good thing. Maybe they
even recognized the Broncos. Plenty of guys in the club knew who they
were. Either way, money was the point and it wasn't stopping. A few players
brandished chunky Super Bowl rings which sparkled even in the scant available light. Piled into knee-high black leather chairs, the Broncos paid for
several lap dances at a time. A collection of patrons stumbled from the men's
rooms with telescoped eyes. They landed hard in the low chairs and watched
the skin flash in the blue-purple lights. Huge chunks of time passed unno-
ticed. Ryan Clement took it all in.

The Broncos soon had enough of Crazy Horse Too. They drove to the
Strip, where they emerged at Flamingo Road. They were going to Drai's.

This was one anachronism that managed to survive amid the Strip's perpetual reinvention. Drai's was supposedly the best restaurant in town, yet it was housed in the Barbary Coast casino, a run-down relic that had seen better days. The Barbary Coast's human analog had terrible dandruff and a job in a doughnut shop. The place didn't make much sense, sitting on the intersection that also contained the Bellagio and Caesar's Palace. The old casino stood on one of the city's most valuable pieces of real estate. The owner steadfastly refused to sell. He wanted to be part of the action.

The Broncos lined up outside Drai's. The place wasn't full of fools like the other Vegas clubs that everyone in their twenties talked about, places with names like Rum Jungle. You went to Drai's if you had cash, or an aspiration to class. It wasn't easy getting in. You had to know someone. Or you had to be famous. Ryan Clement took it upon himself to get his Broncos friends inside. He was Vegas's quarterback. He pulled aside the bouncer. The bouncer didn't know who he was. Clement turned to the guys in the bachelor party. "My name did nothing," he said. Then a member of the Denver entourage tried his valuable hand. Clement watched as the bouncer emitted an ingratiating chuckle. The door opened.

Drai's was a compartmentalized, wood-paneled cloister, stuffed with floozies and guys in gabardine. Cash flew around. So did medication. The Broncos didn't stand out. Everyone's eyes looked like saucers.

Clement joined in, but as he watched the Broncos clink glasses and share old laughs, he couldn't help but feel like a sidekick. This was where he had always seen himself, with deep pockets and a face that opened the door.

By the time Clement left the party, it was well after sunrise. He slipped out the front door of Drai's and into the fresh air. Cars whizzed by on the Strip. The sores and bruises from the L.A. game began to exert their will over his movements. Clement looked at the sparkling Bellagio across the Strip as he walked out beneath the aged Barbary Coast marquee, which flashed vainly against the sunlight. And he crawled into a cab.

15

APRIL FOOL'S

THE TAILGATERS DIDN'T ARRIVE at Sam Boyd Stadium as early on April Fool's Day as they had on February 3, when the XFL was the new circus in town. Nor did they arrive in identical numbers. But they did show up, trading in bratwurst in the parking lot, tossing footballs between cars. Smoke billowed here and there. It still looked like an event. Even if it was just the XFL, this was still the biggest pro sport in Vegas. While many of the summer soldiers who had filled the stadium on opening night were long gone, a solid core of fans remained. After all the talk of must-win situations, everything really did come down to this game between the Outlaws and the San Francisco Demons, who were tied with each other for second place in the Western Division. Only one team would join L.A. in the playoffs, a setup that produced the simplest equation: Win and you're in.

If there was any doubt how the fans felt about this game, this league that had become a laughingstock, it was erased well before kickoff, when two Demons fans walked past a ragged Vegas crowd that huddled around a truck on the edge of the parking lot. Someone said something, someone else wouldn't let it lie, and soon a cloud of desert dust whipped up in front of a Suburban. A couple of rent-a-cops broke up the scuffle, dragging one of the San Francisco fans to his feet. His nose trickled blood on his ripped Demons jersey. Inside the stadium, most of the players still wore street clothes, but the game had already begun.

Just how hale the feeling was among those wearing all-access passes was harder to tell. The XFL rank and file had suffered a crisis of confidence dur-

ing the week. As the cameramen and grips and producers hunkered down for
their pregame meal around several tables in the press box, there was little
chatter. In previous weeks, they had burst with the banter of combat cama-
raderie. This Sunday, the place sounded like they had finally surrendered the
battle. Two production staffers met in the food line. "I'm pyro," said one,
from the fireworks crew. "Oh hey," said the other one, not hearing quite
right. "I'm Bill." Still confused after all these weeks.

Everyone knew what had happened that week, and it was difficult to keep
their minds focused on the day's task of producing Week Nine of the XFL.
Dick Ebersol had finally spoken.

A week earlier, on Sunday, March 25, Dick Ebersol was in Ponte Vedra
Beach, Florida, where NBC was broadcasting the PGA Players Championship. The event was the furthest thing from the XFL. Golf had always
earned consistent ratings, rarely surprising producers with much fluctuation
in either direction. Similarly, its production had changed little over the years.
There were a few updates, such as the "Eye of the Tiger," a camera that Tiger
Woods wore clipped to the bill of his cap while hitting warm-up balls. Generally, though, golf telecasts remained constant: crisp and classy, like a new
hundred-dollar bill. A conservative cadre of golf viewers depended on the
telecasts simply to depict shots as they occurred. More was unnecessary, and
indeed would have been met by wild revolt. It was fitting, then, for Dick
Ebersol to issue what sounded like the denouement of his flashiest under-
taking from the manicured terrain of his most solid property.

A *Washington Post* reporter corralled Ebersol in NBC's golf command
center and asked about the future of the XFL. "We all want to see it work,"
Ebersol said. His comments would appear in the following morning's *Post*.
"The evidence through 75 percent of the regular season is not promising. We
have a two-year commitment . . . but it's going to have to show a marked
swing in the ratings in the postseason for it to have a real shot beyond this
year, just from an advertising standpoint. A decision on whether to go or not
go would be made no later than the end of April. As recently as last night,
we were still hoping there will be a major turn."

As recently as that Sunday morning, Ebersol discovered that there had
been no major turn. The game between Vegas and L.A. earned a 1.8 rating.
It was difficult to say whether Ebersol could find a silver lining in a 1.8.

Maybe a tin lining. Whatever kind, there was a lining in the 1.8: It wasn't a drop from the previous week's 1.6.

Not that the nail biting ceased, even though the two remaining weekends in the XFL would feature games that meant something, when teams pushed to make the playoffs. There was still one week left in the Final Four. After that, of course, NBC expected ratings to pick up for the playoffs. The XFL had escaped the stigma of an awful record. But for how long? On Saturday, March 31, would the Final Four pull viewers away from the XFL? Or could the league fall no further? This passed for suspense.

On the course at Ponte Vedra, Ebersol couldn't understand how he had misfired so poorly. "One of the few minor surprises was that the public and the media did not really respond to the 'Little Engine That Could' aspect of the league," he told the *Post*, speaking as though composing an obituary, or summing up a broken marriage. "It didn't seem to resonate the way I thought it would." Ebersol had produced so many winners that he had trouble dissecting a loser. He hadn't often had the displeasure, and he wanted to make that fact very clear. "I've been in this job for 12 years, and no one other than Roone has had a run like that." Ebersol sought perspective for his career the only way he knew how, by measuring himself against his mentor.

The ratings added up to what looked like an inevitable conclusion for NBC. But the numbers had little bearing on where the XFL might wander for its second season. There were still plenty of TV outlets, and Vince McMahon wasn't about to watch his football league whimper to its death. He had always maintained that the XFL was a long-term proposition. And his hubris led to startling news. The XFL, the butt of endless jokes, was going to expand.

On Tuesday, March 27, XFL president Basil DeVito turned up in Washington, D.C., along with Rich Rose, head of the league's expansion committee, and Mike Keller, vice president of football operations. The group toured RFK Stadium, former home of the Washington Redskins. The trio met with officials of the D.C. Sports and Entertainment Commission. After the tour, DeVito held a news conference at a downtown hotel. He knew what Ebersol had said in the *Post*, and he stated clearly that if NBC pulled the plug, the XFL would continue to operate on another TV outlet. He said the league was considering moving all games to Sundays and regionalizing its TV coverage, like the NFL did, instead of trying to mount huge ratings with a single national game. "We're going to be here," DeVito said. "There was a business plan in place prior to NBC coming in to the XFL, and that business plan still exists, still makes sense." DeVito stated that a decision on expansion would come by June.

How could DeVito possibly talk of expansion? The XFL was in no position to discuss adding teams when the clubs they had weren't pulling the TV ratings on which the league was founded. What next, a Whitesnake stadium tour? A headline in the *Washington Times* summed it all up: XFL EYEING DISTRICT PROVIDED NEW LEAGUE SURVIVES. Vince McMahon explored leasing property adjacent to the WWF location in Stamford. He figured the XFL deserved its own headquarters. Was everyone willfully out of touch?

Past the volcanoes spewing "lava," past the plastic rain forest and the walled wilderness of white tigers, at the back of the Mirage casino a genuine article materialized. Falling off a pit of dice and cards, a hangar was cloaked in towering TV screens and ticker boards. Dark carpeting lent it an underworld glaze. Fishnetted cocktail waitresses navigated a sea of booths and swivel chairs. A roar erupted in front of a bank of monitors.

The cheering was especially loud that afternoon in the Mirage sportsbook. The Final Four was on. Robert Walker, head of the sportsbook, sat behind a desk in his modest office on the other side of the TV bank. He didn't look the part of a Vegas bookie. He was tall and thin, with wire-rimmed glasses, a dark sport coat, and the diction of an English teacher. But he was all figures. Walker expected to handle more than $100,000 in action on the first half of the basketball game. At halftime, he would post a new betting line, which would elicit more action. Another NCAA semifinal game followed in the evening, and the championship game would come Monday night. This was the real action that kept the book in business, though Walker was always looking to expand.

He was one of the first bookmakers in town to take on the XFL. The casinos were initially skeptical about booking a Vince McMahon enterprise. After getting reassurance from the new league, the books provided the XFL with some level of legitimacy, as the sporting public realized that the sportsbooks wouldn't handle anything that was fixed, at least not to their satisfaction. Still, XFL games never generated much action. "The only league I can liken the XFL to is the WNBA," Walker said.

The Duke-Maryland basketball game played on a TV in Walker's office. Every so often he would look at the time clock in the upper corner of the screen. Walker had been at Sam Boyd Stadium that first XFL night, when the Outlaws shutout the Hitmen. He thought the league had a chance. When the press piled on, he could see what was happening. Walker used to write sports for a newspaper, and he knew what a hatchet job looked like. He made a concerted effort to watch the games, but since the Mirage saw so little XFL action, he didn't need to. He couldn't remember the last game he'd seen.

The half was winding down. An assistant poked his head into Walker's office, reminding him of the time on the game clock. Walker nodded calmly. "We would love to see the XFL succeed," he said. "But it'll die its own death. People won't ask about it, they won't care about it, and that'll be the end." He left to post the second-half line for a crowd that registered their team allegiance as much in rooting as in betting. Guys in Maryland hats invariably put their money on Maryland. Same for the Duke fans.

Ebersol and McMahon wanted to arouse the public with the very idea of the XFL—the overarching concept. But real fans aren't interested in an amorphous league. They're interested in teams. Partisanship is what makes people buy officially licensed merchandise. Ebersol and McMahon had created "brand awareness" as though they were selling a logo, overlooking the things that fans find meaningful in the teams that wear them. The XFL's brand identity only came back to haunt the bosses, as everyone knew of the grand defeat.

Down in the stadium locker room, the Outlaws were questioning where it had all gone wrong. They had won three of four games to begin the season. Then they lost three of their next four.

Jesse Ventura didn't come through the locker room for a visit before the game. The UPN cameras didn't stay long. This was straight football, minus the sideshow. Of course, Rod Smart did his bit, striding the locker room without a stitch. Several players washed down pills and concotions with Powerade. Jim Criner got his troops ready. He knew that Clement's shoulder still wasn't 100 percent. Smart's ankle wasn't either. Kinney's foot troubles had kept him out of practice. Criner ran a palm over his face. He was worn out.

The venom from the fight out in the stadium parking lot carried over to the stands as Vegas prepared to take on San Francisco. Fireworks snapped off at the beginning of the UPN telecast; something snapped inside of the crowd, too, and it hung over the stadium, violent and unpredictable.

Brian Bosworth stood up in the broadcast platform, handling the color commentary for UPN. Bosworth had been a college football star. He flashed brightly as a constructed personality, the Boz, but then quickly fizzled in the NFL. He fled to Hollywood, where he acted in B-action pictures with titles such as *Stone Cold, One Tough Bastard,* and *One Man's Justice.* Apparently he still had a few fans out there, including a young guy in a coed–naked lacrosse T-shirt sitting near the TV platform. The kid hoisted a sign reading I LOVE BOSWORTH. Deep in his game preparation, the Boz acknowledged the fan of blessed memory with a clipped wave.

A gusting wind down on the field wasn't going to help either team's passing game. Rod Smart ran well to open the first quarter, scoring the first touchdown on a one-yard plunge. Several dozen fans waved their HE HATE ME towels. A few fights broke out on the far side of the stadium. Yellow-jacketed security swarmed like bees to an intruder. The Outlaws defense stopped San Francisco with less than a minute to go in the half, forcing a punt.

The Demons' punter boomed the ball into the air, where it rode on a stiff wind. Jamel Williams was back deep for Vegas. The wind sent the kick sailing over his head. It landed on the one-yard line for a league-record sixty-seven-yard punt. According to XFL rules, it was a live ball, having traveled more than twenty-five yards. Williams scrambled for possession, but he fell under a heavy Demon rush. The ball squirted loose into the end zone, where San Francisco fell on it for a touchdown. The devastating play tied the game at halftime.

During the half, cameras found four women in the crowd wearing tight white T-shirts advertising Cheetah's strip club. The women were grinding. Then they started climbing on the men who sat near them. A few rows away, a four-year-old girl in a yellow T-shirt and frilly pink socks mimicked the display.

When the game returned, so did the Outlaws' misfortune. Ryan Clement threw an interception, which San Francisco returned forty-nine yards. The Demons connected on a twenty-five-yard touchdown pass a few plays later, near the end of the third quarter. The rest of the period existed in amber, with nothing happening. In the tension of the six-point deficit, another fight broke out in the stands. The yellow jacketed security guards descended.

Play continued on the field, but fans watched the spectacle of five men throwing haymakers in the stands, their beers exploding in cloudbursts. The Cheetah's girls were competing for attention by fondling each other and grinding into a man's lap. The stadium cameraman zoomed in on the Cheetah's logo, providing free advertising to a crowd of seventeen thousand. One of the strippers grabbed the bottom of her T-shirt as if to lift it. The image on the big screen quickly changed to a shot from the field, and a chorus of boos rose from the crowd. The girl in the yellow T-shirt stretched the end of her shirt.

Ryan Clement threw a pass. As he watched the play run upfield, his world was suddenly upended. A Demon linebacker, Jon Haskins, plowed Clement into the turf on his bad shoulder well after he released the ball. The referee whistled Haskins for a flagrant personal foul and ejected him from the game. Haskins protested, but finally made his way toward the dressing room, escorted by jeers from the crowd. As Clement rose to his feet, game but wobbly, hard guitars played over the linebacker's departure. A sideline reporter stuck a microphone in Haskins's face, asking him what happened.

Haskins, red-faced and angry, nearly slammed the reporter in disgust. "What the fuck do you think?" he yelled. "I didn't hit him fucking late. That's fucking bullshit." The league's censor system wasn't designed to insert a five-second delay into the in-stadium audio, as it was for TV broadcasts. Haskins's invectives reverberated through the stadium. The girl in the frilly socks suddenly stopped gyrating. She looked at her parents, sensing that something had gone terribly wrong. Her parents glanced at her, then at each other, not knowing what to do.

On the Vegas bench, a trainer tested Clement for a concussion. Drool hung from Clement's chin as he tried vainly to follow a finger left and right in front of his face. Clement eventually returned to the game, demonstrating that his most lasting ability was a capacity for pain. The Haskins hit revved up the crowd even further.

"Hey," yelled the young fan sitting near Brian Bosworth in the broadcast booth. "Hey. Hey Boz. Hey Boz." The kid gained the announcer's attention, and he flipped around his Bosworth sign. APRIL FOOL's, it read. The kid began to cackle. Then he screamed. "Boz, you suck!" he yelled. "Boz, you're a joke. You're a fucking joke! Fuck you, Bosworth!" The kid galloped several rows toward the broadcast platform, yelling loud enough for Bosworth's microphone to pick him up. He hopped up and down, whooping and hollering until the security bees descended on him. They grabbed him by the arms, and pushed him toward the concourse. The kid raised his arms in triumph, a wide smile glued to his face.

There was a game to finish. The Outlaws' season hung in the balance. They kicked a field goal, closing the gap to 12–9. They stopped the Demons and regained possession of the ball. Starting at its own thirty-yard line late in the fourth quarter, Vegas put together its best drive of the game. With Clement on the sidelines, Mark Grieb relied on Rod Smart, who took one handoff after another, pulling his team up over midfield. Smart caught a flare pass for fifteen yards, putting Vegas in range for a game-tying field goal. There was time enough for a touchdown. The crowd suspended its mischief, concentrating now on what looked like the Outlaws' winning drive.

It was second and goal from San Francisco's six-yard-line. Smart took the handoff from Grieb and scampered around right end. His legs were churning. He had a full head of steam. He was going to score. A San Francisco defender lunged for his ankles. Smart dove for the end zone, stretching his body for the orange pylon in the corner. He reached out with the football, trying to break the plane of the goal line for a touchdown. He reached, stretched . . . and the ball slipped from his grasp. Smart slammed to the turf, and the football bounced out of the end zone. The crowd erupted.

The officials gave no signal. The Outlaws on the field raised their arms, willing the play to be a six-point score. The crowd, the players, the coaches, everyone looked to the refs conferring in the end zone. There was utter confusion. Had Smart scored?

Then the head referee stepped forward. He stiffened one arm and waved it at the side of his body. The Outlaws slowly processed what they were watching, and a groan shot through the stands. Rod Smart hadn't scored a touchdown. He had fumbled. Since the ball had then continued out of the end zone, the play was ruled a touchback. It was San Francisco's ball at the twenty-yard line. The Demons ran out the clock, winning the game and a spot in the playoffs. A drunk guy ran onto field, and a beefy security guard tackled him at the goal line. The crowd roared.

The teams left the field. Some fans clapped and some yelled encouragement. Others weren't so kind. As Rod Smart weaved his way toward the locker room, a hometown graybeard let loose in the direction of the Vegas tailback. He threw his HE HATE ME hand towel in Smart's direction, calling out as the white fabric took flight, "We hate you!"

Smart packed up his belongings in the painful silence of the locker room. He had gained 121 yards on 28 carries. It was his second hundred-yard rushing performance of the season. But it was that last yard that everyone would remember. "I reached out and saw the pylon," he said, his voice barely audible. "They called it a fumble." It was all he could say.

A few hours after the defeat, Kelvin Kinney sat on a bar stool at the House of Blues in the Mandalay Bay casino. Even sitting, he was still taller than most of the guys who comprised the standard Vegas sausage party. He wore a black tank top, and his chiseled arms bulged as he raised a drink to his lips. Kinney closed his eyes to the dancing girls in fatigues who swirled on pedestals nearby, seeing only the futility of the day's performance. The Vegas defense had shut down San Francisco, yet the Outlaws still managed to give away the game. "That's the first time I ever really needed to have something and I couldn't get it, couldn't make it happen," Kinney said. "That hurt. That really hurt." House music assaulted the senses. Images of the dancing girls projected on huge TV screens. "After the game, Coach Criner said we should have won, but we didn't," Kinney said. Lights flashed across his face. "I'm not coming back here next season."

16

THE SAME OLD STORY

WHEN THE *TITANIC* SANK, it dipped gradually into the icy waters of the North Atlantic over a period of nearly two hours. Packed into lifeboats, several hundred survivors could not have been pleased by what they saw, but there was nonetheless something majestic in the ship's measured, serene descent into the deep. It was going, but gracefully. Then the *Titanic* blew apart. Air pressure in the stern ripped the hull to pieces, reminding anyone who could have possibly forgotten that this was a disaster.

On Saturday, March 31, NBC's nationally televised game between New York and Chicago provided punctuation to the XFL's otherwise gradual defeat. The game earned a Nielsen rating of 1.5. There would be no spinning this time. The XFL was the biggest bomb in television history.

In a sign of how crudely the league had been slapped together, no one had quite figured out what to name the title game. They couldn't just call it the XFL Championship Game. Too boring. And what about the XFL Bowl? That wouldn't do, either; it sounded staid and traditional, everything the league's hype had disparaged. There was the Rose Bowl, and the Orange Bowl, and of course that other bowl—all of which had been around since time immemorial. Not to be lumped in with all those reverence payers, the XFL referred to its championship as The Big Game at the End for most of the season. It was a working title, which would eventually be replaced. Months went by . . . no one had any good ideas. Finally, as the championship loomed and ratings resembled a dwindling blood cell count, the XFL, flinching at just what the working title portended (a game at the *very end*?), opted for something else.

The title drew again on the focus groups. Research suggested that of all the new and different components of the XFL, fans most appreciated the fact that the players played for real money. Not the ridiculous money that the big-time players made, the money that had created the likes of Randy Moss, who earned a fat contract but played hard only when his delicate biorhythms allowed. Fans could relate to the XFL players, who were paying bills just like them. "The name switched because people saw that as a way to say, 'Look, we're not all about ratings and naked cheerleaders and Jesse Ventura,'" said one XFL team marketing director. On April 2, the XFL released the new name for its championship game. It would be called the Million Dollar Game, reflecting the dollar amount that the winning team of working-class athletes would split among them.

There are myriad ways to handle bereavement—dissolving into tears, lashing out in violence—any number of ways, really, with the character of the reaction speaking to the character of the disappointment.

During the final week of their season, the Outlaws slipped into a breezy, end-of-school posture. Temperatures hovered in the mid-eighties. A late-spring breeze blew along the clipped turf of the practice field, all tension escaping on the mild wind as resignation overtook indignation. This wasn't happiness but denial. The model airplanes dive-bombed the field for one last set of practices, and several Outlaws traced the arcs with their eyes, semi-conscious of the drills at hand. Reclining on the lawn, they propped themselves on elbows and gazed at the sky. "Those things don't matter much anymore, do they?" one hulking specimen philosophized, gesturing toward the buzzing airplanes. The players seemed sedated, beyond being stunned by what had happened to their season.

"We thought we were gonna be hosting the championship game here. And now . . ." said Trey FitzGerald, the team's PR man, his voice trailing off with the thought that was too present to express. He stood on the edge of the field, his arms folded across his chest as though he wasn't ready to let it all go. "The main reason all the players and coaches and staff are here is 'cause we're all football people. And we were hoping to build something similar to the

NFL, and the NBA, and the NHL. And hopefully we still can." FitzGerald had left a job to take this one, and he wasn't ready to start searching again. He was full of rumors and possibilities. He talked about an XFL deal with FOX SportsNet. He said that UPN was still on board. He mentioned that TNN's XFL contract bonded the cable network to air games as long as the league desired. NBC still hadn't issued an official announcement on the XFL's fate, though Ebersol's *Washington Post* comments—along with the 1.5 rating—only strengthened speculation that the network wouldn't pick up a second season. "Well, if they don't, they'll have to write us a forty-five-million-dollar check," FitzGerald said, his blood rising. "'Cause that's what their fifty-percent commitment is for next season."

For the players, the fire had gone out. Their season was over, save one meaningless home game against the Memphis Maniax. After that it would be waiting on NFL scouts to issue invitations to training camps. All the Outlaws could do now was hope that an NFL coach liked enough of what he saw of them in the XFL. The Outlaws didn't know if they would be involved in the next XFL season, or even if there'd be a next XFL season. It was too much to think about, and the players preferred chasing each other around the practice field like third-graders playing tag. It felt like the last day of school, on the cusp of a welcome new routine.

Out at Destiny's Oasis RV park on the south end of the Strip, it took a minute before the American Eagle rattled and shimmied, betraying inner activity. The door opened and a hair-matted barrel chest poked out. A crew cut followed the chest through the tight doorway. Finally, a face poked out. "You're early," Dick Butkus barked as he toweled the face of pro football.

By the end of the XFL season, Butkus always seemed to be frowning. He wasn't happy about being caught in his boxers, but he didn't forget his manners. "Aw, come on in, then." Butkus's RV was no Madden Cruiser. There were no rec rooms, video games, or roast turkeys with eight legs. It did have the comforts necessary for someone who had logged thirty thousand miles in one year of ownership. There was plush carpeting, cushy couches. There was wood paneling mirrored in crenellated sections, like the corner booth in a '70s diner.

Butkus slipped on a red XFL golf shirt and hit the ignition, setting out for the ride to Sam Boyd Stadium. He slapped his huge mitts on the industrial-size steering wheel and edged out of his numbered parking slot. He winked. "They were all filled up when I called for a space," he said. "They had to squeeze me in." Butkus laughed, amused by the fact that his celebrity had sustained this long. He still got a kick out of being handled with care, though he didn't court the treatment. He slept in an RV. That was why McMahon hired him, for his working class pedigree.

Butkus was always the barometer, and as the season soured, so did he. As he turned on to the Strip, his face carried a frown, a long way from the smile of his first XFL visit to Vegas. "I had discussions with Vince," Butkus said, recalling their initial meetings. "'Don't fool with the integrity of the game.' That's what I told him. You woulda had trouble getting decent coaches and players. I wouldn't be here. If a guy streaks down the sideline, you can't pick up a folding chair and hit the guy over the head with it. That wasn't the idea, and if it was marketed that way, it was a mistake." The RV barreled past a strip mall.

If that wasn't the idea, then clearly Ebersol and McMahon held some cards to themselves. "I don't think the coaches really knew about a lot of the stuff that would happen when they took it on," Butkus said. "I didn't know about the Bubba Cam until right before the first game. They overmerchandised it. Football-wise, we told them it would be difficult to start training camp in January with seventy strangers. It would be difficult to get a cohesive team running smoothly by February first, or whenever they wanted to start the thing. They put the marketing into everything instead of the football. The announcers lost a lot of potential return viewers. They piled up that NBC game with so much equipment. They had more coverage than the Super Bowl."

Butkus ticked off his grievances, as though they had been stewing inside him for months. He flew through an intersection, the RV nearly catching air on a small dip in the road.

"Oh, and then here we go with the 'Burger King at the Half,'" he said, tossing his hands into the air as he cruised past another strip mall. "You see the sign POSITIVELY NO ADMITTANCE, and you go in and catch a coupla guys taking a leak. They should have asked the coaches when a good time was to come in. That way a coach coulda told them, 'Well, I do most of my talking right at the beginning. Or right at the end.' These guys have character, too, and they don't wanna come off bad."

By then, the RV seemed to cruise at a rate of its own will, whipping past several wide-eyed drivers in Ford Focuses. "People wanted to see girls with pasties giving lap dances. And when that wasn't it, they just turned it off."

Butkus made it to Sam Boyd Stadium in something approaching record time. He pulled into the lot, where he had made prior arrangements to have a large gate opened for the RV. When Butkus rolled up, the gate was shut. He grumbled, "aw, Jesus." Through the RV's tremendous windshield, he waved at a parking attendant in a reflector vest. The attendant waved Butkus to the next entrance. "No, no, no," Butkus yelled. That entrance was too tight for the RV. It would require too sharp a turn. "I gotta go through there," he said, exaggeratedly mouthing the words for the attendant. The reflector vest waved a fluorescent flag at the wind. "Aw, Jesus," Butkus said again, resigned to try his luck through the tight squeeze. He steered through the turn, swinging his elbows to steer the huge wheel. He was sweating. He was swearing. And he got stuck, jamming the American Eagle between one curb and another. He let out a yell.

Word circulated through the parking lot that Butkus had arrived. Several fans gathered to watch their football hero find his way out of a jam. A few people walked up to the RV and snapped pictures as Butkus rocked his motor home back and forth. The huge vehicle rolled over one curb and then another. It finally made it over the hump. Butkus was exasperated. "People don't realize that this thing can't turn on a dime!"

It was an ominous day, gray and dark, that marked the Outlaws' final game of the season. Thirty-mile-an-hour winds swirled through the horseshoe stadium. Rain beaded on the players' helmets. The fans stayed home. Slivers of red bleachers showed like gaping wounds. The stadium wore the signs of a neglected neighborhood. A gust tore down a huge XFL banner that skirted the bottom of the bleachers. No one refastened it. When the game began, the sun made an appearance on the Vegas sideline, catching Jim Criner in a yellow shaft. Was it so long ago that his team had been undefeated? So long ago that the stands were packed with fans who were predisposed to endorse whatever they saw?

Following a play on the Outlaws' first defensive series, Kelvin Kinney butted heads with a Memphis offensive lineman. Kinney grabbed at the other player's jersey. There was a lot of milling about. A few plays later, he started another set-to with someone else. It wasn't long before he had to be restrained once more. Frustration overtook action, since the game meant nothing. Kinney had come to care about very little. Apparently, no one else cared, either. Soon the scoreboard read MEMPHIS 16, LAS VEGAS 0. Boos mixed with raindrops to pelt the field. A fan raised several sheets of damp toilet paper with something scrawled in black marker. It was hard to make out what it said. Then it came clear: VENTURA RULES.

At one point, Ryan Clement backpedaled in the pocket, unable to escape Memphis's oncoming rush. A defensive lineman wrapped up Clement and drilled him into the turf on his right shoulder. Clement crumpled, then slowly regained his feet. He jogged toward Criner, and as he did, he waved his hands in the air as if to say forget it. Clement made it to the sideline and Criner invaded his face. They barked at each other. But there was no more vaunted audio. It was the UPN telecast, on which the XFL had scaled back considerably since the first game. An image lingered on the big screen, which waffled in the stiff wind: Criner sending Grieb into the game while Clement hovered over his coach's shoulder, removing his helmet one last time, his eyes reduced to slits. He had finished his Miami career watching from the sidelines, too. Was this how the dream was going to end?

Memphis won the game 16–3, sending the Outlaws further below the .500 mark. They finished the season with a record of 4–6. They lost five of their last six games. The depleted crowd waddled rain-soaked through the exits one last time. In a season with plenty of disappointments to choose from, this was the bottom.

After the game, Jim Criner held his final press conference. There was one reporter. "We were running backwards the whole game," Criner said, his words echoing as though he stood at the bottom of a large drinking glass, looking up an insurmountable crystalline wall. "We can't buy a dad-gum break. If we make a couple of those catches we dropped . . ." His sentences trailed off. His skin was slack and blotchy. He swallowed hard.

The reporter asked about the XFL's future.

Criner sat up. "As long as we sell the league as football, an alternative to the NFL, not as good as the NFL . . ." he said. He trailed off again, this time into the distance between the reporter's eyes, lost somewhere before catching the thread. "We can't compare with the NFL. Once we start promoting on TV that it's football and not fireworks and naked cheerleaders. . . ." He kept on.

The XFL's crossed wires allowed Criner and his fellow purists to spin the debacle their own way. It's the football people want to watch, they said, not the shenanigans. Football is just that good, they said. Maybe in another world. Because this rainy day in the desert was never going to earn the numbers that the boys in New York needed. "I just don't know," Criner said. "We'll have to see." He wandered through the locker room's double doors.

In the parking lot, Rod Smart had nothing to declare. After the fumble against San Francisco and the furor of his nickname, what was left to say? He disappeared into the night. Ryan Clement left in bandages and ice packs. Kelvin Kinney wasn't far behind, steadfastly shoe-gazing.

Ryan Clement looked relieved as he held court in the kitchen of his house several hours after the game. His hair was still wet from a shower. Blackjack at the Hard Rock casino was in his plans for the night. He could take a break from thinking about football.

A few friends were there from back home in Denver. A few teammates, too. And Ms. Sachs. Clement didn't harbor any illusions as he doled out beers, standing on the linoleum in front of the fridge, "I might call up the Arena League," he said. He didn't want to think about football. His friends didn't talk about it, either, realizing the weight of the topic. The closest anyone came was asking about Clement's busted shoulder.

Everyone talked about Vegas, where the girls were, who they would see at the Hard Rock. The whole setup was uncomfortable, and the conversation reached a lull with everyone looking into their beers. It was like every one of Clement's friends had died a little bit watching him come up short again. They knew what it meant. And they knew how much it must have hurt.

Clement was the one who piped up. "Let me tell you something," he said. "I remember my junior year, we're playing Florida State in the Orange Bowl." His friends turned toward Clement, much as the crowd would have done that day at the Orange Bowl.

"They're number three, we're number six. We're both four and oh. We're down early, seventeen-zip. We gave 'em a couple easy ones, turned the ball over. But then we come roaring back." Clement put his beer can on the

ledge, using both hands to tell the story. He didn't have to think about football that night, but he couldn't escape it. He relinquished himself to the
annecdote. "It's third and twenty, and I hit Yatil Green for forty yards. We go
eighty yards for a touchdown, and the place is getting into it. We get the ball
back. And we drive down the field again. And I throw another pass to Yatil.
Touchdown." Clement's friends smiled, but they didn't know what to say.
"Seventy-five thousand people go absolutely nuts. My head just popped off."

How sad the story was, not to Clement but to those gathered around him,
who realized that he didn't know how many times he had told it. Clement
grabbed his beer and swished it around. Everyone watched him. No one
wanted to be the first to move or to say anything. Someone cleared his
throat. The night came to a halt, and it was difficult imagining how it would
pick up again.

The doorbell rang, and the whole room volunteered to answer it. Attention shifted to the new arrival, which left Clement to gulp down his beer. He
didn't know where he would end up, but in his mind he could always go back
to the Orange Bowl.

17

NO BODY CARES

L.A. HOSTED SAN FRANCISCO in NBC's national game on Saturday, April 7, in a match-up of the top two teams in the Western Conference. Announcers billed the game as a possible preview to the Million Dollar Game. The Xtreme won, 24–0. The blowout was not welcome news, since it was about time for the XFL to struggle back to its feet after the three-week deluge of the NCAA tournament. There was no more basketball to hinder die-hard sports fans from tuning in. Trouble was, the weekend of April 7 marked the opening of Major League Baseball. The XFL promptly notched its second straight 1.5 rating, solidifying its standing as the lowest rated program in prime-time network history.

In the week following the final dismal game of the season, the Outlaws' diaspora commenced. Some players went home to their families. Others left Vegas for the CFL or the Arena League. Many rested up for another go at the NFL in the summer minicamps, where they would likely be little more than tackling fodder.

Meantime, the XFL playoffs began, with San Francisco traveling to Orlando and L.A. hosting a Chicago team that had somehow made the playoffs after starting the ten-game season with four straight losses. (Rusty Tillman's New York/New Jersey Hitmen finished at 4–6.) The league office enacted a rule change for the playoffs. After a touchdown, a team would have the option of three different conversions. Officials would award one point for a conversion from the one-yard line, two points from the five-yard line, and three points from the ten-yard line. Enacting its version of the three-point shot, the XFL ripped a page out of the NBA's book. Was this supposed to attract a 4.5 rating?

On NBC's Saturday-night playoff show, San Francisco spotted the heavily favored Rage sixteen points in the game's opening seven minutes. It looked like Orlando was going to win easily and host the Million Dollar Game, with the best record of the four playoff teams. But the Demons battled back in the second half. They tied the game in the third quarter and escaped with an upset win, 26–25, which sent them into the title game. Fewer than fifteen thousand fans showed up for the thriller in Orlando, well below the team's 25,563 season average. It was a pro football playoff, broadcast live on NBC, and an AA baseball crowd turned up. The next day, at the ninety-thousand-seat Los Angeles Coliseum, just 13,081 fans paid to see the hometown Xtreme handle Chicago, 33–16.

Orlando versus San Francisco was a great game, but after ten dog-eared weeks of the XFL, the quality and importance of a contest didn't correlate to the number of people who wanted to watch it. On TV, the game drew a 1.8 rating, a slight increase from the record low of the previous weeks but worse than dozens of no-name programs, including UPN's *Special Unit 2,* about missing-link monsters.

The Million Dollar Game was set: Los Angeles would host San Francisco. The name of the championship left the impression that the game dealt in high stakes. A million dollars certainly was a lot of money. But not when it was split among forty-some people, with each player receiving roughly $25,000. That wasn't bad—it amounted to half of the regular season salary—but it was no million, just another XFL ruse.

Yet it was an inversion of the common illusion, wherein athletes had come to compete for something other than victory in its purest form. A ripple of unease shot through the stomach when Duke won the NCAA basketball title on April 2. As with all recent championships, prestitched baseball hats tainted the players' exuberance, plunked by glad-handers on the heads of anyone whom the camera lens might capture: DUKE 2001 NCAA CHAMPIONS. This was now routine. The once pure collegiate star had become as cynical as the rest. The goal had been obfuscated. It was no longer to win, but to win the right to wear the hat that said you won.

Why a million bucks? Why not $2 million or $5 million? Did everything stem from a dominant cultural theme? A million was exactly how much *Survivor*'s greatest grub pulled in, and also the titular claim of Regis Philbin's quiz show on ABC. *Survivor* creator Mark Burnett couldn't take credit for the denomination, but in this TV context, everything seemed referential, piggy-backing on the success of another. Was it coincidence that the winner of the XFL, a so-called reality program, won the same amount of money as the progenitors of the form?

In the week before the Million Dollar Game, the XFL handed out its Most Valuable Player award to Tommy Maddox, L.A.'s quarterback. Newspapers took great pains to delineate the numbers he'd accrued during several years as a backup quarterback in the NFL: six touchdown passes, fourteen interceptions. Maddox played at UCLA in the early 1990s and left for the NFL after just two seasons. He survived in the league for four years—largely on the misguided faith of Dan Reeves, who, as coach of the Broncos, drafted Maddox in the first round, then took him along to successive jobs with the Giants and the Falcons. Ultimately, Maddox used up his chances and left football entirely to run an insurance business for a few years. There was certainty with insurance: Something would always break, someone would always die, and someone would always want protection against the inevitable.

But in the middle of one work day in September 1999, fed up with the calls that bounced from one phone line to the next, Maddox picked up and left his office. He hadn't scratched the itch on that terrible part of his brain, the one that controls joy and addiction. After watching the Kurt Warner saga, which could not have seemed so dissimilar from his own, Maddox joined up with the very same Arena Football League. Maddox managed to regain the confidence he had lost. Now he was playing on NBC's Saturday night. Too bad no one was watching.

It wasn't Dick Ebersol who made that truth plain. It was Vince McMahon. Maybe he was saving his old friend the trouble. Two days before the Million Dollar Game, Larry Stewart wrote in the *Los Angeles Times* a story straight from the hoarse mouth. "There's nothing official," McMahon said, "but as for NBC showing games on Saturday nights, that's not going to happen." McMahon didn't say that NBC had decided to drop the games altogether, but the implication was clear. He went on to discuss the changes that were in store. "We'll only play on Sunday afternoons, at one and four. That's when viewers are used to watching pro football." McMahon stressed the longevity of his once-revolutionary product, which was beginning to look more and more like the NFL, except for the quality of its on-field personnel. "The way I look at it, next year will be our first year of business. We made mistakes and we have learned from our mistakes. Next season will be the real test. The WWF wasn't built in a year. The same is going to be true with the XFL." McMahon had no guarantee that his other broadcast partners would stay aboard. He didn't produce anyone else interested in diving a sunken wreck. Yet he managed to sound nearly as confident about a second season as he had about the first.

If you could overlook the haze that clouded the buildings downtown, it was another perfect day in L.A. And if the circumstances had been something other than a wake, those in charge of the Million Dollar Game might have considered it an encouraging coincidence that in 1967 the NFL played its first Super Bowl at this very same Coliseum. The NFL sold about sixty-two thousand tickets for that game. But as fans creaked through the turn-stiles on April 21, 2001—some dressed in Xtreme jerseys, some in Demons jerseys, and even more wearing the silver and black of the long-departed Raiders—it was clear that this game would approximate only a sliver of that original championship crowd, about twenty-four thousand. Coincidence didn't end there. The Million Dollar Game would take place on the same day as the NFL draft, an occasion that had once caused many XFL players to dream of a future that involved more than twenty-four thousand fans.

The press box reverberated with cheers before game time, though they weren't so much cheers as a dull, wishful urging. The time for the Million Dollar Game's kickoff had come and gone, postponed by an NBA playoff game that had run late on NBC. The XFL brass suctioned to a TV dangling from the rafters, hoping that the Minnesota Timberwolves wouldn't convert on their final trip up the court, that San Antonio could just finish the game. They watched the clock in the corner of the screen and yanked their cuffs back to peer their watches. This was what a delay felt like, as Lorne Michaels would have gladly explained.

The Spurs pulled it out, and all eyes turned to the football field, which looked like a green horse pill so far down below. The league had the Coliseum operators switch on the Olympic torch, the same flame that flickered above the 1932 and 1984 Summer Games. To a sports fan with notions of history and reverence, this was some kind of blasphemy. The Million Dollar Game quickly proved itself worthy of excommunication.

L.A. and San Francisco met in the first game of the regular season, with Tommy Maddox fumbling on his first play from scrimmage and the Xtreme losing in overtime. They also played each other in the last game of the season, when Maddox led his team to a lopsided romp. This game conformed to recent history.

On the Demons sideline, Ebersol and McMahon beamed as the sun poured down on them. They backslapped each other like Shiatsu masseurs. Could they possibly be celebrating? No, they were just glad to put the XFL's first season behind them. The comedians would have to get along without them.

Dick Butkus shuffled centipedelike to a safer distance. The face of pro football had grown wistful by degrees. He kept his distance from the plastic people nearby, those who traded in the intangible.

L.A. scored its first touchdown in the second quarter. Tight end Josh Wilcox rumbled into the end zone off a play-action pass from the one-yard line. Wilcox's father, Dave Wilcox, was an NFL Hall of Famer. The son moonlighted as a pro wrestler, having twice appeared in the ECW ring as All-American Josh Wilcox. For him at least, the XFL was a perfect fit. After scoring, Wilcox threw the football to the end-zone turf, then dropped on it with an atomic elbow. McMahon cheered from the sideline chalk. In this silly, fleeting moment, the bossman witnessed the closest his league ever came to meshing such disparate worlds. Like an amused father, he let out a grateful laugh at the gesture.

San Francisco couldn't move the ball on offense. Even a quick kick resulted in an L.A. touchdown. Butkus, Ebersol, and McMahon, sideline chalk scuffing their shoes, practically urged San Francisco to get back into the game, with players running and huffing past on the playing field in front of them. Covering a play downfield, a referee ran full-speed into Bruno, the Bubba Cam operator, slamming his funny bone against the cameraman's metal apparatus. Did this qualify as synergy? L.A. led 21–0.

Vince McMahon was thinking ahead, planning for the XFL's second year even as the first one concluded. He had invited the coaches and general managers from every team to attend the Million Dollar Game, and their peanut-popping presence in the press box made the game, even in its dreariness, feel like a group project, as though everyone was in this thing together and through the most dismal times. Even Rusty Tillman showed up.

The first half ended and a fan lofted a placard: NO BODY CARES, the capital letters forming the offending network's acronym. An expletive escaped onto the PA from a player with an open microphone—"Fuck!"—and the crowd emitted its loudest roar of the game.

The halftime show began with cheerleaders from every XFL team dancing at midfield. It was like a high-end strip club. Somewhere you could hear it: "Next on the main stage, Benita from Brazil." Fireworks blasted down the middle of the field, choreographed like the jets in the Bellagio pools, yet they were not enough to distract from Jay Howarth's feeble-witted carping. A blow-up doll bounced around the crowd.

The show didn't run longer than it took to cycle through the restroom line, and the teams soon took the field for the second half. Quickly, the Extreme went up 31–0. L.A. kicked off, and the Demons coughed up the ball. Ebersol and McMahon had ceased their backslapping. They stared into the middle distance. The PA announcer did what he could to keep the crowd into the game, repeatedly revisiting the million bucks at stake. "Remember, fans, they're playing for *one million dollaaaaarrrsss.*" The fans yelled as though they themselves would receive a share. By the end of the third quarter, a third of the crowd had gone home. This was a stinker. "I gotta talk to a couple L.A. linemen I know," said Matt Butkus, Dick Butkus's son, himself a league employee. "Tell them I got the over."

The Xtreme dominated the game so decisively that its first punt came in the fourth quarter. L.A. ran the score to 38–zip. McMahon's now palsied hand clenched and unclenched at his side as the season drew to a close. In the final minute, as what was left of the hometown crowd raised its volume, sensing a trophy presentation, San Francisco managed to avoid a shutout. A third-string quarterback scampered for a touchdown past a distracted defense, with twenty-five seconds on the clock. Final score: 38–6. The XFL could not have found a more fitting end to its season—a blowout, devoid of all tension.

As the seconds counted down, fireworks exploded in the night sky, the crowd buzzed with potential vandalism, and a hodgepodge of cheerleaders gyrated haphazardly to Randy Newman's ubiquitous "I Love L.A.," which rang from the PA. It felt like being the only sober one at an acid get-together. It was all too obvious.

At season's end, the XFL brass had little to do but mourn missed opportunities and lost dollars, much like the throngs fleeing the casinos every night, their pockets turned white to the wind. This bet was a losing bet, and they shipped out the operation to die in L.A., in a long abandoned stadium where pro football could never win out. In the cavernous confines of a colossal bowl, the Million Dollar Game played as Pop Warner, appropriately sized. From the cheap seats, or even the not so cheap seats, it looked like a game within a game, a stadium within a stadium, little ants scurrying along the grass, ringed by fans who were themselves ringed by endless fields of empty seats. Where was all the action?

A man in white gloves appeared carrying an odd-weighted X-shaped slab of gold-plated plastic. It looked like a brass bed melted down. The white gloves handed the eyesore to Vince McMahon. "Let's get the reporters down here," said McMahon, flicking his head toward the scoreboard that registered an absurd blowout. "So they can see we scripted every play." Nervous chuckles filtered in from the gathered handlers.

For a game named after money, the trophy couldn't have looked any cheaper. It was as though its purchasers chose not to extend themselves on a grail that might not see much sipping. The Million Dollar Game trophy looked like a Seiko watch, ungainly and plated and millennial baroque like the Trump Tower, yet with hollow walls, like the Venetian or Caesar's.

McMahon started to hand the trophy to Dick Butkus, who was charged with the presentation. Butkus looked at the thing oddly, trying to figure it out. There was no helmeted figurine anywhere to be seen, no football. This didn't look like a football trophy. It was just a big shiny "X," referring to nothing except its own flash. What the heck was it? Butkus grabbed the trophy. And the top of it promptly crashed to the ground. A dozen hands reached for the hunk as it tumbled, and then everyone bent over and made a grab for it, scrounging on the grass like caddies lifting the master's flung putter in exchange for a buck tip or a pat on the head. The piece went back on top.

The game's final gun sounded, and McMahon's throng made for the center of the field. Butkus lugged the trophy. Hundreds of people crowded around—players, coaches, family, photographers, reporters, fans. Rent-a-cops pulled yellow rope across a V-shaped swath of turf at midfield. Within seconds, everyone had broken the line. The security guys yelled in vain. It was chaos.

McMahon grabbed a microphone and addressed the crowd. He thanked the fans. He thanked Ebersol and the coaches and players. He vowed that the league would return for a second season. "See you next year," he said. L.A. coach Al Luginbill grabbed the trophy from Butkus. "Here stands a man's man," said Luginbill, taking the microphone and gesturing toward McMahon. "He stands for what is good in this country." It was time to weep in underdog solidarity.

The microphone then made its way to MVP Tommy Maddox. His team-mates reached above the crowd and smacked the trophy, which pinged like an empty tin of olive oil. *Ka-blong!* Frustrated by the crush, the L.A. players pushed their way toward the trophy like barbarians, insulting bystanders, tossing racial slurs, comments about fat people, short people, those deemed too ugly. "Get outta my way, Chinaman," said one player. "Move it, shorty," said another. It was a swirling sea of people, with a great disparity in size. They were wearing pads.

In the melee, Ebersol and McMahon got separated. McMahon looked up and waved a forlorn palm to his partner, who was shipwrecked on the far side of the crowd. They stood separated and separate, and as the crowd grew and distended, they lost complete sight of each other in the crush. Silently, Ebersol walked off stage left.

Tommy Maddox grabbed the trophy and trotted to the stands, where he held it over his head, as the remaining fans cheered him on. This was L.A.'s first pro football championship since the Raiders won the Super Bowl in 1984. The stands were empty. And the majority of attention was lavished not on the Xtreme but on Vince McMahon, who found himself swarmed by fans, players, and cheerleaders.

An Xtreme linebacker hustled up to McMahon with the flushed face of a kid who'd had too much recess. "I wanna thank you for the opportunity," he said, effusive in his praise of the boss man, trying to catch his breath and contain his excitement. "It's a dream come true for me. I decided not to resign with Green Bay for this." Was the NFL practice squad really that miserable?

McMahon administered to the cheerleaders huddled around him. They gazed into a face that couldn't possibly return all their stares. They beamed in a certain available way. McMahon was hounded, surrounded. The throng grabbed for him as though doubting his existence, as though their hands might have gone through McMahon and exited a hologram on the other side. Until you laid a hand on him, it was hard to know if Vince McMahon was real.

By this time, Butkus was marching off the field under the cover of the melee at midfield. The season was over. A fan noticed him slinking toward the stadium tunnel. "Dick Butkus!" the fan called out from the seats. "The best linebacker ever!" Butkus just kept on going.

The crowd still clung to McMahon as Al Luginbill opened the floor for questions in a cramped, stuffy meeting room in the bowels of the Coliseum. "We couldn't have scripted it any better," said the coach. "It was a dominating effort." A small crowd of a dozen reporters listened to the title game's press conference. A sad indicator, as even the crows had lost interest in swooping down for a stab. A reporter asked Luginbill how he ended up in the XFL in the first place, inadvertently drawing the coach's ire. "I have not been a coaching gypsy," Luginbill said, a little riled. "I didn't have to take this job. The one reason is Vince McMahon. The guy is a man's man. I've never met a man so direct, can-do, as this man."

What about next year, did Luginbill see a next year? "We're gonna be here," he said. "For whatever reason, we're gonna be here. We're not asking for handouts. We'll earn our way." The room echoed with his words, the empty scene reducing Luginbill and his dogma to something from a high school gym. Who could possibly care about what he had to say, and who would sit here and take it except these golf-shirted few?

It wasn't so serious in the L.A. locker room. The thirty-eight players on the regular Xtreme roster had voted to share the million bucks with the seven players on their practice squad. The forty-five-way split worked out to $22,222 per player. Everyone was happy. Thirty minutes after the trophy presentation, the Xtreme players were still in uniform. They horsed around like kids in pajamas, spraying one another with what was left of the champagne. They sang sawed-off songs. A group of linemen huddled in one corner of the locker room, near the stalls draped in protective plastic. "Bling, bling," they sang, "we're getting a fucking ring." Whether they would ever see any jewelry was in serious doubt.

Jerseys and pizza crusts lay in huge puddles of acrid champagne. Pictures of football legends loomed on the walls. Marcus Allen hung there in a USC jersey, making a cutback against Washington State decades ago. He was watching this XFL party go down, cigar smoke hanging in the air and clouding his vision. The room wrapped in a vociferous din. The money subsided, size didn't matter, victory at last was the thing.

The season had mercifully concluded, and on this evening, the Los Angeles Coliseum had the hoary stench of a sepulcher. The predominant sentiment mandated vacating the premises as quickly as possible, before the gloom consumed everything. It was even worse out in the parking lot, where except for a few flickering streetlamps, the lights had been extinguished. Must. Leave. Now.

The fans had fled a long time ago. The only noise in the parking lot was the recorded PA announcer. "The Los Angeles Xtreme appreciate your support during this inaugural 2001 season," he boomed in a cheerful voice, OD'd on some antidepressant. "Make sure you keep in touch with us at XFL.com. And look for us to return in 2002, right here at the Coliseum." The message ran on a loop, blasting itself again and again over the dark, rubbish-strewn evening. On the way out of the stadium lot, the words from the PA blended into one loud, indistinguishable blast of white noise. It dissipated toward the corner gas station on MLK Boulevard, near the freeway entrance, where a car fire raged out of control.

Up on the 110 Freeway, southbound side, a billboard for *The Mummy Returns,* The Rock's Hollywood debut, perched above the blurred SUVs. Here was possibly the single biggest reason that Ebersol and McMahon had entered into their football league: The Rock as movie star—suspension of disbelief—wrestling's coming hegemony. Applying the polish of the WWF production to the spontaneity of genuine competition: Did that seem such a far-fetched idea, even in its ultimate failure? In a recent TV segment, an interviewer had asked The Rock what he would like most in life. "A time capsule," The Rock had said. He went on to say that he considered himself a "timeologist." The XFL and the Los Angeles Coliseum shrank in the background, along with the leaping flames from the gas station. It had become abundantly clear that some people were well served by scripts, but fire fascinated only in spontaneity.

18

THE VAMPIRE SLAYER

THE XFL SEASON WAS FINISHED, and one question remained: Would there be another one?

The rating for the Million Dollar Game, a 2.1, was lower than any other network show for the week. Overall, viewers preferred ninety-two other programs to the XFL championship. The Million Dollar Game earned the sixth worst rating of the XFL season, a number that was just 22 percent of the league's 9.5 opening rating. Over the season's twelve weeks, the XFL averaged a 3.1. Only the first two weeks had hit the promised mark of 4.5.

The ratings, predictably, measured poorly against those of established sports leagues. The NFL averaged a 10.7 during the 2000 regular season and earned a 40.4 for the Super Bowl. Major League Baseball's regular season averaged a 2.6 on FOX in 2000 (most of the games aired outside of prime time), while the World Series scored a 12.4. The 2000 NBA regular season averaged a 3.3, mostly during weekend afternoons, and the NBA Finals rose to an 11.6. Even the NHL, which routinely scored low ratings in the U.S., notched a 3.7 for its 2000 Stanley Cup Finals on ABC, those six games easily averaging out to surpass the Million Dollar Game.

This wasn't the final humiliation. The Million Dollar Game had fallen on the same weekend as the NFL draft. ESPN slogged through the interminable, multiday event as it always did, beginning at noon on Saturday and continuing until seven P.M., when the coverage switched to ESPN2. During that seven hours of coverage on the flagship station, the NFL draft pulled in a rating of 2.65. If ever there was a thing called active disinterest, this would describe it—several million football fans opting to watch NFL executives gum doughnuts and slurp coffee—call it the Coffee Bowl—instead of a living, breathing football championship. The XFL began by beating the Pro Bowl; it ended by losing to a board meeting.

Nonetheless, NBC execs had to be grateful. Their long national nightmare was over. They could finally lay low again on Saturday nights, resume broadcasting the programming that no one had much cared about in the first place. It was okay if no one drove by to have a look. At least they wouldn't egg the house.

On April 28, the week after the Million Dollar Game, NBC aired something safe, the movie *Goldeneye,* a charmless James Bond rehash starring Pierce Brosnan. Appearing in the same Saturday-night time slot as the XFL, *Goldeneye* drew a 4.6 rating. This number would have guaranteed the league's success. How could the movie have done so well? Maybe people wanted to feel what it was like to punch in NBC's Saturday night on the remote, having avoided it for months.

Two and a half weeks after the Million Dollar Game, Vince McMahon and Basil DeVito invited all the XFL coaches and general managers to Stamford for meetings. There were plenty of topics on the agenda. The second XFL draft. Expansion. Proposed rule changes. Football stuff. Vince McMahon was handling the TV end.

Some XFL brass were heartened by the fact that the league was coming down from NBC. That had been the business plan from the beginning—start small and work up to the big time, the "brand building" that McMahon intoned at every chance like a string-activated doll. Establish a name, give the teams time to gel, the quality of the play an opportunity to develop. Most importantly, grant the production crew time to streamline the telecast and make it worthy of the many gadgets lavished upon it. After the nosedive of the first season, a year or two on UPN and TNN didn't look so bad. In fact, it was looking pretty perfect. It was just a matter of money, since ad revenue on UPN was only a fraction of NBC's.

The media giant Viacom owned UPN, and from its standpoint, an XFL deal couldn't have looked so bad. Sunday afternoons were almost throwaway slots for UPN as it was. The ratings for XFL games weren't complete horror stories. The XFL appeared to work on UPN and TNN. While the league's .7 average rating among adults aged 18–49 tied for 158th, at the very bottom of the UPN's prime-time shows, it managed to expand the network to a sixth night of the week with roughly the same ratings of regular programming but at a lower cost. On TNN, the league's Sunday-afternoon games averaged a .93 rating, which was up 48 percent over the same period in 2000, and a .71 among adults 18–49, a 92 percent increase in the time slot.

There was something else at work. In the history of both UPN and TNN, neither network had ever operated in the black. The problem was a lack of identifiable programming. *Seinfeld* said NBC, but no program screamed UPN. Even with all its difficulties, the XFL was still a recognizable property among viewers. It had the kind of visibility that a hundred sitcoms could never have collectively. Viewers may not have liked it much, but at least they knew what it was.

UPN execs understood their problem, and for some time they were bent on rectifying the situation. While the XFL was setting records over on NBC, UPN entered into discussions with Twentieth Century Fox TV to finally land a well-known program. The UPN brass had something particular in mind to put their network on the map. They wanted to steal *Buffy the Vampire Slayer* from the WB. Viacom had spent enough time in the land of anonymous programming.

During the week of May 7, XFL coaches and general managers met with Basil DeVito in a conference room in the Stamford WWF offices, as well as in a similar meeting space in Stamford's Westin Hotel. Meanwhile, Vince McMahon held discussions with UPN executives, where they hammered out a deal for Season Two.

To celebrate the close of the spring meeting, DeVito, Dick Butkus, and most of the coaches planned to see a game at Yankee Stadium the night of Thursday, May 10. The coaches cleaned up in their hotels. Then they returned to the WWF offices, where they were scheduled to pile into vans and drive down to the stadium, where the Yankees would play the Minnesota Twins. This was as much a reward for the hard work of Year One as it was a send-off until the next meeting. The coaches gathered in the conference room, and there they received an unexpected visitor. Vince McMahon walked into the room, finally disgorged from the UPN talks. Was he going to the Yankees game with them?

"Guys, I got something to tell you," he said. "There's not going to be a second season. The XFL is finished."

Viacom agreed to pay nearly $2.5 million per *Buffy* episode, which prevented the company from being able to take a chance on the XFL. In order to make a deal to broadcast the XFL's second season, UPN execs demanded that McMahon cut his WWF *Smackdown!* by 30 minutes. This would allot the network real estate for a new program, with a valuable lead-in audience. Without that concession, UPN just couldn't pay McMahon what he needed to cover the costs of a second season. TNN's ad rates weren't high enough. McMahon refused to slash *Smackdown!* and relinquish a half hour of ad revenue. In the end, *Buffy* slew Vince.

"We just thought it was okay, let's go, type of thing," said Dick Butkus's son, Matt. "You can't be mad. It's a business decision. They started stepping on the toes of Vince's main money maker, the WWF. So what can you do?" Several coaches went along to the Yankees game, though Matt Butkus and his father couldn't stomach it. "We said, 'Shine that.' We went out and put one last dinner on the company."

Ebersol and McMahon opened a conference call with the press. "You don't often have the ability, and it is to be applauded in this wonderful country we live in, to take a calculated risk," said McMahon. "Some of them pay off, some of them don't. This one didn't. But nonetheless, I don't regret for one moment attempting this. Especially considering NBC and Dick stuck with us all the way through this." He couldn't get through his opening remarks without tipping his hat to his partner, continuing the pageant.

Ebersol returned the smooch. "I don't know how to thank Vince. NBC has enjoyed a lot of partnerships through the years, but I'd be challenged to find a more decent, trusting, or accommodating partner and friend than Vince McMahon." It was like listening to an old friend give a hard sell on his new girl.

The teleconference continued, and to their credit, both men gave forthright answers. "The buck stops with me, principally," McMahon said. "I think we let NBC down in terms of holding up our end of the deal. . . . [Blame] clearly rests on my shoulders. This was my vision. And it did not work, for whatever reason."

"I think the first week showed that there was an appetite, and we just didn't answer it in a way that the public wanted us to," said Ebersol. "Bottom line: We didn't deliver what they wanted to see. 'Cause they came and they just didn't come back. . . . And the responsibility lies on us."

On the teleconference that dropped the eight XFL clubs into the circular file, McMahon took great pains to speak of the bright future of the WWF: "There's a film out now called *The Mummy Returns*. Universal has graciously stated how much help we were for the success of that, not just with the performance of one of our characters, The Rock, but the promotional effort, our promotional machine. So obviously we're growing in film. Our growth is boundless. . . . We're in the publishing business. We're in the licensing business. We're in the live-event business. We're in the home-video business. We're in the pay-per-view business. . . ."

It was time to hang up. It was also time to remember that first teleconference back in November 2000, when there was one more baritone on the line.

Jesse Ventura's enthusiasm for the XFL had run it course. Out in Minnesota, reporters caught up with the governor after he delivered a speech to the Urban Land Institute in Minneapolis. What did he think of the XFL's demise? "I don't care," he said. "I don't work for them anymore."

EPILOGUE

WHEN THE XFL FOLDED, Rusty Tillman was glad to step away from the spotlight. But after several months at home with his family, he realized he needed to get back to work. "I'm about out of honeydews," he said. Tillman met with several NFL teams and quickly realized how hard it was to reenter the fraternity, even as an assistant coach. "I may have to wait till next year."

Kelvin Kinney led the XFL in sacks. But he knew that his injuries and the NFLPA's salary requirements would combine to keep him out of the NFL. He signed on with the CFL's Toronto Argonauts, the team that could have belonged to Vince McMahon. The Argos finished the season with a dismal 5–11 record, and Kinney went home to Columbus, Ohio, to spend time with his family. He operates a trucking company and is contemplating a return to Canada for another season of football.

Aside from an appearance on NBC's short-lived sitcom *Inside Schwartz,* Dick Butkus returned to the quiet tasks he had performed before the XFL came along. He manages his seven-year-old insurance business, Bear Paw, as well as the Dick Butkus Football Network, an Internet repository. Approaching his sixtieth birthday, the face of pro football writes a recurring online column called "On the Sideline."

As Jesse Ventura considered running once more for governor of Minnesota in 2004, the sting of his XFL experience persuaded him to limit his moonlighting. "We have turned down a lot of stuff," said one of his advisors. But by his very nature, Ventura couldn't avoid making headlines.

He appeared regularly on news programs and talk shows, offering his unfiltered opinions on a wide array of topical issues. He made a guest appearance on *The Young and the Restless*. A playwright continued work on *The Body Ventura*, a musical based on Ventura's life that was targeted for Broadway. And when Major League Baseball raised the specter of eliminating the Minnesota Twins as part of its proposed contraction plan, Ventura arose as one of the sanest voices in the debate over baseball's purported insolvency.

Sitting alongside baseball's commissioner, Bud Selig, during a December hearing of the House Judiciary Committee, Ventura sounded off. "I have a hard time believing it, Mr. Selig, that [baseball owners] are losing that kind of money and still paying the salaries they're paying. That's asinine. These people did not get the wealth they have by being stupid. Baseball might be a fair game, but its owners have set their own rules." Once again, he delivered the straight message that no other bureaucrat could manage to give.

On a January 2002 telecast, CNN's Aaron Brown asked Ventura if he had any regrets, referencing his wide array of experiences, notably the XFL. "Never!" Ventura shot back. "I don't live life with regrets. You can't go into this life and regret things you have done, because you can't relive them over again. I don't do that. I don't regret anything. I'm who I am."

Ryan Clement moved back to Denver, where he began clerking at a law firm. He was finally getting his house in order. He submitted several law school applications and got engaged to Melissa Sachs.

In January 2002, the Miami Hurricanes took an 11–0 record into the Rose Bowl for the national title game, against the University of Nebraska. Clement watched from the stands as his old team clobbered Nebraska, 37–14. The game abolished his emotional ambiguity. "I was elated. I teared up. One thing I realized is I bleed orange and green," Clement said. Miami's quarterback, Ken Dorsey, finished third in balloting for the Heisman Trophy, restoring the luster of Quarterback U. "Better timing than me, that's the way I look at it," he said.

Clement decided to study law back at his old school, Miami, where his name still carried some weight among the well-heeled booster club. Then football got in the way again. Clement took a job as player/coach in the French Federation of American Football, where players smoke cigarettes on the sidelines. Before he joined his newest team, the Ironmask de Cannes, Clement said it was merely an extended vacation before law school. "But when I go over to Cannes, who knows what happens? If I start feeling it again, I may give the agent a call and say, 'Hey, get me a couple workouts.'"

In August 2001, Rod Smart signed with the Edmonton Eskimos of the CFL. He wore his surname on the back of his jersey. The Eskimos cut him after just one game. He returned to his apartment on Nellis Boulevard and waited confidently for a call from an NFL team, since he had finished second in XFL rushing. Nothing came.

For all the attention HE HATE ME had earned for the XFL, Smart never saw an extra penny. XFL brass had spoken with his agent, and they promised to bump his pay for a second season. That plan was long gone. But Smart didn't have any hard feelings. "Nothing but good came of HE HATE ME," he said. In September, he appeared in a degrading skit on Fox's NFL pre-game show. His role: a pizza delivery man. "It got me noticed once again, so it was fine with me."

A month later, he finally got The Call. The Philadelphia Eagles invited Smart for a workout, then signed him to their practice squad. Six weeks later, the Eagles cut the running back above him on the depth chart. HE HATE ME started dressing with the big boys, although he didn't execute his standard pre-game rituals. "I'm still trying to get comfortable. I can't just open up yet," he said. Philadelphia players (including wide receiver Freddie Mitchell, his first cousin) gave Smart a new nickname, Heat, an abbreviation of his old one.

In November, he played in his first NFL game, running down kicks on special teams. And in the last week of the regular season, during a game in Tampa Bay, Florida, thirty-five miles from Lakeland, Rod Smart got his first NFL carry. Valerie Smart was off house arrest and watching in the stadium. Smart gained six yards off-tackle. On his second carry, he broke his ankle.

But it wasn't a serious break. HE HATE ME was determined to stick in the NFL and had nothing but positive thoughts about his time spent in that other league. "It was a stepping stone, playing on the pro level before the NFL. It was like going to a junior college before you go to a big college. And it was a lot of fun."

In January 2002, the NBA left NBC, signing a six-year, $4.6 billion TV contract with ESPN, ABC, and TNT. In all practicality, NBC opted out of any new agreement, adhering to its strategy in the 1998 NFL negotiations, when it offered the NBA nearly $500 million *less* than it had been paying in the current deal. In just a few years, NBC had lost the NFL, Major League Baseball, and the NBA. But it was hard to argue against the fiscal wisdom of this latest move. The NBA's ratings had dropped 35 percent since Michael Jordan retired from the Bulls, and NBC claimed losses of more than $100 million per year during the life of the contract. Dick Ebersol sounded his refrain. "We won't subsidize big-time losses in sports."

The NBA deal gave ESPN a hand in each of the four major sports leagues. Meanwhile, NBC Sports, with a collection that included auto racing, rodeo, and thoroughbreds, looked very much like early-'80s ESPN, when the fledgling cable channel struggled to fill its twenty-four-hour format. The *Hollywood Reporter* dubbed NBC's new look as "profit over prestige," reflecting a general trend for over-air networks.

With 83 percent of America's TV households hooked up to cable or satellite service, there was no longer much difference between broadcast and cable in the eyes of advertisers. In the softest ad market in memory, broadcast networks reliant exclusively on advertising revenue struggled to compete with cable networks, which received proceeds from both advertisers and subscriber fees. Sports rights fees continued their lofty ascent. According to industry estimates published in the *Washington Post,* the broadcast networks collectively lost roughly $1 billion in 2001 on contracts with the NBA, NFL, Major League Baseball, and NASCAR. NBC's XFL folly didn't look so irresponsible in comparison.

NBC still had the Olympics. For the 2002 Winter Games in Salt Lake City, Dick Ebersol altered the network's human-drama format, airing more events and fewer features. NBC averaged a 19.2 rating over two weeks of coverage, 18 percent better than CBS's number for the 1998 games, and almost 14 percent higher than the rating NBC had guaranteed advertisers.

Even though NBC benefited enormously from the domestic venue, it was clear that Ebersol solidified his standing as Olympics czar. Like Vince McMahon, he failed to broaden his reputation with the XFL.

Just before the Olympics, Ebersol attended a screening of TNT's adaptation of *Monday Night Mayhem,* a behind-the-scenes look at *Monday Night Football.* Roone Arledge asked Ebersol to moderate a discussion panel at the screening, which took place at the Museum of Television and Radio. Ebersol was honored to oblige, especially since his seventy-year-old mentor was too ill to attend, stricken with bone and prostate cancer. After the screening, Ebersol took a ride to the New York Times Building, where he briefed writers about the upcoming games. A reporter asked him what he thought would be his legacy. Ebersol danced around the question, then finally answered, saying he thought he would be remembered as "someone who loves sports but is ultimately a businessman who has a responsibility to shareholders."

Two months later, in March, Ebersol announced NBC's latest pro football venture. The network signed up the Arena Football League. Ebersol said that the AFL was "the most exciting, fast-paced, high-scoring game you have ever seen in your life."

"This Sunday," read a WWF release hyping a July 2001 event, "for the first time in history, WWF Superstars will stand opposite WCW and ECW in a battle for sports-entertainment supremacy. The course of history will be changed forever!" Not quite. Vince McMahon's plan of pitting wrestlers from the WWF and WCW against one another in a Super Bowl of his own design never got off the ground. Wrestling viewership sank in a cyclical dip, and with no one left to battle, the WWF struggled to find its identity. Vince McMahon realized there was something missing, and in one of many changes, he welcomed back Jerry Lawler, who rejoined Jim Ross at ringside.

It was fitting that McMahon's XFL vision began in Las Vegas, and it made sense that at the end, he walked away having lost a pile. The WWF declared a $36 million loss on the XFL, identical to NBC's figure. During the league's three-month season, WWF shares fell 32 percent. The company posted a fourth-quarter loss of $20 million, while full-year earnings in 2001 totaled just a third of 2000 numbers. In November, the WWF, like many other companies struggling in a depressed economy, cut its work force. McMahon fired the company's president, along with thirty-nine employees. That didn't stop Linda McMahon from singing the familiar chorus, claiming that the WWF was "really poised for growth." The company made plans to open an office in London.

Vince McMahon was determined to put the XFL experience behind him. In the Macy's Thanksgiving Day Parade, he waved from the WWF float that trundled down Fifth Avenue. It was further evidence of his inclusion in the Entertainment Business, though all it really took was a check. And in May 2002, when a court case brought by the World Wildlife Fund forced the WWF to change its name, there was really only one option: World Wrestling Entertainment.

The XFL's technical legacy was evident during the 2001 World Series, when Fox Sports miked Arizona Diamondbacks manager Mike Brenly. When Brenly yanked pitcher Curt Schilling late in a thrilling seventh game, fans could hear his words from the sacred territory of the pitcher's mound. "We took viewers places they've never been before," said John Gonzalez. "And to have that kind of access to other professional athletes would be a huge benefit to viewers, who seem to be turning away from sports." In November, Gonzalez found himself in Austin, Texas, directing NBC's coverage of the Bud Light World Challenge Rodeo.

NFL ratings did not improve in 2001. Super Bowl XXXVI duplicated the substandard numbers of the previous championship game. *Monday Night Football* continued its decline, dropping another 9 percent in average viewership. In February 2002, ABC jumped at the chance to hire John Madden, the respected former CBS and Fox announcer. The Dennis Miller experiment was over—it was back to straight football.

Undoubtedly, some other collection of individuals will undertake the task of creating a renegade pro football league. Whoever it is would do well to examine the fundamental failure of the XFL.

It was a league of empty promises. The cheerleader cam, the abolishment of the fair-catch rule, placing announcers in the stands: these were just a few examples of the XFL's corrupt sales philosophy. Ebersol and McMahon gained access to places that had always intrigued fans, but there wasn't much happening when they got there. The bosses promised a measure of Rabelaisian wit, a look inside the charnel house of the WWF, but the closest they came were a few cuss words boomed over the PA. They believed too eminently in their own mystique. They overpromised and undersold. It was all a shell game. And that was odd, since McMahon knew the danger of promising a steel cage match and delivering a scuffle between two unknowns.

All of this was a sign of a lost age, circa 2000, when boom times and bull markets afforded the chance to throw blind handfuls of money at "concepts" and "projects," without a vague notion of whether they might succeed. For Ebersol and McMahon, the XFL was little more than that—a concept that lacked the innovative thinking attendant to all things truly different. In the end, nothing worked, and their cavalier approach couldn't obscure the vast and echoing empire of their failure.

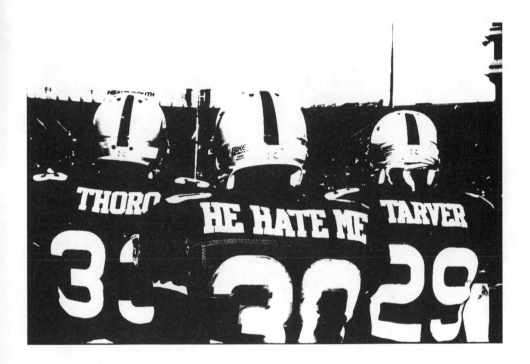

ACKNOWLEDGMENTS

The difficulties of writing an unauthorized book are clear. As I began my reporting on *Long Bomb*, XFL lawyers issued a letter explaining that they would "exercise all available remedies in both equity and law to prevent the publication. . . ." When the league folded, conditions were exacerbated by the Severance Package and its inevitable rider, the Confidentiality Agreement. Nonetheless, I conducted the majority of reporting for this book on the ground, and I must thank the players and staff of the Las Vegas Outlaws, and also Dick Butkus, John Gonzalez, Rusty Tillman, Jesse Ventura, and many others who gave freely of their time and insights. I conducted more than eighty interviews and obtained quotes from those who chose not to be interviewed from press conferences and teleconferences, or from periodicals, where noted in the text. The memo on page 129 comes from *Monday Night Mayhem*, by Bill Carter and Marc Gunther.

As for the pitched battle of committing it all to paper, thanks are due foremost to my editor at Crown, Pete Fornatale, who bought my proposal when no one else wanted it, then did the old, unfashionable work to make sure the book came out right. Thanks to Matt Bialer at Trident Media Group, for landing my first deal. To Dorianne Steele at Crown and Cheryl Capitani at Trident for their vital aid. To Cicero DeGuzman and James Westman, for what should have panned out. And thanks to Ju, for those fragile few minutes before hitting the wall . . . and for all the rest of it.

INDEX

ABOUT THE AUTHOR

Looking for the perfect place to blow his book advance, BRETT FORREST packed up and moved to Las Vegas. His research on the XFL involved four months of close association with the Outlaws—shooting dice, drinking bourbon, and eventually getting tossed out of Diva's. His articles have appeared in *Spin*, *Salon*, *Details*, and the *New York Times Magazine*. He lives and works in Brooklyn, New York. This is his first book.